The Ethical Subject of Security

While critical security studies largely concentrates on *objects* of security, this book focuses on the *subject* position from which 'securitization' and other security practices take place.

First, it argues that the modern subject itself emerges and is sustained as a function of security and insecurity. It suggests, consequently, that no analytic frame can produce or reproduce the subject in some original or primordial form that does not already reproduce a fundamental or structural *insecurity*. It critically returns, through a variety of studies, to traditionally held conceptions of security and insecurity as simple predicates or properties that can be associated or not to some more essential, more primeval, more true or real subject. It thus opens and explores the question of the security of the *subject* itself, locating, through a reconstruction of the foundations of the concept of security in the modern conception of the subject, an irreducible insecurity.

Second, it argues that practices of security can only be carried out as a certain kind of negotiation about *values*. The analyses in this book find security expressed again and again as a function of value cast in terms of an explicit or implicit philosophy of life, of culture, of individual and collective anxieties and aspirations, of expectations about what may be sacrificed and what is worth preserving. By way of a critical examination of the value function of security, this book discovers the foundation of values as dependent on a certain management of their own vulnerability, continuously under threat, and thus fundamentally and necessarily insecure.

This book will be an indispensible resource for students of Critical Security Studies, Political Theory, Philosophy, Ethics and International Relations in general.

J. Peter Burgess is Research Professor at PRIO, the Peace Research Institute Oslo, where he leads the Security Programme and edits the interdisciplinary peer-reviewed journal *Security Dialogue*, and Senior Research Fellow at the Institute for European Studies of the Vrije Universiteit Brussels.

PRIO New Security Studies
Series Editor: J. Peter Burgess
PRIO, Oslo

The aim of this book series is to gather state-of-the-art theoretical reflexion and empirical research into a core set of volumes that respond vigorously and dynamically to the new challenges to security scholarship.

The Geopolitics of American Insecurity
Terror, Power and Foreign Policy
François Debrix and Mark J. Lacy (eds)

Security, Risk and the Biometric State
Governing Borders and Bodies
Benjamin Muller

Security and Global Governmentality
Globalization, Governance and the State
Miguel de Larrinaga and Marc G. Doucet

Critical Perspectives on Human Security
Rethinking Emancipation and Power in International Relations
David Chandler and Nik Hynek (eds)

Understanding Securitisation
The Design and Evolution of Security Problems
Thierry Balzacq (ed.)

Feminist Security Studies
A Narrative Approach
Annick T. R. Wibben

The Ethical Subject of Security
Geopolitical Reason and the Threat against Europe
J. Peter Burgess

The Ethical Subject of Security
Geopolitical reason and the threat against Europe

J. Peter Burgess

Routledge
Taylor & Francis Group

LONDON AND NEW YORK

First published 2011
by Routledge
2 Park Square, Milton Park, Abingdon, Oxon, OX14 4RN

Simultaneously published in the USA and Canada
by Routledge
270 Madison Avenue, New York, NY 10016

Routledge is an imprint of the Taylor & Francis Group, an informa business

© 2011 J. Peter Burgess

The right of J. Peter Burgess to be identified as author of this work has been asserted by him in accordance with sections 77 and 78 of the Copyright, Designs and Patents Act 1988.

Typeset in Baskerville by FiSH Books, London
Printed and bound in Great Britain by CPI Antony Rowe, Chippenham, Wiltshire

British Library Cataloguing in Publication Data
A catalogue record for this book is available from the British Library

Library of Congress Cataloging-in-Publication Data
Burgess, J. Peter.
The ethical subject of security : geopolitical reason and the threat against Europe / J. Peter Burgess.
    p. cm.
1. National security–Moral and ethical aspects–Europe. 2. Internal security–Moral and ethical aspects–Europe. I. Title.
UA646.B87 2011
172'.4–dc22

                                                                        2010038602

ISBN13: 978-0-415-49982-8 (hbk)
ISBN13: 978-0-415-49981-1 (pbk)
ISBN13: 978-0-203-82894-6 (ebk)

Voor Karen, hart en geest van het werk

Contents

Acknowledgements

I am indebted to many people for the ideas that take form in this book. Some are close collaborators, others are distant inspirations, others still are anonymous interlocutors with whom I have debated in conference and workshop settings. Those perhaps most present in these pages are Claudia Aradau, Thierry Balzacq, Endre Begby, Didier Bigo, Pinar Bilgin, David Campbell, John Carville, Simon Chesterman, Carol Cohn, Bill Connolly, Christopher Daas, James Der Derian, Mike Dillon, Cynthia Enloe, Serge Gutwirth, Lene Hansen, Paul de Hert, Jef Huysmans, Vivienne Jabri, Oliver Kessler, Jennifer Klot, Mark Lacy, Anna Leander, Luis Lobo-Guerrero, Cristina Masters, Jean-Christophe Merle, Emilio Mordini, Rens Van Muster, Andrew Neal, Taylor Owen, Mark Salter, Mike Shapiro, Ole Wæver, Cynthia Weber, Annick Wibben and Mike Williams.

My collaborators at PRIO, the Peace Research Institute Oslo, have been invaluable in my efforts. I have enjoyed the continuous support and friendship of Stein Tønnesson, former Director of PRIO, and the continued confidence of its new Director, Kristian Berg Harpviken. I am grateful to my closest collaborator and irreplaceable managing editor of *Security Dialogue*, Marit Moe-Pryce. Valuable research assistance was also provided in particular by Jonas Gräns, Monica Hanssen, Mareile Kaufmann and Christa Waters. PRIO's uncommonly competent administrative staff gave support throughout.

I am happy to acknowledge previous use of some of the material that appears in this book. The Introduction develops ideas present in a variety of settings, some of which appear in the 'The value of security', in *Europe's 21st Century Challenge: Delivering Liberty* (Bigo, Guild, Carrera and Walker (eds), London, Ashgate). An early draft of Chapter 1 was presented in a workshop on the *Biopolitics of Value(s)* at the University of Keele in early 2010. A first sketch of Chapter 2 was presented at a conference in Rome the Military Centre for Strategic Studies (CeMiSS) in 2004, and parts of Chapter 4 were presented at a conference on *New Landscapes of Justice and Security* at the Faculty of Law, University of Oslo, in spring 2010. Chapter 7 was presented at a conference on *The Globalisation of Justice*, at the University of Zürich in 2006. Chapter 8 is an early draft of a chapter appeared as 'The ethical core of the nation-State. Zizek's contribution to the Nationalism Debate' in *Ethics,*

Nationalism and Just War: Medieval and Contemporary Perspectives (Reichberg and Syse (eds.), Washington: Catholic University Press). Chapter 9 was presented as a lecture at the Watson Institute for International Affairs, Brown University, in the spring of 2009. Parts of Chapter 10 were presented at the Theory Seminar of the Norwegian Institute for International Affairs in 2009. A slightly different version of the Chapter 11 appeared first as 'Modernity and political culture: Ulrich Beck's theory of a cosmopolitan Europe' in *United in Diversity? European Integration and Political Cultures* (Ekavi Athanassopoulou (ed.), London/New York: Tauris). Chapter 12 is an abbreviated version of an article that appeared in *Geopolitics* 14, in 2009. Chapters 13 and 14 appeared in the volume *Globaliserung der Öffentlichkeit?* (Berlin: Akademie Verlag). Finally, the book's conclusion builds on material published as 'There is no European security, only European securities', *Cooperation and Conflict*, 44(3), 309–32.

Attentive readers will notice at once that this book fits poorly into the discourses of international relations theory, security studies or security theory. This is not an accident: a philosopher by training, I am not formally schooled in any of these fields and only began to study them in 2001 when I assumed my current position at PRIO. This fact, and the style, assumptions and perspectives it engenders, may prove to be an annoyance for some, but hopefully an inspiration for others. For readers will also notice the presence of a conviction running through these pages, that security, as both concept and practice, is among the central issues of our era, a structuring quest of human experience, a social frame, and a political discourse.

Consequently, it is only consistent with this avowal that the hypotheses of this book should be set out from a position of insecurity. The risks in undertaking this book project have been many and the insecurity considerable. Bracketing for the time being the 'personal' insecurities that follow from sending these pages from me, the most significant analytical risks are those associated with conceptual re-tooling of the notions of security and insecurity that have been necessary in order to maintain a coherent account of a certain discourse of security.

Finally, this book is dedicated to my wife, Karen Lieve Ria Hostens. Convention will have it that loved ones be thanked for the sacrifices they have made for the author's scholarly ambitions. Her contribution to the book, however, has not been one of a sacrifice. Rather, it has been the constant reminder of the sacrifice that would be made by *not* completing the project under difficult circumstances and a heavy workload. Her presence in the project has been a gift of vitality and vigour, in particular when the midnight oil was burning. Nothing less would have sufficed.

Introduction

Security as *ethos* and *episteme*

Few concepts encapsulate the depth and breadth of human experience like *security*. This brave concept, noble in its aims and solemn in its aspirations, strives simultaneously to embody what we most cherish and to mobilize the means and modes of thwarting its threatened loss. Both *ethos* and *episteme*, it purports to both feel and to know, to identify the thing we cherish, to look ahead toward the danger that threatens it and to mobilize a campaign of stalwart normativity, setting out in the most scientific terms what action should be taken, what must be suffered in order to prevail and what can be sacrificed in the name of averting the threat.

Security reflects our knowledge of the past and our aspirations for the future, draws upon our experience and the experience of others. It reflects what we know while simultaneously authorizing us to delve into the unknown, legitimating action based on a certain understanding of future life. It mediates, structures and regulates forms of uncertainty that we consider increasingly inescapable, unavoidable, or inevitable in our lives. The discourse of security makes uncertainty an incessant certainty. When called upon, in the right setting, with the right reserves and humility, with the right measure of consideration for the sublime dangers on our Earth, it aspires to touch the very frontier between faith and reason. Security is called to cast itself into the metaphysics of the unknown, into implicit, and sometimes awkwardly explicit, concerns for the other-worldly.

Security as a concept is historically determined and, as such, a very young concept. Moreover, since its first widespread circulation in the mid-20th century the concept has evolved considerably. Yet even from its earliest traces, security was inseparable from religion, starting in ancient Greece and running to the superstition of the Middle Ages, to the Enlightenment philosophers and onwards (cf. Wæver, 2008). The sciences of security, from the frivolousness of the pre-modern scholarship to the challenge of probability and statistical uncertainty, to the new sciences of security management, all conceptualize insecurity as something to overcome, an experience whose time can and should be put to an end, as though security, in an anti-Hobbesian way, were itself some kind of natural state of things, the beginning and and end of humanity. Like other social-scientific frameworks the evolution of security studies has closely followed the profound changes in our physical understanding of the world. Yet the need for security insistently recurs, approaches and withdraws, the science of security, hysterically repeating the fantasy of its own end, then transforming and nearly re-tooling itself through a breakneck logic of disciplinarity, into the operations, protocols and etiquettes of social science (cf. Buzan and Hansen, 2009; Burgess, 2010b). From pragmatic to theological, the short history of security has taught us as much about ourselves, about our relation to our self-knowledge, to our values and indeed to our own being, as it has taught us about our relation to the dangers of the world. Yet if the efforts to eliminate insecurity have varied, the need to take a human, and thus ethical, attitude toward it has been unchanging. Through its brief but rapid evolution, the concept of security has sought to legitimate its scientific status, attaching itself to the social sciences and the long-standing, stalwart discipline of International Relations, latching onto the scientific traditions that provide the political sciences with their own disciplinary import and institutional anchoring.

Security knowledge

More recently, a certain engagement of security studies with risk studies has become visible, itself drawing force from a scientific tradition growing out of the actuarial sciences. The reliance of security studies on science and technology, easily adapting to both the gadget fetishism of technological security management and to less material techniques of governance, is both odd and disquieting. For the epistemological lineage of the natural sciences is organized by a straightforward logic of the *episteme*, the opposition between the unknown and the known. Science derives its rationality, but also its normative force and legitimacy, from the primacy of the known or the immediately to-be-known. And yet, security is by definition excluded from this field. For security concerns precisely what we do not know. Its entire rationality, politics and normativity revolve around just this epistemological aberration: security is by nature a relation to what is unknowable. The moment the unknowable becomes known, it ceases to be a question of security.

Scientists, political scientists among them, are notoriously poor prophets. They are merchants in knowledge of the here and now. Knowledge of the future is, to put it mildly, cut from a different cloth. This is, of course, among their charms. It is odd, then, and symptomatic of the state of our scientific – and security – culture, that we turn in reflex to the means and methods of the sciences, preferably the natural sciences, to analyze security, to cast light upon what we not only actually do not know, as it happens, but more importantly upon what-we-do-not-know as such, upon the unknowable itself, upon necessary, structural, imminent unknowability, a field charged with meaning and consequences. We are trained to appeal to science, not only for answers about what we do not know but also about the unknowable itself, not about that which, through proper analysis, will become knowable, but rather about what is *structurally unknowable*.

What do the scientists know about this? Well, nothing, to begin with. Still, we can hardly reproach them for knowing nothing about the unknown. This is only their tautological reality. However, to their credit, let us recall that knowing nothing is not the same as knowing nothing about nothing. Far from it. In the scientific canon the ordinary dialectical logic of knowledge ensures that the unknown remains discretely inscribed in the field of the known. The unknown is in this sense not *radically* unknown, but rather something to become known, something that we know we will know once the ordinary processes of scientific assessment are applied. It is like flotsam scavenged from a beach, lying on the examination table, awaiting identification. No, we don't exactly know what it is, but we are not in doubt that we will find out. All that stands between us and that knowledge is a known, practiced and, above all, institutionally legitimated process of scientific discovery. This object of 'knowledge' is also famously (known as) the 'known unknown' (cf. Daase and Kessler, 2006; Burgess, 2007b). This is the situation that makes any natural scientist itch in the fingers. The task consists not in 'discovery', in any strong sense, but rather in the controlled combinatorics of known facts, tested methods and lived experiences. By contrast, were the found object somehow radically unknown – beyond the sphere of the simply unknown-but-to-be-known – we would be unable to establish its object-ness; we would not even *see* it as an object on the examination table. We would be unaware of which properties establish its it-ness.

The structural misprision involved in Cartesian scientific enquiry is, however, that one believes that the finality of the scientific enterprise is to transform, more or less without epistemological residue, the unknown into the known. The 'nothing' that the security researcher knows about the future is, in the eyes of science-as-usual, only a temporary condition. One might even be tempted to characterize it as 'bad' knowledge (as Hegel might have put it) – faulty, defected or flawed – if only such artificial unknowns, as Kuhn argued decades ago, were not the artificial and massive support and guarantee for the existence of scientific institutions (Kuhn, 1972: 34–6). The deferral of knowledge in knowledge of the pleasure it will inevitably bring – the pleasure not being in the discovery but rather in the deferral, a kind of Freudian epistemological pleasure principle first exposed in his essay on the infant play of *fort-da* in 1920 (Freud 1961) – is not what is at issue as far as security is concerned. What is at issue is that science is ill-equipped for *not-knowing*. While science is impeccably capable of generating, manipulating, packaging and disseminating knowledge, it has no tradition for not-knowing, non-knowledge, no tradition for managing ignorance (through science) into the field of understandable, meaningful, significant, communicative, useable objects.

Security epistemology concerns knowledge that will never be knowledge, properly speaking. For inadequate knowledge is not the starting point but the very theoretical variable of security. A negative epistemology orders and regulates what can be asserted or carried out in the name of security. It is not a matter of mobilizing the security discourse *in spite of the fact* that we do not know what is to come; it is far more a matter of mobilizing *because* we do not know. Once the danger or threat that is set out by security is known, it ceases to be a matter of security, is transformed into knowledge of real existing danger, no longer merely likely or probable, but imminent, thereby transforming the foundation upon which any ethics of action is undertaken.

Security ethics

A long tradition in philosophical thinking insists on the difference between epistemology and ethics as a sub-set of the distinction between what is and what should be. The basic premise of this distinction is a metaphysical insistence on the distinction between what is and what is not, even if what is not actually exists in the form of a judgement about the future or the formulation of a normative claim. Security thinking in our time transcends this option. Security analysis, management and communication, today more than ever before, is confronted with a future that lives itself out fully and powerfully in the present. More than ever before, value judgements involved in security reasoning not only reflect our past and characterize our present, but also reach into our future, and link not to what we know as a basis for what we should do, but rather what we do not or cannot know.

We are here *not* referring to certainty *about* normative statements (for example, what it is that I should do if I acquire knowledge that I should clean the garage). We are referring to the certainty or uncertainty of knowledge itself, which itself has normative effects, but which itself mobilizes action. The force of not knowing something has, itself, enormous power, power of a kind that is more forceful than what we do know. As Taleb argues in *The Black Swan*, it is not the case, as our grandmothers told us, that 'what we don't know can't hurt us'. On the contrary, what we don't know can indeed hurt us. It forces us to act, but without a complete picture of what we are going to (Taleb, 2007). The unknown in its essence, by virtue of being unknown, is the foundation of ethics.

This is the space where ethics 'happens'; between necessity and randomness. Ethics, from a certain point of view, is nothing other than making decisions in the absence of certainty. If there were certainty about our actions, if we actually knew without doubt what to do, then this could be many things, but it would not be called ethics (Derrida, 1987). It might not even be called human. Ethics is meaningful in the world of inadequate knowledge and randomness. *This* is also the home of security studies. Yet we are not suggesting that the study of security would be served by incorporating ethics into risk analysis. The study and procurement of security *is* an ethics, from start to finish. If we define ethics, as we do in this book, as the disquieting task of making decisions under conditions of inadequate knowledge – decisions where it is the incalculable, the unforeseeable, the passionate, zealous or perhaps even apathetic, that counts; the mobile, instable or fragmented stuff of our humanness – then the ethics of uncertainty, like the epistemology of the unknown, will have to serve as its basic science.

The still expanding insurance industry butters its bread by being a security provider. Yet when insurance providers carry out assessments based on statistical profiles, likelihoods and probably backgrounds, they are not increasing security but rather eliminating the demand for it, not because the car will not crash, the chain-smoker won't contract emphysema, but rather because the negative *value* of the danger, should it exist, is henceforth reduced to zero. In the sense of determining the way it will affect human lives, the consequences will have already taken place through the calculation of an adequate compensation. In the insurance logic, the accident has already happened, (human) value assessments have already been made, actions already taken.

Yet a portion of insecurity is not assimilatable to the value calculus of security analysis. It is the part that *counts* in our lives, precisely because it *doesn't count* in the scientific calculus. It cannot be reduced to nil through analysis and planning. It cannot be pulverized. This indestructible radical insecurity is important precisely *because* it is unforeseeable and because it is this 'eventuality' that forms the only available basis for judging how we should lead our lives in the face of threat. This sense of insecurity is therefore the site of a *decision* about what we value in human terms, and therefore it is a decision about our own identity, about who we are and what we want, what is dispensable and what is indispensable.

How has the security *ethos* evolved and how is it backgrounded in the variegated and evolving field of security theory? The claim of this book is that ethics and security must be considered together. Ethics and security grow out of the same logic or discourse of humanity, in all its fears and frailties. It argues that they are both profoundly metaphysical, that they are both discourses of the unknown and they both make invisible, intangible but nonetheless meaningful reference to the human. Finally, it argues that they are both related to the deep, abiding philosophical problem of contingency, that is the question of whether the here and now is somehow necessary, whether it could have been otherwise, or maybe even not at all.

Insecurity of the subject of security

In a 1992 interview at Oxford University on the subject of human rights and the deconstruction of the subject, Derrida was asked by the interviewer, Alan Montefiore, whether he might 'reassure' those critics of deconstruction who fear that it undermines the rationality of the subject. Derrida began his reply by emphasizing:

> I'm not here to reassure anyone. [...] In order to think or to do something political, you do not have to be reassured. On the contrary, you have to be anxious and sometimes scared by the task in front of you.
>
> (Derrida, 1992c)

The experience of the subject of thought, of language, of action, is one of insecurity. To open a thought, to put pen to paper, means running the risk of getting it wrong or being misunderstood. Both the assertion of insecurity, the anchoring of securtization theory, and the very experience of insecurity, stem from a subject whose position is already insecure and at risk. The subject of security is already subsumed to the question of the security of the subject, with all the ethical consequences that this implies for the subject. Derrida, again, from one of his earliest essays:

> It is because writing is inaugural, in the fresh sense of the word, that it is dangerous and anguishing. It does not know where it is going, no knowledge can keep it from the essential precipitation toward the meaning that it constitutes and that is, primarily, its future. However, it is capricious only through cowardice. There is thus no insurance against the risk of writing.
>
> (Derrida, 1978: 11)

This insecurity of the thinking, acting, perceiving, speaking, writing subject, we argue throughout this book, is primordial in a complex and multi-level way, taking a variety of forms, projecting and countering along several trajectories and flows simultaneously.

Insecurity's *practical* dimension links it to a practice of thought, speech and action. The condition of possibility, of coherence and meaningfulness of these practices, presupposes the risk of one form or another of contingency, of the possibility of interruption, of failure, of misunderstanding, of misprision, malfunction, breakdown or even catastrophe. What would 'secure' thought actually look like without the insecurity of contingency? Secure thought, if such a thing were thinkable, would only proceed from a necessity, an absolute coherence without ambiguity, based on a presupposed unity between the thinker and the thought, between the subject of thought and its object, without variance or temporality, a necessity linking subject and object, a presupposed completeness, the thought somehow already complete, and full, total, accomplished and integrally meaningful. Such a pre-thought, pre-reasoned, pre-structured and pre-fulfilled activity of thought would not be what we would or could think of as thought. Thought, as Heidegger points out, cannot be an ordinary object of thought among others. Thinking is a kind of call from the future, a call to think about what has not yet been thought and thus will have been thought some time in the future: 'We never come to thoughts. They come to us', reads the exergue to this lecture *What Is Called Thinking* (1952) (Heidegger, 1993: 365). Security is operating as an analogy to thinking itself, profoundly linked to what is in store for us in the future. The insecurity of our time is not the security event, the catastrophe itself, though this can be corroborating factor, but the *thought* of the catastrophe, the fantasy of harm, careening toward us from the future and carrying with it the responsibility to act guided by the only ethics available, an ethics of the unknown:

> The question 'What calls for thinking? asks for what wants to be thought about in the preeminent sense: it does not just give us something to think about, nor only itself, but it first gives thought and thinking to us, it entrusts thought to us as our essential destiny, and thus first joins and appropriates us to thought.
>
> (ibid.: 391)

Thinking itself attests to an imbalance, a precariousness, a kind of ontological normativity whereby the *status quo* tends toward another state. Thinking itself is the expression of a misalignment of subject with object, a reordering of things in order to set the subject in alignment with the object. Thinking is action whose movement and meaning repose upon disparity, discrepancy, disproportion. If there is thought, it is because the subject *as such* is under duress, under pressure or stress to realign with the objective world. This is the fundamental insight of the Hegelian historical world spirit: its perpetual dissatisfaction is the normative force that presses forth the progress of universal rationality so brazenly advanced in Hegel's *Phenomenology of Spirit* (1806).

The subject is, in other words, unstable, exposed, threatened and at risk. This endangerment is not, however, to be understood as a contingent property, but rather as the subject-ness of the subject, its enabling, enhancing quality. The subject position is one of implicit anguish as an expression of this exposure. Here again, Heidegger exposes the insight through the notion of 'ecstatic temporality', the being of *Dasein* is its experience of being thrown in the face of the indifferentiatable future. In *Being and Time* (1927), he analyzes this ecstatic nature of *Dasein* from several angles, among them the 'mental state' called *fear*:

> Fear discloses something threatening, and it does so by way of everyday circumspection. A subject which merely beholds would never be able to discover anything of the sort. But if something is disclosed when one fears in the face of it, is not this disclosure a letting-something-come-towards-oneself [*ein Auf-sich-zukommenlassen*]?
>
> (Heidegger, 1962: 391)

Fear and the insecurity it generates are modes of existence in time, modes of temporality, of being-in-time. The experience of being in the present, of self-presence as subjects, is already shaken, disrupted or displaced by our existence in the future, in the face of the danger of the unknown future. This insecurity is the *Dasein* of the present.

To the status of the subject thrown into a risky and unforeseeable future can be added the dimensions of the linguistic communication and the logic of the assertion about the insecure subject of security as the subject of language. Austinian speech act theory first distinguished between felicitous and infelicitous speech acts as the basis for assessing the 'success' of speech act (Austin, 1975). In an often-cited critique of Austin, Derrida answers by putting into question the opposition between the felicitous and infelicitous speech act. The very felicitousness of the felicitous speech acts, he suggests, presupposes the unresolvable contingency of meaning. Not only are there no guarantees, he argues, but the very meaningfulness of speech – its felicitousness – depends on this contingency, this risk, this lack of guarantee, a type of linguistic insecurity (Derrida, 1982). The insecurity of the speaking subject is the condition of successful speech. In short, the possibility of a 'failed' speech act, of the message that does not arrive at its destination, or does not arrive in an understandable form to the intended addressee, is the un-removable horizon of any speech act.

What does it mean for the subject to face danger? The fundamental insecurity of the subject stems from the pragmatic character of the subject and its relation to itself as self-certainty. Any number of accounts of the western modernity will place a distinct notion of the *subject* as at its *alpha* and *omega* of human history. This tacit notion of the subject structuring the very idea of rationality, anchoring politics, and setting the premises for moral reflexion, grows out of a Cartesian philosophical universe that has thrived for centuries. The critical re-readings of Marx, Freud and Nietzsche, at the close of the 19th century, followed by many others, began to expose and analyze the assumptions of this distinctly Cartesian subject: it is rational, autonomous, sovereign, self-conscious, self-present, unified, stable and, above all, free. More recent research in gender studies, critical anthropology, and subaltern studies have added awareness that the subject, passed on through the Cartesian heritage, is also male, Eurocentric, and northern. By extension, a wide range of critical accounts of the modern subject have in the last decades emphasized the historical situation of the subject, its social and cultural setting, its politics and its inscription in a field of power.

The heritage of the Cartesian tradition transmits a conception of the subject as the subject of certainty. This subject, in its most unadulterated, most authentic form, issues from the Cartesian methodology of purification. This methodology proceeds through a systematic and uniform application of doubt, a process that powers the ejection of all properties and objects subject to doubt. The result is a subject that is certain of itself, a secure subject, for which all doubt has been purged.

Certainty, however, as we will see, is not the primary mode of security. On the contrary, it is *uncertainty* that enables, structures and regulates security. The notion of *uncertainty* occupies a remarkable position in our experience of security. It is remarkable because, even though we would most often associate it with *truth* or *facts*, it has a more complex relation to these than we might expect. Certainty is never just about the facts, never just about what is true about the world, what is in the world, etc. Certainty is always somehow different than truth, something beyond us, held by others, in a different time, in a different place. As we know, it is possible to be entirely certain and at the same time entirely wrong. Therefore, as a first conclusion, we can say that certainty is not bound by the facts, by the world, by the truth.

Why is it that risk analysts and risk managers are so concerned with certainty when it, in objective terms, is so undependable? As mentioned, the concept of certainty is closely connected to the absence of *doubt*. A perfectly certain state is one in which doubt is absent. Doubt is, in this respect, the enemy of certainty, but it is always lurking, always close by. Moreover, as we all know, doubt takes us down another road all together. It links the analysis to emotion, confidence, even spirituality or religion. Certainty implies knowledge *about* the knowledge, meta-knowledge, a way of saying that not only is what is true true, but also that my knowledge of that truth is true. Finally, certainty involves a certain conception of *perfection* in knowledge. It carries with it some aspect of completeness or wholeness. Certainty means without imperfection. Certainty is related not only to true knowledge but also to full or complete knowledge. It is knowledge that from one objective point of view or another is true, and it is not this truth or true-ness that lies at its core. Certainty has in this sense both an *outer* existence and an *inner* core.

Certainty is (most certainly) about truth, about getting it right, about knowing or saying what is true. But it is neither merely about the facts, about what or how the world is, nor about the 'subjective' experience of the world, about me and you who are interested in the facts. It hovers in an untouchable space in between these positions. Certainty is the position of embodying the danger of uncertainty in speaking, thinking, acting, etc. And yet this danger, this risk, is variable not only according to knowledge about the world, about the perils of the future and about what can be objectively undertaken to objectively forestall harm – though it is about this too – it is also about what Aristotle would call 'moral substance' of political being. It is about dealing with the *anthropos*, that irreducibly human in-between, not merely fact, not only experience. It is both a richly human experience of the danger of not knowing and the creative energy and inspiration that prepares us for that unknown danger and for the response and the human resilience that withstands the catastrophe. Yet the imagined ability to withstand catastrophe, beyond any certainty-based preparation that may be thinkable lies at the very core of what it means to be human (Burgess, 2010b).

Security is inseparable from uncertainty, yes, but from an awkwardly post-Cartesian, perhaps something more like Kantian, certainty, an experience of the close proximity between a state of the world and a state of the mind, the soul, and the person. Whether or not we find it reassuring, security situates itself at the intersection of distinct logics. These logics, or discourses, vary in time and space and along multiple and variable axes, historically determined, culturally programmed, deployed and governed across fields of social networks and relations. This conception of security status and practice presupposes a subject that somehow precedes security, to which security is a meaningful but not non-essential predicate. This book develops the hypothesis that the subject is in general always a subject of security. That by virtue of the logic of subjectivity itself, the subject – be it the subject of knowledge, of law, of morality, etc. – is already involved in a logic of security and insecurity, a logic that, if it does not indeed precede the subject, will certainly share its finality.

The return of the return of ethics

Values and subjectivity are not foreign to security studies. Something calling itself ethics has for over a decade been on the rise in the field of International Relations, the mother discipline of security studies, and a large number of works have contributed to a certain debate about the norms and codes that can and should be involved in international politics.[1]

The traditional absence of ethical reflection that preceded this movement is consistent with the predominant orientation of the field: political – and thus ethical – realism. A basic tenet of political realism is that politics supplants ethics. To assume the realist standpoint in the analysis of international relations is to adopt the posture that the political dynamics of security national interests on the international playing-field contains no moral dimensions. It is neither moral nor immoral. Instead, it is amoral (Campbell and Shapiro, 1999; Hutchings, 1992; Donnelly, 1992; McElroy, 1992). Based upon a Weberian-inspired understanding of interest in international politics, the realist and neorealist branches of IR theory have built upon the more or less coherent conclusion that differences between opposed international entities are to be resolved based upon questions of power understood as a strategic, military and technological dimension and connected to the security of a given nation-state. Indeed, international politics is considered an adept device for translating the perilous metaphysics of values – be they religious, cultural, ethnic, etc. – into the universal language of military power. In other words, the essential differences between states may derive from metaphysical value differences, but they are negotiated on the secular field of international politics.

Some ten years ago, Walker pointed out the growing canon of literature on 'ethics and international relations' (Walker, 1993: 50). 'Ethics and international relations', he suggested, is indeed a meeting place, but one where two completely heterogeneous fields of thought come together and interact in a way that does not disturb or problematize either one. 'Ethics' remains a codified set of principles and norms to be applied to any given object. 'International relations' remains a crystallized set of assumptions and methods about the make-up of the relation between two or several states. Neither is in any sense in a situation of mutation or development based upon interaction with the other. The various narratives of the one are simply applied to the narratives of the other, only to withdraw to their stable and entirely incongruous domains.

Walker responds ingeniously by questioning and re-construing the concept of international relations as something distinct from ethics, developing instead an analysis considering the degree to which claims of ethics are compatible with claims of international relations, 'the spatio-temporal articulation of political identity and community' (ibid., 1993: 51). In order to do so he proposes three innovative readings of international relations as embodiments of ethics. The first reading concerns the parallel trajectories of ethics and international relations as they emerge from similar parallel states of modernity. According to this reading, the dichotomy announced in Weber's version of modernity between instrumental rationality and value-based rationality is problematic and troublesome, though certainly not unwarranted. The second reading of the connection between ethics and international relations criticizes the identification of political sovereignty and thereby political community with conventional territoriality. The questions of ethical relations are, according to this model, inevitably framed in terms of the differentiation of political space. In his final reading, Walker questions the classical conception of international relations as a negotiation of the opposition between state and anarchy advanced in the 1970s by Hedly Bull (Bull, 1977).

These arguments are also related to, but do not address directly, the work of a small group of authors interested in articulating and exploring the notion of 'normative power Europe' (Manners, 2002; Manners and Whitman, 2003; Rosencrance, 1998; Smith, 2003). This line of thought grows out of an older argument, also by Headly Bull, about the European Union's 'civilian power' in international affairs, itself derived from François Duchêne's conception of the EU as a civilian power (Duchêne, 1972).

In its most useful form, this fledgling literature forms a set of principles about the nature of power and influence, about how international organizations and sovereign and quasi-sovereign entities exert influence on the international scene. It is about how political will is translated into impact. In its less coherent incarnations it is an attempt to conceptualize a *particular* kind of power – European power – to show that the historical, cultural and geographical *particularity* is the basis for a certain kind of power in the world, European power. The particularity of European power in this literature is based on it being inseparable from a certain cultural-moral content. It is a power that empowers a certain set of values, European values, giving them validity, strength and influence, and giving those who adopt them access to a certain civilizational substance. In one sense, this type of argumentation comes uncomfortably close to the notion of a kind of European *mission civilisatrice* – the EU's role in the world is to spread European civilization. In another sense, it misses something of the fundamentally ethical nature of security and power.

All power has an ethical underside. All power promotes implicitly a set of values, if only clandestinely. There is no act of foreign policy that does not simultaneously put forth in the world a value or set of values as an alternative – a forced alternative – to what is the case. If the point were not to change the world, to make it more compatible with the interests and values of the state or state-like entity that is acting, it would not be foreign policy, nor power. All power is normative. It belongs to the essence of a state to exert its own *alternative* values in the world, its own form of ethical being in the world. If it were not a value-alternative to other states, it would not be a state.

On the other hand, however, it is precisely the fact of this universality of values in power that leaves the normative power theory quite naked (leaving aside the anthropological problems associated with the notion of a European civilizational mission). Yes, Europe is a normative power, but it is not by virtue of being Europe. It is by virtue of exerting power. Suggesting the alternative – that Europe has no normative thrust, no influence, no impact – is to say that it is simply not a state or state-like entity (cf. Sjursen 2004).

Securitization theory and the concept of security

In the field of International Relations, the concept of security itself has been relatively invisible. Until the publication of Buzan's *People, States and Fear* in 1983, security as a concept was relatively underdeveloped. In his survey of extant literature of the moment, most of the work on security came from the field of empirical strategic studies for which 'security' was the core concept. Discussions are, by and large, limited to measuring the limits and stability of national security (Buzan, 1991: 3). Since 'security' was the tacit foundation of security studies, it was rarely problematized. More general studies on security institutions and their role in International Relations hardly scratch the surface of this central concept.

Buzan's book is a milestone in the sense that it opened the concept of security to a more penetrating analysis of the nature, structure and extension of the concept. It was also the first contribution to the increasingly sophisticated literature on the nature of security, generally taking its point of departure in a strict interpretation of security as 'military' security. The productive problematization of the concept of security has become a field unto itself. Among the most innovative contributions to understanding the concept of security are the Copenhagen School of security analysis, itself building upon and enveloping Buzan's earlier work (Buzan *et al.*, 1993, Buzan *et al.*, 1998; Wæver, 1995) and the poststructuralist critique of traditional security thought (Der Derian, 1992; Der Derian and Shapiro, 1989; Der Derian, 1987, 2001; Campbell and Shapiro, 1999; Campbell, 1998a; Campbell and Dillon, 1993; Campbell, 1993, 1998b; Connolly, 1991, Walker, 1993; Weber, 1995).

The durability and the widely productive later critique of the Copenhagen School is a testament to its validity as a theory. Its fundamental originality is double: first, and in general, it develops and systematizes the notion of security as a system of reference. According to this approach, the meaning of security lies in its formulation and communication whereby, 'the exact *definition* and *criteria* of securitization is constituted by the intersubjective establishment of an existential threat with a saliency sufficient to have substantial political effects' (Buzan *et al.*, 1998: 25). This methodology of analyzing security discourse as a set of strategies of securitization redefines the concept of security as a pragmatic *function*, as the transitive *act*, of 'securitization'. Indeed in the latter years it has become more strongly construed as a 'speech act' carried out by a 'security actor' (Buzan et al. 1998: 40) inspired by Austin's speech act theory.

The main axis for identifying the *subject* of security is fundamentally intersubjective. It is based on the movement of meaning and perception between the individual and the social setting. But the *identity* of the securitizing subject, the securitizing actor, the author speech act, lies in the very 'organizational logic' of the speech act. Securitization theory thus identifies the *locus* of the ethical subject of security in the logic of the speech act. And yet this approach is ultimately too narrow, precisely because this 'organizational logic', like the subject itself, is not neutral, not objectively given. Rather, it is itself organized and structured by the uneven relations of power implicit in the categories of individual, group, state and society. By taking the individual embedded in an organizational logic as a given, we miss the ethical nature of the subject.

Still, to reiterate the principle set out above, the ethical is not some endogenous property of the subject. On the contrary, it contributes to constituting the subject. Therefore, the speech act theory of securitization needs to be supplemented by attention to an analysis of the *subject* of security. The *actor* of security is not the same as the *subject* of security. What does their difference mean? While the speech act theory of security teaches attentiveness to the object of security and to the dynamics of reference that connect security actors with objects of securitization, a value-oriented approach underscores the multivalent nature of the security actor as an ethical subject.

The value of security and the security of values

A threat to security is implicitly linked to what has value for us. It is linked to the possibility that what we hold as valuable could disappear, be removed or destroyed. Objects of no value cannot be threatened in the same sense as those that do have value. The key to understanding threat therefore lies in understanding the systems that link human values and things. A threat is not simply an unknown danger lying in wait, ready to be launched upon us in some unknown way at some unspecified time. Threat is not incidental or accidental, or at least not entirely so. Nor is the effect of a threat independent of those targeted by it. Threat is not determined by others alone. It is co-determined by those who are under threat. It would be impossible to threaten us if we were not already projecting the catastrophe itself, and with it the dread fear, into the imminent future.

Terrorism, for example, goes well beyond targeting what has value. It aims, in addition, to produce a signal effect of meanings from the very insecurities we already possess, insecurities that lie deep within the psyche of our societies. These insecurities often have their origins in other contexts, from other historical moments. They breed and mature in the collective imagination of our culture. They have their roots in both past events, current vulnerabilities and future fears.

How are value, threat, and fear linked? The ideal terrorist act would seek to find the fit between what we value, the fear of its loss implicit in that value, and the political interests sought by those who carry out the act, though this link is never perfect or ideal. While infrastructure experts, for example, know and understand technical weaknesses in infrastructures, threat analysis must also take into account the human dimensions of loss associated with these infrastructures. This naturally includes the consideration of how our lives would be practically changed by the death of citizens or the destruction of institutions, buildings or infrastructure. However, it also includes consideration of how our lives would be changed by the fear and insecurity created by such events, and how such fear asserts control on our lives and implants insecurity into our relation to both other potential targets and other aspects of our daily existence.

In other words, it is not the disrupted trains service, or oil production, not even the poisoning of a local water supply, in themselves, that have significance for the 'terrorist'. Rather, it is the *loss of confidence* in rail service, oil production, water supply and infrastructural services in general. It is not the reality of a computer virus in itself that we have to fear, and which a terrorist might use as a tool, but rather the *fear* of the release of a virus, the presence of a kind of symbolic virus, the contagion of insecurity, that disseminates distrust and fear, both in the world of private commercial services around which society is organized, and also in terms of international trust and faith in a globalized market system. Nonetheless, it is in the meeting with these material values and the threats against them that the intangible values of the European project are validated.

There is a wide range of theories of value. Perhaps not surprisingly, the classical modern concept of *value* emerges from the experience of World War I (Joas, 2000: 34–6), though the basic questions to which it responds are formulated in the texts of Nietzsche, Freud and Marx. By opening the question of values, we are touching upon a lively and important contemporary debate originating in Nietzsche's *The Genealogy of Morals* (1887), which we deal with in Chapter 1. The classical *sociological* positions to which we refer in Chapter 12 originate in Simmel's turn-of-the-century work on the basic principles of moral science (1989) and Durkheim's sociology of values (2004) (cf. Joas 1997, Mesure 1998, Edel 1988, Kuhn 1975).

For our purposes, we wish to simply differentiate between an economics-based notion of value and a culturally or socially based notion. According to neoclassical economics the *value* of a thing is identical to the *price* it would bring in an open market. It is the worth of something relative to the other things. Historically, the debate on economic value has revolved around the degree to which things have *intrinsic* value, and such value can be added or transformed. According to more culturally or socially based conceptions of value, the value of a thing is based on the particular *quality* of the thing that makes it valuable, i.e., either principles or standards that are socially accepted or moral ideas about what is good and right.

Thus, in social terms, it is not the *materiality* of threat that determines its value to society, and thus to terrorism, it is rather the social, culturally determined *ideas* of value, historically, geographically, environmentally, and also economically determined standards and measures. It is therefore not sufficient to refer solely to material or economic measures of value when considering critical infrastructures.

The value-laden nature of security and insecurity has contributed to a fragmented evolution in European approaches to the challenge. The adaptation of European institutions to this new reality has been difficult, thwarted by the wide variations in cultures of law enforcement, border control, intelligence, diplomacy and, not least, new cultures of fear and prudence. This shift to a new security environment has at the same time brought a shift in the areas of focus of security thinking in Europe and, accordingly, a re-tooling of the roles of security institutions, the scope of their responsibilities, the European partners they work with, the international rights regimes they answer to and the source and nature of the threats they are confronting (Bigo, 2000; den Boer and Monar, 2002; Grabbe, 2000; Haack, 2006). This new continuum of internal and external security has created a novel situation whereby concepts and institutional arrangements traditionally aimed at internal security challenges (police, national and local information and administrative authorities, social agencies, etc.) become increasingly challenged to address matters traditionally reserved for the external security professionals (military and international police forces, foreign affairs officials, international legal agencies, diplomatic corps, etc.), while the latter are increasingly required to deal with matters reserved for the former.

What then is left of *Realpolitik* on a continent where wielding power is no longer simply a matter for external affairs, but is inseparable from internal affairs? How are we to understand this value-based security concept relative to the canon of objective security? What impact does the notion of 'security values' have on a deeply entrenched world of 'hard' security institutions?

The threat against Europe

It nearly goes without saying that the attacks of 11 September 2001 changed the way we understand and communicate 'security' and 'insecurity' in Europe. First, in relation to the US-led 'War on Terror', then following the Madrid bombings of March 2004 and the London bombings of July 2005, Europe has embraced a new global discourse of security. However, despite common assumptions, security has not always been a central concern for European politics. Security, which has quickly evolved to become the baseline discourse of our time, assuming an uncanny naturalness and self-evidence, is actually not naturally occurring, and its self-evidence is a call to suspicion. Like many things European, the idea of security has had a unique history in this part of the world, bound to a certain set of traditions, a distinct historical experience, and a repertoire of ideas, customs and values.

European values are widely evoked, in official EU documents, political debates and, not least, the discourse of security. And yet there is little clear consensus about the concept's content and reference. What are the values that are apparently so central to the European project? How is it that European values have evolved to play such a central support role in the constitution of the European security landscape? An essential starting point for answering these questions must lie in the EU's official self-constitution as founder and purveyor of values. But at the moment of the birth of the European Union, the threats to Europe were of a different kind than those we face today. The core issues that have marked European construction over the past 55 years have been dominated by economic concerns and largely organized by a kind of economic rationality.

Moreover, the European Union we see today was conceived and has evolved largely as a project of peace. With the horrors of the World War II freshly in mind, the founders of the European house formulated the basic idea that the only sure way to prevent future armed conflict on European soil – and, in particular, between France and Germany – was not to shelter the nations from each other, but rather to integrate them. The path to that integration was economic.

In this sense, Europe's most clear historical enemy was not some external other, most commonly embodied today by the migrant, nor an internalized external other, i.e., the non-'integrated' migrant; but rather Europe's own historical divisions. European 'security' politics in the early years of the EU's construction was formed around the 'insecurity' caused by Europe's own internal oppositions, cultural differences and historically shaped animosities. The quest for peace and security was based on a perceived need for overcoming these divisions.

Is there something distinct in European history and culture with implications for how we confront security challenges? Is there a European particularity that makes the European experience of security and insecurity singular? What indeed is 'European security'? What does it mean to say that Europe is insecure? What does it mean to say that Europe is threatened? Is it the subways, bridges and railways, nuclear plants, and other buildings that are under threat? Is it the ships and harbours, the sea-lanes from the oil-exporting Middle East that are in danger? Is it the oil and gas installations in the North Sea? Is it Europe's communications infrastructure that is exposed to attack? Is it Europe's 'borders' or its political leaders who are endangered? Or do threats concern something else, something more fundamental?

The challenge in answering these questions lies in our basic understanding of what threat is, what it means to predict it, what it means to react to it and what special challenges are brought by the new era of transnational terrorism. Security is fundamentally a question of value and the 'new' security challenges faced by Europe are not merely technological challenges of the kind we associate with improved surveillance, reinforced border protection and other kinds of fortress measures. Rather, the challenges emerge from the meeting between the human values that make European life what it is and the security technologies required to secure it.

This book

This book advances a number of perspectives revolving around two basic arguments. First, it argues that the modern subject emerges and is sustained as a function of *security* and *insecurity*. It suggests that no analytic frame can produce or reproduce the subject in some original or primordial form that does not already reproduce with it a fundamental or structural insecurity. Second, it argues that the *practice* of security can only be carried out as a certain kind of negotiation about *values*.

The development of the first argument about the *subject of security* takes place along two axes. On the one hand, it returns, through a variety of avenues, to a set of commonly held conceptions of security and insecurity as simple predicates, as contingent properties that can be attached, or not, to some more essential, more primeval, more true or real substance. On the other hand, it examines the *security of the subject,* following the traces of theoretical and applied notions of the subject itself, locating in the modern conception, a fundamental insecurity.

The study of the value function of security also follows a double approach. On the one hand, security is understood as a function of value. Thus the analyses in this book find security expressed again and again in terms of an explicit or implicit philosophy of life, articulating a certain philosophy of life, of individual and collective anxieties and aspirations, of expectations about what may be sacrificed and what is worth preserving. On the other hand, its sees values as fundamentally insecure, continuously under threat. This insecurity seems to stem from the very root of value. The complex social, cultural, and political operations that converge in the formulation of value assertions are themselves structured in terms of a threat against values, in such a way that the very essence of the value seems to be inseparable from the threat against them.

This book organizes material into three basic *approaches* to the ethical subject of security, corresponding to three main sections. The first section, *Theory of the ethical subject*, works out four components of a theory of the subject of security by developing the insights of four proto-theoreticians of security. Chapter 1 develops the relation between uncertainty, security and subjectivity in Nietzsche; Chapter 2 examines the link between the ethical and the subject in Foucault; Chapter 3 analyzes central texts of Lacan on the fundamental insecurity of the psychoanalytical subject; Chapter 4 develops Butler's concept of the precarious subject in terms of security.

The book's second section, *Holding together*, turns to the question of the self and security by examining the relationship between identity, community and security in a variety of contexts. Chapter 5 thematizises security in the identity-community nexus; Chapter 6 analyzes tolerance as a function of threat and insecurity; Chapter 7 analyzes the tensions between discourses of justice in political, legal and moral spheres; Chapter 8 analyzes Žižek's Lacanian interpretation of nationalism; Chapter 9 attempts to conceptualize 'security culture' in relation to an expanding culture of risk.

The third section, *Geopolitical rationalities of Europe*, turns to Europe's own self-understanding and its relation to a perceived landscape of geopolitical threat. Chapter 10 reviews and analyzes the range of value statements constitutive of the European political order; Chapter 11 examines Beck's theory of a cosmopolitan Europe as a historically determined reaction to the discourse of the global other; Chapter 12 takes up Schmitt's theory of the European public sphere, analyzing his concept of the European *nomos* as a re-thinking of Europe in the world; Chapter 13 revisits the European federalist movement in order explore the link between value, culture and European community; Chapter 14 examines the arguments legitimating war in the name of the European collectivity, concretely those made in the 1994 Kosovo crisis.

We should, perhaps, have avowed at the outset: this book is not *about* security. In other words, it does not take its starting point in a more or less universally recognized and recognizable notion of security in order to show, through theoretical demonstration or empirical findings, that the world as it nakedly presents itself to us is populated by objects to which the property 'security' can be ascribed or which carry out practices and procedures understood as 'security'. On the contrary, it pursues the hypothesis that the meaning of security is not only far from self-evident, but also that the moral and political force of its mobilization derives – sometimes directly and blatantly, sometimes circuitously – from its very ambiguity, instability and unpredictability. Anything more or less would simply not fill the criteria that security sets for itself.

Note

1 (Hutchings, 1992; McElroy, 1992; Crawford, 2002; Smith and Light, 2001; Seckinelgin and Shinoda, 2001; Oppenheim et al., 2001; Appadurai, 2001; Bleiker, 2001; Gasper, 2001; Sutch, 2001; Thomas, 2001; Smith, 2000; Barkan, 2000; Finkielkraut et al., 2000; Shaw, 1999; Jabri and O'Gorman, 1999; Cochran, 1999; Harbour, 1999; Hutchings, 1999; Robinson, 1999; Segesvary, 1999; Barry, 1998; Gregg, 1998; Lefever, 1998; Doyle and Ikenberry, 1997; Graham, 1997; Hurrell, 2002).

Part I

Theory of the ethical subject

1 Nietzsche, or value and the subject of security

Scholars have often analyzed Nietzsche as a kind of exit from modernity and entry into postmodernity. He provides an immensely powerful critique of the modern era, its fascination with science, with metaphysics and morality. In this sense, he is a historian of mentalities. A sharp-eyed observer of his culture and an analyst who critically documents historically anchored changes in the way we see and experience the world.

Less visible but equally important are Nietzsche's astute insights not into history and the ebb and flow of changes it brings, but also into the temporality of experience, of our relation to what *is* as a function of what *has been*. Nietzsche understands and tries to express not only the changes of human culture in time. He studies not only the difference between what is and what has been, but also digs into the far more elusive pathos of that change, the troubling and contradictory experience of what is lived through the thought of what is not, what has been, or what could be.

A certain *pathos of temporality* is thus at the core of Nietzsche's critique of values and of valuation. It is not, the regret of nihilism that is Nietzsche's primary concern – as so many read him – but rather the notion that values are inhabited, even caused, by the possibility of the exhaustion of values.

Thus, in a fragment from early 1887, Nietzsche says the following about what he considers 'the ambiguous character of our modern world':

> Feelings about values are always behind the times; they express conditions of preservation and growth that belong to times long gone by; they resist new conditions of existence with which they cannot cope and which they necessarily misunderstand: thus they inhibit and arouse suspicion against what is new.
>
> (Nietzsche, 1968: 69)

The well-rehearsed Nietzschean thesis about the decline of values in modernity – nihilism as a kind of character fault of the modern personality – builds, in effect, upon a certain evolution in the subject. The modernity of modern subjectivity is, in this sense, inseparable from its negotiation of values.

Morality and security

A first-cut approach to Nietzsche and security must be worked through and put behind us. An essential line needs to be drawn between morality and values. For Nietzsche, moral values are just one of several possible value systems. He regularly thematizes other values, such as aesthetic values, cognitive values and religious values, in addition to moral values. His well-known argument in this context is that the moral values are unrightfully given privilege relative to other values. Much of his philosophical project is dedicated to genealogically sorting through the origins of this privilege. The genealogy of morality, which is unfolded in several of Nietzsche's works, is the history of a relation to customs, traditions and a notion of significance and worth based upon repeated action in a collective setting. Morality is understood as one's obedience or sacrifice to customs whose origins are too distant to permit a clear understanding of where the essential value premises of the values might lie.

For example, in *Daybreak* (1881), he argues that:

> morality is nothing other (therefore *no more!*) than obedience to customs, of whatever kind they may be; customs, however, are the *traditional* way of behaving and evaluating'.
>
> (Nietzsche, 1997: 10)

In this sense morality is linked to a kind of determinism. It corresponds to a set of principles of predictability, of security understood as knowledge of where we are going. Morality, according to Nietzsche, provides *protection* against the unknown. Thus, in Nietzsche's reconstruction, all that is linked to the unknown has been gradually assigned a moral character. *Contingency*, the *undecided* and *undecidable*, is conceptualized through history of the West as immoral.

This sense of the moral has as a consequence a pragmatic function. It provides what Nietzsche calls 'security' agains the unknown. Knowledge, determinism, predictability and the security they bring is supplanted in human history by morality. Morality fills the gaps and provides security. Since the lack of knowledge is the human condition, its supplanting through morality is our curse and our bane.

In this, its most general form, 'morality', is, for Nietzsche, a provider of security, a protection.

> It was morality that protected life against despair and the leap into nothing, among men and classes who were violated and oppressed by *men*: for it is the experience of being powerless against men, not against nature, that generates the most desperate embitterment against exist-ence. Morality treated the violent despots, the doers of violence, the 'masters' in general as the enemies against whom the common man

must be protected, which means first of all encouraged and strengthened.

(Nietzsche, 1968: 36)

Morality, in this sense, is a means of mobilizing human energies in situations of material weakness or vulnerability. Where physical inferiority or impotence cannot be overcome by physical means, morality can be mobilized as an inner or natural superiority, attached to a deeper, more essential and thus more authentic, strength.

Much has been made of Nietzsche's nihilism as a kind of appeal to general, banal acceptance of the notion that nothing has value, and that by asserting that nothing has value, somehow values will thereby be abolished. This simplification does not hold up to a careful reading of Nietzsche's texts. It is less interesting for Nietzsche whether transcendental values exist, as is the position from which evaluation – the ascription of value and its insertion into the social, cultural and political – is made. Thus in *Human, all too Human*, he insists that: 'All judgements about the value of life have developed illogically and therefore unfairly.' This is true, he says, for four reasons.

> First, what is evaluated is never complete, its scope and boundaries, both ontologically and epistemologically, cannot be ascertained or fixed prior to the evaluation; second, and consequently because falsity in the way evaluation totalizes its object; third, because all evaluations are based on incomplete or inadequate knowledge; finally, because the standard by which we measure, 'our own being', is not an inalterable magnitude, we are subject to moods and fluctuations, and we would have to know ourselves as a fixed standard to be able justly to assess the relation between ourself and anything else whatever.
>
> (Nietzsche, 1996: 28)

This is the meaning of Nietzsche's 'nihilism': the origin or foundation of nihilism is not nihilistic. On the contrary, it is the consequence of a subjective evaluation. It is rather that all ascriptions of value, including the ascription of nihilism, are fundamentally incoherent. This is not some unfortunate empirical chance, it lies necessarily in the structure of evaluation itself: 'All evaluations are premature,' says Nietzsche, 'and must be so.' In short, Nietzsche's thesis is not an ontological claim about the existence (or even being) of values. It is far more an assertion about the ambiguity, ambivalence or incoherence of the subject position of value ascription. The position from which values are ascribed or assessed is not outside of values.

Moreover, it is not controversial to say that in Nietzsche's thought there are no objective master values, and that all effects of such values flow from one conception or another of the will to power. This is made quite clear in many of Nietzsche's texts, particularly in the fragments collected and published under the title *The Will to Power*. The logic of valuation, however, remains incompletely explored. A certain conception of security is the key to it. For Nietzsche, the critique of morality is a particular case of his critique of values. All evaluation, all practice of conceptualizing, determining and applying values, fits into the kind of genealogy Nietzsche carries out on morality. 'All evaluation,' he says, 'is made from a definite perspective: that of the preservation of the individual, a community, a race, a state, a church, a faith, a culture' (Nietzsche, 1968: 149).

Four axes of value subjectivity

For Nietzsche, value does not emerge from outside truth, being and valuation. Its movement is in complex ways co-terminous with these fundamental preoccupations of modernity and the modern subject (Sleinis, 1994). Clearly, the interdependency between security and subjectivity in the discourses of truth, being, and value will differ in nature. However, in very general terms for Nietzsche, the search for truth, for being and for morality is a search for security.[1]

In Nietzsche's reading of modernity, the subject of security is differentiated in at least four interlinked sub-positions: ontological, epistemological, aesthetic and axiological. *First*, the security of humans requires a steadfast reality, a world in which an indivisible essence is concentrated, an essence that opens and lets itself be known by human subjects, where insecurity derives not from appearances, but from real situations that may be concretely dealt with. *Second*, the modern security subject requires a stable, durable and, above all, *knowable* truth about this reality and a clear distinction between what is known and knowable, and what is unknown and unknowable. *Third*, the security of humans presupposes an appropriate bearing toward this world and knowledge about it, a clear system for orienting oneself in relation to the world and knowledge of it. *Fourth*, the play of surface and depth, appearance and reality, is the place of the frivolousness and danger of meaning. In Nietzsche's view, this four-point structure is both the anthropological necessity of humans and the illusionary veil that condemns them to ignorance and ineffectiveness (Klossowski, 1997: 58–71).

In short, for Nietzsche, the thing in itself (the Kantian heritage), the absolute stability of the world, the rational instrumentality of knowledge about the world (the Cartesian tradition) and stable values of self-orientation (the mono-theological tradition) are all the main symptoms of a disease called *insecurity*. The general metaphysics of human responses to them have the function of producing or, to use the more contemporary jargon, constructing security (cf. Deleuze, 1983: 61–5).

Security as certainty

In Nietzsche's philosophy, the concept of security is the key to an important consideration of the epistemological subject. This stems, to a large degree, from an ambivalence in the German term 'security' (*Sicherheit*). In line with the central conceptions of his time, Nietzsche most often – though certainly not always – understands and uses the word 'security' to denote what we today would call 'certainty', and the term is translated in kind. 'Security', is thus often seen to refer to an *epistemological* property, a state of knowledge held above all doubt, perfect, true, factual or objective.

At the same time, by necessity or chance, the concept of security in Nietzsche's work finds itself at historical conjuncture (Conze, 1984; Wæver, 2005). Nietzsche's work emerges approximately at the moment of a linguistic return from security as certainty, to security as a moral or spiritual dimension, denoting a relation to danger, fear, awe, etc. This is the *historical* meaning of security at the close of the 19th century, which English language translators have contributed to masking by consistently rendering *Sicherheit* (security) as 'certainty'. In general, this translation is superficially correct, but does not catch the crucial transition that I would like to argue is taking place in Nietzsche's work.

The evolution of the notion of certainty is a complex and intriguing story of its own. Common philosophical wisdom distinguishes a number of types of certainty. *Epistemological* certainty can be said to deal with the structure and character of given assertions. *Psychological* certainty refers to the strength of conviction about the truth of claims about reality, and is thus linked to epistemological certainty. *Moral* certainty also relates to the strength of conviction.

As Karl Jaspers explains in his classical reading of Nietzsche,

> scientific certainty is not security in terms of what is important. Certainty is linked to methodological knowledge, in all its determinacy and relativity. The drive for security, on the other hand, seeks on the whole, harmlessness. Not, however, says Nietzsche, against the scientific, methodological certainty, but against the whole desire for security. Certainty, says Nietzsche, is better than uncertainty and the open sea.
>
> (Jaspers, 1981: 177)

In other words, certainty easily translates as a search for security, where danger and peril are cast as the stakes of the struggle. Moreover, If there is a moral struggle, a moral drive, in Nietzsche it corresponds to the search for philosophical security, security which itself is dangerous indeed: 'The will to truth that still seduces us into taking many risks, this famous truthfulness that all philosophers so far have talked about with veneration: what questions this will to truth has already laid before us!'. (Nietzsche, 2002: 5)

Much of our reading of Nietzsche will pivot on this ambiguity. It is most often, though not exclusively, an epistemological one. Security understood as certainty of knowledge. And yet when it is values that are in question, the picture will change. Long before knowledge is in hand, in our books, journals, databases and registers, long before the material of the world out there is raised to the status of knowledge, it becomes implicated in risk, in the kind of dangers we are willing to run in order to hold, control and regulate it.

Subjectivity and security

According to Nietzsche, the instrumentalization of subjectivity in modernity results in a belief in the singularity or atomism of the subject. The subject is regarded not only as the author and intention of thought, but subjectivity is also seen as a process whereby thought is a consequence or product of thinking and whereby thought is transparently exhausted in its thinking. Nietzsche's project is in one sense to announce the decline of this conception. However, he announces it before his contemporaries have even fully understood it.

Among the many arguments, explanations and reconstructions that Nietzsche advances in his genealogy of the subject and the more or less scandalous discovery of its subversion, the most prominent assertion concerns the multiplicity or multivalence of the subject itself. In a nutshell, according to Nietzsche, the subject cannot be a singular author of thought or of predication since the subject is quite simply not singular. Thus in 1885 he observes:

> The assumption of one single subject is perhaps unnecessary; perhaps it is just as permissible to assume a multiplicity of subjects, whose interaction and struggle is the basis of our thought and consciousness in general? 'My Hypothesis: The Subject as Multiplicity'.
>
> (Nietzsche, 1968: 270)

The postulate of the multiple subject is partially built upon the observation of the multiplicity of perception, of the vast field of inputs to individual experience, impossible to generalize or universalize.

The fictitious world of subject, substance, 'reason', etc. is needed – there is in us a power to order, simplify, falsify, artificially distinguish. 'Truth' is the will to be master over the multiplicity of sensations – to classify phenomena into definite categories (ibid.: 280).

Two essential elements of Nietzsche's philosophy will grow out of this notion of multiplicity: a complex intersubjectivity, inseparable from the constitution of the subject and the unique notion of corporality. The platonic Christian tradition downplays the meaning and value of the body: the danger of the direct questioning of the subject about the subject and of all self-reflection of the spirit lies in this, that it could be useful and important for one's activity to interpret one's self falsely. That is why we question the body and reject the evidence of the sharpened senses; we try to see whether the inferior parts themselves cannot enter into communication with us (ibid.: 272).

Not only is the subject not self-originating, self-producing, autonomous, essentially an effect of action, it is also inescapably intersubjective, both proactive and reactive, relative to internal multiple voices and between subjects on a social plane.

This implies that the experience of the subject is not an endless, resistance-less flow of subjectivity, a kind of pure exteriorization of the will. Subjectivity is an experience of the bumps and bruises of the heterogeneity of internal multiplicity on a psychic level and the antagonism in its most basic form on the external, social or anthropological level.

The logical-metaphysical postulates, the belief in substance, accident, attribute, etc. derive their convincing force from our habit of regarding all our deeds as consequences of our will – so that the ego, as substance, does not vanish in the multiplicity of change.

Theory of the subject

Nietzsche's critique of modernity is inseparable from his critique of the modern subject. Indeed, his critique of modern subjectivity has been so influential that to rehearse it often seems to produce only commonplaces. Returning to Nietzsche reveals prototypes of the central ideas that we have come to associate with Foucault, Latour, Butler, Rancière and others.

In *Beyond Good and Evil* (1886), Nietzsche also identifies a crossroads in the history of the notion of the subject. Modern philosophy since Descartes, he claims, has been out to 'assassinate' the traditional notion of the soul, most commonly linked with the Platonic and Christian traditions, attacking simultaneously the very structure of predication of which it forms the foundation:

> People used to believe in 'the soul' as they believed in grammar and the grammatical subject: people said that 'I' was a condition and 'think' was a predicate and conditioned – thinking is an activity, and a subject must be thought of as its cause. Now, with admirable tenacity and cunning, people are wondering whether they can get out of this net – wondering whether the reverse might be true: that 'think' is the condition and 'I' is the conditioned.
>
> (Nietzsche, 2002: 49)

Insofar as the subject is understood as the seat of the soul, self-present and morally autonomous, with value, depth, memory and meaning, the Cartesian moment is a fundamentally antimoral and anti-Christian moment. The pre-Cartesian subject was one in which the 'I' was also the seat of the soul, origin of value in absolute terms, an instrument capable of deploying value in the world, embedding acts with value that far transcend their own instrumentality.

The modern philosophical project of epistemological scepticism, canonically associated with Descartes, becomes in its essence, according to Nietzsche, a project of amoralism, a project in which the possible relationship between subjectivity and value is fundamentally changed. The modern project understands epistemology as soul-less as value-free, as superior to axiology, to rationalities of moral value. The value substrate of knowledge is occluded and undervalued. Modernity in Nietzsche's eyes understands knowledge in general and knowledge of truth in particular as detached from spirituality and value or, at best, as having less value than what can be attributed to the pre-Cartesian subject. This subject understands the 'I' as the foyer of the soul, as the reflection of value, meaningfulness, holiness, i.e., morality, and seat of intention.

The new orientation that Nietzsche observes is a reversal of the Cartesian formula. Instead of the subject being the cause of 'the thought, thinking is now construed as the cause, and the subject is in some sense understood as the effect of thought. The subject, and therefore the soul, has now only apparent existence.

'Subject', 'object', 'attribute' – these distinctions are fabricated and are now imposed as a schematism upon all the apparent facts. The fundamental false observation is that I believe it is I who do something, suffer something, 'have' something, 'have' a quality. (Nietzsche, 1968: 294)

In short, predication itself, understood as a simple grammar of subject and predicate, is understood as false. In the mechanism of subjectivity, the subject is essentially generated together with the objects or attributes with which it is associated. Furthermore, consciousness itself follows the same course. The post-Cartesian notion of transparency and clarity, distinct categories of truth and illusion, reality and appearance, cannot, according to Nietzsche, be sustained in the light of this understanding of the modern subject. In a note from around 1887 he declares:

> That which becomes conscious is involved in causal relations which are entirely withheld from us – the sequence of thoughts, feelings, ideas in consciousness does not signify that this sequence is a causal sequence; but apparently it is so, to the highest degree. Upon this *appearance* we have founded our whole id of spirit, reason, logic, etc. (none of these exist: they are fictitious syntheses and unities), and projected these into things and behind things!
>
> (Nietzsche, 1968: 284)

Psychoanalyst *avant la lettre*, Nietzsche links the formation and mechanisms of consciousness together with the effects of the formation of the subject. He continues the same reasoning again in *Beyond Good and Evil:*

> ...a thought comes when 'it' wants, and not when 'I' want. It is, therefore, a falsification of the facts to say that the subject 'I' is the condition

of the predicate 'think.' It thinks: but to say the 'it' is just that famous old 'I' – well that is just an assumption or opinion, to put it mildly, and by no means an 'immediate certainty.' In fact, there is already too much packed into the 'it thinks': even the 'it' contains an interpretation of the process, and does not belong to the process itself.

(Nietzsche, 2002: 17)

This use of the term 'it' (*es*) presupposes the Freudian use of the same term to denote the *id* almost 25 years later. Access to the 'it', that is the source or origin of thought or action is only possible through an interpretation of signs, out of manifestations and events.

Nietzsche's theory of value

An essential and immediately provocative starting point for Nietzsche's theory of value is that there is no primacy of one type of value over another. Nietzsche's theory of value is not normative. On the contrary, it is merely descriptive.

Nietzsche's theory of value distinguishes itself by two distinct character-istics. First, it is, of course, post-transcendental, post-Christian or even atheist. It locates value not outside the individual subject but within the individual, within individual experience, within subjectivity. There are no values without valuing or valuating beings. Second, and more importantly, it is far more (though not exclusively) interested in *valuation*, in the judgements and processes by means of which objects acquire value, distribute, exchange and transform value.

Nietzsche's approach to values is ironic, deconstructive: he asks, 'What value do value's have?' In the preface to the *Genealogy of Morals*, Nietzsche explains:

> We need a critique of moral values, the value of these values should itself, for once, be examined – and so we need to know about the conditions and circumstances under which the values grew up, developed and changed (morality as result, as symptom, as mask, as tartuffery, as sickness, as misunderstanding; but also morality as cause, remedy, stimulant, inhibition, poison).
>
> (Nietzsche, 1994: 7)

In Nietzsche's theory of value, values are not objective, empirical, universal nor generalizable. There is in Nietzsche's system no natural or necessary attachment or link between subjective positions of an individual and the values they might enable or mobilize. Subjectivity or subjective responses do not produce values.

Value, for Nietzsche, is not cognitive, neither the object of thought nor the simple product of subjectivity. In general, it precedes thought, channels and orders it, but is not exhausted by it. It has effects, moral, aesthetic and intellectual, yet is not an autonomous cause.

The primary correlate of value is power. It is a condition of perception and of experience. More importantly, it is the condition of life. It is in this sense that the concept of value first communicates with a kind of fundamental security. Value as a condition of the preservation of life. Thus Nietzsche, in a note from 1887:

> The *valuation* 'I believe that this and that is so' is the essence of '*truth.*' In valuations are expressed conditions of preservation and growth. All our organs of knowledge and our senses are developed only with regard to conditions of preservation and growth. Trust in reason and its categories, in dialectic, therefore the valuation of logic, proves only their usefulness for life, proved by experience – not that something is true.
>
> (Nietzsche, 1968: 275–6)

Valuation is a relationship to meaning needed, in Nietzsche's optic, in order to preserve meaning. That the epistemological, aesthetic, religious value of a thing sets it apart as valuable is at the same time its intrusion into existence, its marking or signalling, its position in the scope of experience. Value, in this sense, sets the thing apart, thereby enclosing it in its apart-ness, protecting and preserving it. This is the primordial security function of value in Nietzsche.

'We have senses,' says Nietzsche,

> for only a selection of perceptions – those with which we have to concern ourselves in order to preserve ourselves. Consciousness is present only to the extent that consciousness is useful. It cannot be doubted that all sense perceptions are permeated with value judgements (useful and harmful – consequently, pleasant or unpleasant). Each individual color is also for us an expression of value.
>
> (Nietzsche, 1968: 275)

In what we experience, the ability to exercise a kind of phenomenological bracketing enables the meaning or the meaningfulness of the experience. Simultaneously, in an equally phenomenological movement of insecurity it provides the framing for preserving the experience. It is the boundary, the frame of the video screen that simultaneously excludes a world to include and image, protecting while threatening.

By the insecurity of the surface of things – the unsure or even fleeting meaning – we create meaning. Insecurity is the hermeneutical moment, the interpretative moment, the presence of the possibility that *this* understanding may not be the 'right' one. It is thus the risk of thinking at all, the risk of getting it wrong. Or worse, of getting it wrong and not knowing that we *are* getting it wrong.

This experience of the contingency of meaning, of the presence of misprision as danger, of hermeneutics as insecurity, happens only at the surface of things. The deeper we penetrate toward the stable and fixed, the more contingency is corralled, narrowed down, focused in to necessity. Necessity, in Nietzsche's terms, is not only not meaningful, it is not life. It is, however, secure.

> But its intelligibility, comprehensibility, practicability, and beauty begin to cease if we refine our senses; just as beauty ceases when we think about historical processes; the order of purpose is already an illusion. It suffices that the more superficially and coarsely it is conceived, the more valuable, definite, beautiful, and significant the world appears. The deeper one looks the more our valuations disappear – meaninglessness approaches.
>
> (Nietzsche, 1968: 326)

The value of the world lies in interpretations, in the confrontation with meaning as contingency. Value lies in contingency, in choice, in facticity, in insecurity.

Meaning arises when action is uncoupled from intentionality:

> From time immemorial we have ascribed the value of an action, a character, an existence, to the intention, the purpose for the sake of which one has acted or lived: this age-old idiosyncrasy finally takes a dangerous turn – provided, that is, that the absence of intention and purpose in events comes more and more to the forefront of consciousness.
>
> (Nietzsche, 1968: 351)

The value subject of security

The modern subject is thus inseparable from a certain practice of valuation, from the ascription of value, from setting standards, from assigning gradations of sense or meaning. These ascriptions and assignations are performed by the subject and yet they both precede and exceed it. They precede it in the sense that subjectivity itself stems from value predicates that distinguish the 'spirituality' of the subject from its 'materiality'. The subjectivity of subject requires the predication of its own value from an other, external, source. The valuation of the subject exceeds it in the sense that the value created or ascribed to the phenomenon grows from it, derives from it, extends its logic and core principles or mutates from them.

(This ambivalent position of the subject, somehow between being both the source of value ascriptions and the result of them, corresponds to a certain ambivalence in the very concept of 'quality'. The term refers to both the property of a thing, the distinctive characteristic that makes it identifiable relative to something else and to the standard or excellence of a thing measured against other things of a similar kind. The attribution of properties, which we would commonly think of as 'objective' or 'factual', indeed the performance of predication itself, is in this sense a valuation, an ascription, assignation or determination of value.)

Subjectivity as it is understood in our time consists in a triple movement of seeking value, affirming value, and organizing a defence against the loss of value. These three movements make up subjectivity as a movement of insecurity. The value dimension of subjectivity is the enactment of the experience of potential loss, the experience of the potential of fragility, frailty, weakness, exposure. It is the experience of *passivity*, of living in the world, and its potentially valuable properties as subject to threat, to compromise or to corruption.

The subject is thus a subject of valuation, and as such it is an enactment of the boundaries of what has value, what is valuable. For this reason the discourse of ethics cannot be 'ethical', cannot belong to the order of ethics.

The subject is not simply 'ethical', but is a kind of hub of values, a processor. The possibility of normativity – the possibility of normative judgement – cannot itself be subject to anything other than pure facticity. The value core, if we can talk of such thing, does not, cannot, belong to the subject. It has to be outside, yet attached, essential and baroque.

The critique of the exteriority of values, the critique of ethics understood as the search for the transcendental origin of values, is a recurring, even obsessional, theme in Nietzsche's work on the modern subject. It is an impossible quest, this impossible but necessary exteriority of values.

We argue above that if something called ethics can be asserted – understood as a structured moral code of values, guidelines for determining right and wrong, standards of action, etc. – then it follows that the foundation of such an ethics cannot be regulated, in a circular fashion, by those very same principles. Values are by their nature self-transcendent. Or to speak like Nietzsche, morals are 'extra-moral'. Says Nietzsche: 'We do not consider the falsity of a judgement as itself an objection to a judgement' (Nietzsche, 2002: 7).

Thus one of the building blocks of Nietzsche's 'revaluation of all values' is his deconstruction of the oppositional character of traditional value metaphysics. Values are conventionally conceived in a reference system relative to their diametral others. Nietzsche, however, lets values play out on two levels, as both truth and valuation.

Human subjectivity has been, up until his day, understood as the creation of values external to humans, justified or explained by reference to a cultural genealogy of forgetting, of habit and of utility, corresponding more or less to the position of English moral psychology at the time of Nietzsche. Thus the error of conceptualizing moral values as transcendental, the 'good' as external and normative, has been carried forward on its own. In Nietzsche's eyes, construing values in this way does not serve us well, since their coherence depends on something extra-human, something that transcends and thus diminishes humans.

This again turns us back to the unusual meaning of nihilism in Nietzsche's work. It is not in any sense an evacuation of existing values, loss of faith in their transcendental force. Rather, it is the name for the structural process by which values self-destruct, self-decay, revert and recede according to their own premises. Nihilism does not refer to the values, it refers to the experience of life that would permit an unproblematic evocation of them:

> Radical nihilism is the conviction of an absolute untenability of existence when it comes to the highest values one recognizes; plus the realization that we lack the least right to posit a beyond or an in-itself of things that might be 'divine' or morality incarnate.
>
> (Nietzsche, 1968: §3)

The basis of this realization concerns neither the status of values themselves, nor the humans who would possess them, but the nature of subjectivity itself:

> The feeling of valuelessness was reached with the realization that the overall character of existence may not be interpreted by means of the concept of 'aim,' the concept of 'unity,' or the concept of 'truth.' [...] all these values are, psychologically considered, the results of certain perspectives of utility, designed to maintain and increase human constructs of domination – and they have been falsely projected into the essence of things.
>
> (Nietzsche, 1968: 12)

Conclusion

The human sense of value is inseparable from the security of humans, and this security is, in turn, inseparable from a classically understood human search for truth. 'In valuations,' says Nietzsche,

> we express conditions of preservation and growth. All our organs of knowledge and our senses are developed only with regard to conditions of preservation and growth. Trust in reason and its categories, in dialectic, therefore the valuation of logic, proves only their usefulness for life, proved by experience – not that something is true.
>
> (1968: 275–6)

The pathos of this seemingly impossible disposition of security is arguably present in the very dramatic force of Nietzche's *Thus Spoke Zarathustra* (1883–5), which dramatizes the voyage of discovering the particular type of blindness that Nietzsche sees as the product of the search for security. This search, he suggests there, is a disingenuous search, one based on the pretext that a search for truth and knowledge about reality and the scope of authentic values can only, by necessity arrive at failure. That is, the logic of the search is already the kernel of the answer.

Zarathustra's journey towards a reinvention of humanity begins by the destruction of the 'table of values' that provides the security not only in the sense of emotional wellbeing, but also in the sense of the stability of correspondence between word, thing and truth (2006: 14). The desire for things is coupled with the desire for knowledge based on the conviction that the truth of the thing is in the thing, and the truth of the world is in the world. Those who come to Zarathustra for reassurance find only a reproach for their complicity in the lack of values inherent in values. The search for security presupposes values, puts them forward, defends them, only to discover that they are projections and that these projections become the threat itself.

Nietzsche's contribution to understanding security and insecurity in our time revolves around his systematic assertion that the modern quest for truth, authenticity and moral value is a search for security.

The security discourse draws its force from the ethos of certainty, authenticity and values. Security is not assured and insecurity does not arise through the *certain*, the *real* and the *right*. Insecurity in all its forms is generated through a sense of disruption or weakening of these three discourses.

As a consequence, the modern discourse of security – the concepts, logics, value premises and argumentative paradigms available to anyone who seeks to conceptualize security today – unavoidably touches upon three primary meta-threats: the threat to the certainty of knowledge, the threat to the stability of authentic reality relative to appearances and the threat to the coherence of values.

Thinking security today, and mobilizing social, moral, economic and political forces in its name, inevitably draws upon the available pathways and discourses surrounding the four meta-discourses evoked here. Thinking security today must start by addressing what would seem to take the form of a disruption of the default spheres of these axes of experience. Yet working through the terms of such a disruption assumes that they were ever stable. Nietzsche's work bears witness to the sense that this assumption is not only dubious, but also life-affirmingly dubious. Thus we are not talking about a fall from the True, the Real, the Right and the Beautiful. If we were, according to Nietzsche, life would have little to live for. What is observable, however, is a double movement clinging to them through a *return* itself inspired and driven by the a sense of irrevocable *loss* of security reference.

From a certain point of view this argument may be less audacious than at first sight. It is, to be sure, inspired by a certain kind of analytical posture advanced some time ago in the field of discourse theory by pioneer thinkers like Foucault (1971, 1973), Bourdieu (1990, 1991, 1998), Lyotard (1984) or Laclau and Mouffe (1985). And yet the historical rise of the discourse of security underscores the continued relevance of these approaches.

Our readings suggest that the subject becomes the subject of security in the moment an object is discerned and its value as object is claimed, asserted or projected. Object valuation, the act of assigning reference to the transcendent source of value, is always a gesture directed toward the peril of insecurity apparently implicit, embedded in the very experience of subjectivity itself.

The subject position of value judgements is always occulted from the source or origin of value. This occultness is the guarantee for the meaningfulness and, the value, in absolute terms, of the value. The value misfit between value subject and value object, the impossibility of the subject, completely accounting for the value of an object, is in Nietzsche's eyes, the guarantee of meaning.

'No experience of another person,' says Nietzsche in *Human, all too Human*, 'however close he is to us, can be so complete that we would have a logical right to evaluate him *in* toto' (1996: 28). The impossibility of objective value assessments applies to the subject as well, to self-knowledge. And yet humans are driven to this need for value assessment, for valuation. This ambivalence inherent in value subjectivity, the necessary occultness of the origin and the blind spot in the subject's gaze upon the world are necessities. The value ambivalence, the contentiousness or antagonism of values lies at the core, if one might speak of a core, of the human subject. In *Human, all too Human*, Nietzsche reminds us:

> Among the things that can reduce a thinker to despair is the knowledge that the illogical is a necessity for mankind and that much good proceeds from the illogical. It is implanted so firmly in the passions, in language, in art, in religion, and in general in everything that lends value to life, that one cannot pull it out of these fair things without mortally injuring them.
>
> (Nietzsche, 1996: 28)

Note

1   In view of the breadth of Nietzsche's thematization of the concept of security, it is notable that so few within the field of security theory or security studies have taken up the question. The oft-cited exception is Der Derian's 1995 essay 'The Value of Security', which builds on Deleuze's remarkable *Nietzsche and Philosophy* (Deleuze, 1983), and a very few other adjacent analyses in the theory of security (Burke, 2002; Dillon, 1992, 1996; Williams, 1998). In his essay, Der Derian focuses mainly on the notion of security as a correlate of sovereignty in a comparative 'genealogy' starting from Hobbes.

2 Foucault, or genealogy of the ethical subject

As we have seen, the Nietzschean theory of the subject situates subjectivity within a constellation of power and value. Taking on the position of subject of knowledge, experience, politics, law, etc. implies situating oneself within a complex of power relations in which subjectivity is a practice of exercising power, channelling and repositioning it, and an assignment of social, cultural, political and moral values. Already in Foucault's early work on the history of madness from 1961 (Foucault, 1989: 25), and on the birth of the clinic from 1963 (Foucault, 2003a) we can clearly detect the Nietzschean imprint upon the theses about the subject as an effect of power, its theoretical development and its traces in the archival discoveries of his historical empirical research.

In this chapter we will examine three fundamental conceptual insights from Foucault's thought of particular relevance for our theory of the ethical subject of security. They stem from three general Foucaultian genealogies of the subject in general. The *first* concerns the general historicity of the subject. By this we mean the historical variation in the way both the subject is perceived and understood, by itself and by others, as holder and purveyor of truth. The *second* concerns the evolution in the way power regulates the terms under which the subject constitutes itself as subject. This is the specific genealogy we have been considering so far in our analysis of Nietzsche. The *third* genealogy, in some ways the conjunction of the first two, regards the evolution of the subject as the seat of the ethical, the centre of the correlation of values and the position from which ethical judgement is translated into action.

Historicity of the subject of security

What is the subject of security? What does it mean to say that a subject is both the effect and transmitter of values that are inseparable from its own security? Had Michel Foucault (1926–84) lived to know the securitization theory so widely discussed within international relations theory, he would perhaps agree that a securitizing actor is the subject of its securitizing speech acts. At the same time there is reason to suggest that he would also have insisted that the environment in which the securitizing actor acts is more complex, multi-layered and composite than theorized by the speech act theory of security. The lacuna in the speech act theory revealed by a Foucault-inspired history of subjectivity is that, while the actor of the speech act is characterized by its ability to deploy power – military, social, economic, environmental, etc. – in the name of the security of its object referent, that actor is itself the effect or product of power and the result of its own ethical constitution.

Foucault's project of a genealogy of the subject is in many ways a return to the traditional philosophical question: 'What is thinking?' The assumptions upon which this question rests are perhaps far from uniquely self-evident as a rigorous philosophical starting point. The question itself assumes that thinking is a structural association between subject and object. The *subject*, according to this assumption, is the position from which thought is emitted, assertions are enunciated, law is adjudicated, political power is legitimated and moral value is ascribed. The *object* is structurally positioned as the addressee, referent, beneficiary, adjudicated, judged, served, etc. The logic of the transfer of meaning is linear, etiological and metaphysically homomorphic.[1]

Foucault's approach to the question of knowledge takes this subject–object axis as its own starting point, then focuses on an interrogation of the conditions of possibility of subjectivity itself. He does so by asking what the conditions of a possible relation between the subject of thought and the object of thought actually are. In his self-presentation, 'Foucault', from the 1980s, Foucault describes his understanding of what thinking is, starting from a critique of an associational or correspondence theory of knowledge, where thought is defined or understood as the association or correspondence between subject and object.

> If what is meant by thought is the act that posits a subject and an object, along with their various possible relations, a critical history of thought would be an analysis of the conditions under which certain relations of subject to object are formed or modified, insofar as those relations constitute a possible knowledge. It is not a matter of defining the formal conditions of a relationship to the object; nor is it a matter of isolating the empirical conditions that may, at a given moment, have enabled the subject in general to become acquainted with an object already given in reality. The question is to determine what the subject must be, to what conditions it is submitted, what statute it should have, what position it should occupy in the real or the imaginary in order to become a legitimate subject of any given knowledge.
>
> (Foucault, 1999: 459–60)

The associational theory of knowledge would have it that the conditions of thinking are themselves subject only to the rules, categories and specifications of thinking. Foucault's position is that the subject–object association at the heart of conceptualization is itself subject to extra-conceptual, extra-intellectual strictures. It is less a matter of what the conceptual terms of association are than the political terms. The question of legitimate and illegitimate associations, authorized and unauthorized, acceptable and unacceptable subject positions, is the object of Foucault's project. It is, as Foucault puts it, a matter of determining the mode of 'subjugation' of the subject as a function of the categorical placement (genre or type of text, object of the text), but also the conditions under which the object is assigned its status as object of 'possible knowledge', the procedures by which it is selected, the criteria of relevance and appropriateness, and the implicit or explicit assessments of its knowability. In short, the study of the formation of knowledge, of determining the act of knowing, is also a study of the conditions of 'objectivation' and the conditions under which this varies (Foucault, 1999: 460).

Taking account of both a certain process of 'subjectivation' and a process of 'objectivation' are necessary but not adequate to understanding the 'politics of truth' that underwrite both the history of knowledge and the history of 'knowledge' (that is, the history of the concept of knowledge). The history of the subject is the history of its experience of itself as subject. Experience – be it the experience of insecurity and security – must also be understood in a relatively broad sense as 'the correlation, in a culture, between domains of knowledge, types of normativity and forms of subjectivity' (Foucault, 1994b: 540). An understanding of the politics of their interconection, their 'games of truth', as he puts it, is essential. It is not about the story of truth but the story of the story of truth:

> It is the history of 'veridictions,' understood as the forms according to which discourses capable of being declared true or false are articulated concerning a domain of things. What the conditions of this emergence were, the price that was paid for it, so to speak, its effects on reality and the way in which, linking a certain type of object to certain modalities of the subject, it constituted the historical *a priori* of a possible experience for a period of time, an area and for given individuals.
>
> (Foucault, 1999: 460)

The history of verdictions is the history of the forms, conditions, limitations, provisions, stipulations and suppositions under which 'truth' can be generated and accepted as truth in particular social settings. In the wake of Foucault's insight we might also suggest a derivative history of the forms and conditions under which the 'truth' of security (and insecurity) can be exerienced, assessed and made actionable as function of the interconnection of security 'subjectivation' and security 'objectivation'. A history of *securidiction* would plot the evolution, emergence and disappearence of discourses assumed to be capable of generating 'true' statements about security: *security truth*.

Truth in Foucault's terms can, of course, not be regarded as a refined or pure status, timeless and placeless. It is co-determined by power. In his 1975–6 lectures at the Collège de France, Foucault examines the relation between the subject as position of truth, and the power that structures and organizes that status.

> In a society such as ours – or in any society, come to that – multiple relations of power traverse, characterize, and constitute the social body; they are indissociable from a discourse of truth, and they can neither be established nor function unless a true discourse is produced, accumulated, put into circulation, and set to work. Power cannot be exercised unless a certain economy of discourses of truth functions in, on the basis of, and thanks to, that power.
>
> (Foucault, 2003b: 24)

In Foucault's analysis, truth and power exist in a reciprocal dependency. Like truth, power is not pure or refined, stemming from a kind of singular force and flowing from power holder to another. On the one hand, thus, power demands truth, just as truth demands power. Power requires a discourse of power, accepted as truthful, in order to maintain its status as power. Power is not idle but 'institutionalizes the search for truth'. Power makes truth into a matter of production. The effect of power on the subject is to interrogate, to open up and question, to intrude and to insist. Foucault understands these functions as the production of truth through the reaches of power. On the other hand, the discourse of truth has a certain power over us. We are subjected to the power of the discourse of truth. Truth does not only describe what is true but prescribes what *shall* be true. The power of the discourse of truth penetrates every aspect of our daily lives: 'We are judged, condemned, forced to perform tasks, and destined to live and die in certain ways by discourses that are true, and which bring with them specific power-effects' (Foucault, 2003b: 25).

Few would doubt that 'security truth', the truth of security, the subject of security knowing itself as secure, is an immensely powerful discourse of truth in just the sense that Foucault is suggesting. Moreover, such an approach would to some extent plot onto, but not have the same function as, a history of securization. As suggested in our introduction, both the subject position from which Copenhagen School securitization is operated and the conditions under which an object is fixed as threatened, are fixed along a number of axes by the theory, though more recent critical studies of securitization are continually bringing more nuance to the theory (Balzacq, 2005, 2010; Stritzel, 2007). The speech act theory of security, like Austinian speech act theory writ large, takes the subject of speech as given, bracketing the question of its genealogy, or the conditions and under which it can coherently can be said to purvey truth, and the frame within which it understands itself as telling the truth about security. In short, it suspends the question of the subjectivity of the securitizing subject, in particular in relation to the power that constitutes it and in its relation to itself.

Power of the state and the subject of security

It is well known that Foucault draws our attention to the way that power circulates in all aspects of our lives. Less discussed in the literature on Foucault is the fact that he in particular draws our attention to the way that power also circulates in our conceptualizations of power. Parallel to the re-insertion of power in the analysis of the subject of security, Foucault gives us the means to understand the implicit ethical nature of the subject in general and the subject of security in particular. Whereas Kant opened our eyes to the relation between rationality and power, Foucault makes possible the insight that the organizational logic of securitization is, by its very rationality, already caught up in a power struggle. For Foucault, the essential questions of the subject proceed from the determinations of power, knowledge and ethics. It is a question that concerns implicitly and explicitly all theories of international relations: What is then power?

Cleary, this question of power is operative in virtually all of Foucault's writing. In his late work, however, he begins to engage a more direct analysis of the notion of power in terms of the history of the institutions that make up the modern state. In the first volume of *The History of Sexuality: The Will to Knowledge* (1976) Foucault describes how he understands power as resisting common political institutions, in particular those that characterize more or less completely the concept of power used by International Relations theory. Power, he suggests, should not simply be understood as the institutionalized rules that are commonly called state power. Nor should it be understood as a systematized domination of one group against another. For this reason one must not begin, as do the vast majority of theories of International Relations, by postulating the state or the general juridical 'forms of law' or 'general domination' as the basis for the analysis of power (Foucault, 1981: 92). Instead, power should be understood as:

> the multiplicity of force relations immanent in the sphere in which they operate and which constitute their own organization; as the process which, through ceaseless struggles and confrontations, transforms, strengthens, or reverses them; as the support which these force relations find in one another, thus forming a chain or a system, or on the contrary, the disjunctions and contradictions which isolate them from one another; and lastly, as the strategies in which they take effect, whose general design or institutional crystallization is embodied in the state apparatus, in the formulation of the law, in the various social hegemonies.

> (Foucault, 1981: 92–3)

According to Foucault, it makes no sense to search for the key to power in a central, sovereign anchoring point, one which organizes some hegemonic set of sub-powers. There is no radiating centre of power, which could be seized and analyzed. There is no base of power; or rather the base is a moving set of relations, from which emerge local, heterogeneous, indefinite powers. Power is everywhere. It is not that it encompasses everything. It is that it comes from everywhere. And 'the' power, in the sense that it is permanent, repetitive, inert, self-producing, is merely the effect of the ensemble (ibid.: 93). In Foucault's eyes, power thus resists all forms of categorization, compartmentalization, instrumentalization, institutional-ization, etc. Power is not a thing, nor a substance. It is a matrix of domination. It is not something that can simply be seized or taken, shared and transmitted along the channels of objective communication.

More importantly for the question of security and the subject of security, power is never exterior to other forms of relations, not even to those that are customarily taken as the objects of the social, human and political sciences. Where international relations most commonly conceptualized power as a quantifiable good, discretely transferable from one subject that possesses it – be it a citizen, a sovereign, an institution, a state, etc. – to another subject that does not. Power for Foucault does not respect this simple arithmetic. Power, in other words, is intrinsic to economic processes, to knowledge, to social and cultural associations and to sexual relations. Such institutionalized objects of study, of cognition or of understanding, are, according to Foucault, already effects of power. The conundrum of the subject is that power precedes both its experience of the world and of itself. Power is dispersed, has no unique or singular source. Indeed the opposition between oppressor and oppressed in a traditional schema of political violence is, in Foucault's optic, a false one, since power cannot simply be directed from one position to another. Instead, multiple relations of force form and play themselves out in different mechanisms of production, in families, groups, and cultural organizations. Power relations can thus never be entirely intentional, never entirely objective.

Foucault takes up this critique of traditional political theory of interna-tional relations in the *Society Must Be Defended* lectures, in the same sequence where he theorizes the reciprocal relation between power and truth. In his 'Résumé' of the lectures, Foucault poses the central question of his teaching and research of that year. In many ways it can be viewed as the basic question of the field of International Relations:

> How has war (and its different aspects, invasion, battle, conquest, victory, relations of victors to vanquished, pillage and appropriation, upheavals) been used as an analyzer of history and, in a general way, of social relations?
>
> (Foucault, 2003b: 207)

The red thread of the analysis of *Society Must Be Defended* is a questioning of the conventional notion of what he calls the juridical model of sovereignty. The implicit assumption of this model is canonical and well-rehearsed: the individual is regarded as the subject of natural rights and a primitive empowerment. This basic power is the seed of the power of the modern state such as it is conceived in the Renaissance. According to this classic concept, the state is the repository of law and law is the fundamental manifestation of law. Standard analyses and histories of the state take the concept of power as a given. Foucault's project is to open the concept of power, to explore and draw out the consequences of its many facets, layers and aspects. Foucault's genealogy of the state thus takes up the analysis of the tacit relationship between power and the subject outlined above:

> We should be trying to study power, not on the basis of the primitive terms of the relationship, but on the basis of the relationship itself, to the extent that it is the relationship that determines the elements on which it bears: rather than asking ideal subjects what part of themselves or their powers they have surrendered in order to let themselves become subjects, we have to look at how relations of subjugation can manufacture subjects.
>
> (ibid.: 265)

This way of analyzing the state is in conformity with Foucault's general strategy for studying the subject and subjectivity in general. The political subject of the state is not taken as an *a priori*. Rather the subject is seen as an effect of an effect of power, a by-product of the relations of power. Power always precedes the subject. Power is never simply a creation of the political subject, much less its political instrument. There has never been a power-free subject that served as the origin of power, the creator or even the first user of power. However, just such a conception of the state dominates political history and political philosophy, exemplified by the Hobbesian model of state sovereignty. It is Foucault's intention, in *Society Must Be Defended*, to retell the history of the state in terms of the history of the subject.

In Foucault's eyes, political history and political philosophy are centred upon a presumed identity between sovereignty and power. This theoretical assumption dates from the Middles Ages when, in western societies, the development of legal thought was naturally attached to the monarch. By the same token, power is essentially royal power. This constellation of power, law and monarchy was, according to Foucault, the consequence of the 'reactivation of Roman law' in the mid-Middle Ages (Foucault, 2003b: 34). Accordingly, legal theory has, since that time, had one central aim, namely to secure the legitimacy of power. Law and sovereignty work at the service of each other. Theory of law works out the theoretical legitimacy of the state and, inversely, the sovereign legitimates legal theory. The consequence is a kind of categorical stronghold or paradigm: the only legitimate form of legal reflection is that which reduces all forms of force or domination to the logic of sovereign power, either in terms of sustenance of the *status quo* or in its contention. Consequentially, all forms of domination are inevitably reduced to one form or another of sovereign power. As we shall see, it is precisely Foucault's project to separate these two domains in the aim of reconceptualizing power.

The recurring 'source' of the notion of sovereignty in political theory is, of course, the *leviathan*. The theoretical motif of the Hobbesian state, which has essentially dominated political realism to this day, envisages the sovereign as an idealized concentration of power equated with legitimacy. Through the philosophical support of juridical systems of the type just mentioned, all power, and all conceptions of power, are conceived as referents of the sovereign. All power is channelled into a closed economy with the sovereign, either flowing to it or from it. Foucault's project resists this closed and bi-directional model of power. The 'body', of which leviathan represents the concentration, is, according to Foucault's reading, a polymorphic composite of power that does not flow in linear ways through the state. Rather, it circulates through and around different groups and individuals, not simply aligning them with the sovereign's logic of unified power. As Foucault puts it, 'Power transits through individuals. It is not applied to them' (ibid.: 29).

According to the theory of sovereignty that dominates the western history of the political subject, the subject of sovereignty – and thereby the subject of security – is part of a cycle of subjectivity. A political subject is, in line with the norms and values of the European Renaissance and the European Enlightenment, an individual who is naturally endowed with certain rights and principles, yet these rights and principles are only coherently under-standable within the framework of power linked to the unified sovereign. The state, in turn, is organized as a vast multiplicity of political powers. Such powers are, however, not properly political, but rather what Foucault calls 'capacities, possibilities, and authorities', all integrated as moments in the general unity of power. This unity takes the form of the sovereignty within the original framework of legitimacy. The constitutions of the political subject is therefore a kind of cycle: from sovereign subject to individual subject, all as part of one and the same legitimization of law and legalization of power. This cycle itself is considered by Foucault as 'primitive'. It seems impossible to conceive of any organization of power that precedes it, that is more fundamental or more original.

Oddly enough, Foucault's opposition to the Hobbesian model is not based on a theoretical reasoning, but rather on an empirical assessment. In his archival work, Foucault uncovers a fundamental political sub-culture in the late 17th and early 18th centuries, what he calls a 'new mechanics of power' (ibid.: 15), featuring a social organization, which circumvents the traditional conception of sovereignty. While this is not the place to present this material, it makes for extraordinary reading, suggesting that Foucault's theory of subjectivity is based on a largely empirical demonstration of the failure of the Hobbesian model of sovereignty. Foucault is clearly of the conviction that this conception of power and subjectivity is incorrect. However, the remarkable rigour of his project lies in the fact that he uncovers a mutation in the conventional model that would ordinarily empirically disprove the theory of sovereignty:

> In short, we have to abandon the model of Leviathan, that model of an artificial man who is at once an automaton, a fabricated man, but also a unitary man who contains all real individuals, whose body is made up of citizens but whose soul is sovereignty. We have to study power outside the model of Leviathan, outside the field delineated by juridical sovereignty and the institution of the State. We have to analyze it by beginning with the techniques and tactics of domination. That, I think, is the method-ological line we have to follow, and which I have tried to follow in the different research projects we have undertaken in previous years on psychiatric power, infantile sexuality, the punitive system, and so on.
>
> (ibid.: 34)

Security and the ethical

The first volume of Foucault's planned four-volume *History of Sexuality* appeared in 1976, the same year as the lectures *Society Must Be Protected*. The second and third volumes appeared only in 1984, just prior to his death (Foucault, 1981). The fourth planned volume, *Avowals of the Flesh*, was never published. The *History of Sexuality*, is, of course, only tangentially concerned with sexuality in a behavioural sense, taking up instead the thread of his work on the history of the subject. It thus continues to build upon an analytic framework set out in Foucault's understanding of the subject of psychiatry and medical practice in the *History of Madness* (1961) and the *Birth of the Clinic* (1963), the subject of the human sciences in *The Order of Things* (1966) and *The Archaeology of Knowledge* (1969) and of the subject of disciplinary practices in *Discipline and Punish* (1975). As he notes in the opening pages of the second volume of the *History of Sexuality: The Uses of Pleasure:*

> ...to speak of 'sexuality' as a historically singular experience also presupposed the availability of tools capable of analyzing the peculiar characteristics and interrelations of the three axes that constitute it: (1) the formation of sciences [*savoirs*] that refer to it, (2) the systems of power that regulate its practice, (3) the forms within which individuals are able, are obliged, to recognize themselves as subjects of this sexuality.
>
> (Foucault, 1981: 4)

The tools for understanding the first two fields having been developed in his work on medicine and psychiatry, the second in his work on the systems of power that regulate the subject and its discourses, Foucault now turns to the way that subjects of sexuality recognize and understand themselves. This takes place at a time when gender studies was only just a vague notion, when the concepts and approaches to the study of discourse and sexuality were all but inexistent. Indeed, it was Foucault who, in many ways, paved the way for the analysis of gender familiar to us today.

> ... when I came to study the modes according to which individuals are given to recognize themselves as sexual subjects, the problems were much greater. At the time the notion of desire, or of the desiring subject, constituted if not a theory, then at least a generally accepted theoretical theme.
> [...]
> Thus, in order to understand how the modern individual could experience himself as a subject of a 'sexuality', it was essential first to determine how, for centuries, Western man has been brought to recognize himself as a subject of desire.
>
> (Foucault, 1981: 4, 5)

Understanding the subject's relation to sexuality is, even more than for the other disciplines and categories Foucault studied, a matter of the subject's relation to itself. To study the regulation of the subject of sexuality is to examine the available means of self-knowledge, self-presence and, to borrow the title of the third of volume of the *History of Sexuality*, the 'care of self'. This reflexive posture at the heart of sexuality is the centre of what Foucault methodologically calls 'ethics'. In this sense, Foucault's work on sexuality will allow us to ask the question of degree to which the subject of security relates to itself reflexively and the degree to which this reflexivity regulates the core question of the ethical itself. What are the procedures by which the subject can observe, analyze and understand itself? (Foucault, 1999: 459). As he clarified in 1981, when asked in an interview whether his *History of Sexuality* contained an 'ethical concern':

> If you mean by ethics a code that would tell us how to act, then of course *The History of Sexuality* is not an ethics. But if by ethics you mean the relationship you have to yourself when you act, then I would say that it intends to be an ethics, or at least to show what could be an ethics of sexual behavior. It would be one that would not be dominated by the problem of the deep truth of the reality of our sex life. The relationship that I think we need to have with ourselves when we have sex is an ethics of pleasure, of intensification of pleasure.
>
> (Foucault, 1997a: 131)

Foucault thus distinguishes between an ethics in terms of moral codes and an ethics in terms of the action people undertake in the name of moral codes. Such action and the positive or negative valence they are assigned to and network to, the constellation of premises and implications they presuppose or draw upon, are arranged and ordered according to determined discursive logics. These logics are both external moral codes and yet implicit in the way that such codes are brought to both make sense in the world and mobilize action through an array of logics of normativity.

> It is the relation to oneself that I find moral and which determines how the individual must constitute itself as a moral subject of his or her own actions. [...] I am writing a genealogy of ethics. The genealogy of the subject as subject of ethical actions or a genealogy of desire as an ethical problem.
>
> (Foucault, 1994a: 394, 397)

When we say 'ethical subject' we are thus not referring to a traditional system of morality, ready-made norms and principles of right and wrong, suited for application to any arbitrary situation. Foucault differentiates between ethics understood as the deployment of moral codes and rules, which are imposed externally, and the attitude one has toward oneself. It is the relation to one's self that determines the ethical nature of the subject.[2]

According to Foucault, the ethical nature of the subject is historically a key to its relation to truth about the world. Through the *History of Sexuality*, not only behaviour itself but also *access* to experience and knowledge, ethically determined. To be immoral was implicitly understood as a hindrance to true experience and true knowledge. Before Descartes, one could not be impure or immoral and possess truth about the world. Descartes' contribution was to demonstrate that immorality was not relevant, that the ethical nature of the subject – the relation to self in view of moral norms – did not determine knowledge. The rationality of proof was sufficient (ibid.: 410). This rational proof, however, remained a phenomenological one, an individual experience of rationality. Kant took the ethical subject further, postulating a kind of universal subject, defining knowledge as a universal aspect of rationality, detached from ethical consideration.

Foucault develops his thinking on the ethical nature of the subject toward the end of his life, in his lectures and writings surrounding the publication of the second and third volumes of the *History of Sexuality*.[3]

> The word of the Delphic oracle: 'Know thyself' is, despite its force in traditional histories of philosophy, not the real guiding key to Western self-consciousness. The more relevant question is not how to know oneself, but rather what to do with oneself, what actions are relevant in order to maintains one's identity.
>
> (Foucault, 1997: 87)

It is not the fact that one violates or obeys an ethical principle that constitutes the ethical subject, it is one's relation to one's self that is ethical. This ambiguity lies closer to the surface in the term 'ethics' (*'la morale'*). By 'ethics' we understand, on the one hand, a set of values and rules of action given to individuals or a group by different kinds of prescriptive mechanisms like the family, schools, the Church. On the other hand, however, we understand the actual behaviour or reaction of individuals or groups to the values and rules given. Foucault continues:

> We are thus designating the way in which [individuals] submit more or less completely to a principle of behaviour, according to which they obey or resist an interdiction or a prescription, according to which they respect or neglect a set of values. The study of this aspect of ethics must determine how and with which margins of variation or transgression, individuals or groups behave in reference to a prescriptive system that is explicitly or implicitly given in their culture and of which they are more or less clearly conscious.
>
> (Foucault, 1994b: 555–6 (my translation))

In Foucault's understanding of the ethical and the subject, the ethical subject constitutes itself not by precisely carrying out the code of conduct prescribed by one authority or another. The subject constitutes itself, becomes itself, through its reaction to the code of conduct, through its particular adhesion, partial resistance, variation and mutation. Given a code of conduct, there is clearly a multiplicity of possible ethical reactions to it, a multiplicity of modes of ethically experiencing it, through sympathy, aversion, etc. Foucault calls these differences the 'determination of ethical substance', that is, 'the way in which the individual constitutes one part or another of itself as the basis, as the 'raw material', of its ethical conduct (ibid.: 556).

This range of differences also determines the 'mode of subjugation' of the ethical subject. The degree of harmonization between the code and the subject is the measure of the dimension of power necessarily in place in order to subjugate the subject. It is the measure of the resistance of the subject to conformity to the code, the degree of contrariety to the will, collective or individual, of the subject. It is thus, in this sense, also the measure of the 'ethical labour' the subject is forced to perform on itself in order to render its conduct in conformity with the code (Foucault, 1994b: 556–7).

Lastly, this difference, this space of variation between a given set of codes or values, concerns what Foucault calls the 'teleology of the moral subject'. Any given ethically determined act may seem singular, but it is, in effect, inserted into the ensemble of values and rules that constitute the code. A single ethically determined act is also an element in the evolution of the ethical code. It marks the continuity and durée of the ethical subject. It tends toward its own fulfilment in the sense that through its fulfilment the constitution of the ethical conduct, which leads the subject to behave in one way or another, also contributes to the future determination of the essence of that subject – to its always new constitution (ibid.: 557).

While the speech act theory of security teaches attentiveness to the object of security and to the dynamics of reference that connect security actors with objects of securitization, the Foucault-inspired approach underscores the multivalent nature of the security actor as an ethical subject.

The approach to security has thus been widened along two axes, adapted from Foucault's history of the subject: *power* and the *ethical*.

The analysis of the subject of security in terms of *power* shows that the security subject is not a simple agent of power, that power is not simply an instrument of the subject. The subject of security is already the effect of power, already involved in a flux over power, which precedes it and determines it even while it is trying to manipulate the field of power for its own protection. This understanding of the subject of security rejects the notion of state sovereignty as the fundamental category of security concerns. There is little innovation in the claim that the sovereign state, as the most relevant object of security, has been weakened.

The analysis of the subject of security in terms of the *ethical* has confirmed the relevance of ethics to security studies, but in an unexpected manner. By innovating the understanding of the concept of ethics according to the model proposed by Foucault, we can see that there was never a question that the 'new ethics' in international relations is only 'new' if one accepts the notion that they were never intrinsically related. Yet we have suggested that the ethical is deeply constitutive of the subject in general and the subject of security in particular. Understanding the ethical subject of security as a function that resists fixed categories of ethics and power in an age when these categories are more complex than ever helps us to gain a clearer picture of the dynamics of security in our age.

Notes

1 We recall Deleuze and Guattari's critique of these assumptions (Deleuze and Guattari, 1994: 85).
2 This ethical 'attitude' translates Heidegger's concept of *Befindlichkeit* in our analysis of the relationship between time, fear and security (Burgess, 2011).
3 Foucault's 1981–2 lectures at the Collège de France, re-edited as *The Hermeneutics of the Subject*, develop the same themes, as does the planned general introduction to the three final volumes of the *History of Sexuality* (including the unfinished *Avowals of the Flesh*), 'The Use of Pleasure and the Techniques of the Self' (Foucault, M. (1994b).

3 Lacan, or the ethical subject of the *real*

In a 2008 lecture entitled 'Beyond the False Promises of Security', Jacques-Alain Miller, one of the central heirs to Lacanian psychoanalysis, pointed out that the experience of psychosis is one that concerns the scope and range of meaning itself. For the psychotic, at the onset of psychosis, he explained, *everything* has meaning. There is, in other words, not a deficit of capacity for interpreting and understanding the empirical world, but rather a surplus. While for non-psychotics, only a certain fraction of the empirical world functions as semiotic signs, for the psychotic there is what a semiotician would call a 'dysfunctional semiosis'. This has immediate consequences, says Miller, for the notion of security.[1]

Psychosis has two primary characteristics. On the one hand, it is surcharge of signification or an over-interpretation of the signification of objects. It is a failure to access the 'healthy' experience of the arbitrary, of contingency, of the existence and persistence of things *devoid* of any meaning whatsoever. On the other hand, it is a multiplication of *threat*. Not only do all experienced objects have meaning, but this meaning is also threatening. Signification itself, its generation and circulation, becomes a matter of menace and danger. The psychotic is thus the ultimate subject of security.

In this context the basic principles of Lacanian psychoanalytic theory draw on the link we discussed earlier between security and epistemology. The link between the unknown and what is dangerous about the unknown *per se*, that which, regardless of what the unknown actually is, lies at the core of Lacan's work on the theory of the subject and constitutes a fundamental dimension of the recent strategies for conceptualizing security and insecurity (cf. our discussion of the 'unkown unkowns' in Chapter 9). At the risk of adopting the psychotic discourse ourselves, we might suggest that the link between the new rationality of security and the logic of psychosis is revealing: in the security logic of the unknown no object is banal or meaninglessness, nothing is arbitrary or random, all objects have inherent meaning. This hidden or unattainable meaning is, in our time, most often associated with threat. The undisclosed significance of ordinary objects, by virtue of their hidden secrets, is the foundation of the threat they implicitly correlate and the source of the legitimacy they mobilize.

Normativity and subjectivity

Our pursuit of the subject of security has begun with a more fundamental pursuit of the subject itself. One of the most remarkable contributions to understanding the structure, function and implications of the subject of security in a post-Cartesian optic is the psychoanalytic theory of Jacques Lacan (1901–81). If it is true that security and insecurity frame life, that at their extremes there is the existential question of survival, be it of the state, certain social, culture or political sub-groups, or the individual itself, then the psychic life of the individual will be a key to it. Lacan's contribution to our reflexion on the basic structures and functions of the security subject is to chart and map the immensely complex drama of psychic life as one of aggression and defence, desire and need, rejection and repression, fear and anxiety.

Lacan was a clinician and teacher. His aim was to develop a set of theoretical principles to be applied in clinical settings. He never sought to draw out the political and social implications of his own doctrine in a systematic way, as did, say, Freud or Firenzi and their disciples. Yet the implications of Lacanian psychoanalytic theory for our understanding of the political are, arguably, quite significant. They could have played a clear role, for example, in the French humanism debates of the 1970s, the heartbreak of decolonization in the 1980s and the European growing-pains of the 1990s, particularly surrounding the Kosovo bombings, which we discuss in Chapter 14.

Lacan was primarily concerned with mental illness, and his basic insights stem from the particularities of the subject of illness. His early work dealt with the nature of paranoid psychosis, the experience and speech of the psychotic, the relation between the psychotic subject and the subject position of the clinician. What emerges from his earliest reflections on mental illness is a sense of the striking split between subjectivities. From this starting point his social, cultural and political references are multiplied to include, in his writing and seminars, a vast horizon of contemporary phenomena.

Lacan saw the Cartesian subject, dear not only to Western philosophical, theological and political traditions but also to medical doctrines from the advent of 'scientific' medical practices in the 19th century, as problematic from the point of view of clinical psychology. Other contemporaries of Lacan – Canguilhem and later Foucault – came to scrutinize the situation of the medical subject in its cultural, historical, social and political environment (Canguilhem, 1988, 1999; Foucault, 2003a).

The subject position, for Lacan the position from which mental illness is operative, is not the place from which the subject of speech is produced. The two positions are different, though not entirely distinct. This difference is the core insight of psychoanalysis, and much of Lacan's work surrounded the effort to systematize and understand this difference. Who or what is speaking when the patient is speaking? What is the place from which the fear, paranoia or insecurity of the patient comes to be expressed? What is the cause of unrequited desire or frustrated fantasy? What logic links these psychic 'spaces' and the voice that speaks? Starting from these basic questions we can see a distinct contribution of Lacanian psychoanalysis to our understanding of the subject of security today.

In Lacan's work and psychoanalytic theory in general we find the subject of security, at its most individual human level and in its most pathological form, as a primary function whose finality is addressing a primary need: the subject of security as a subject under pursuit of itself. In this sense the experience of the psychotic over-meaning pointed out by Miller would imply that there is a logical counterpart in the totally arbitrary, in an experience of the utterly meaningless, without any knowledge content, political valence, moral charge or any other residue that might carry meaning. This counterpart would be a situation where objects enable no interpretation, and even resist it. This would be both the moment of security presumed and idealized by many today. In the logic of psychoanalysis, and maybe in our everyday experience, it would be akin to death itself. Insecurity and security are, in this sense, the poles of life. Absolute security is both impossible in life and the object of a certain kind of desire.

In other words, from a certain point of view, Lacan's project begins and ends with the insecurity of the subject. His basic postulate, formulated early in his career then developed through a variety of forms and phases, is that the subject never occupies the position ascribed to it by the Cartesian theory of subjectivity. On the contrary, its default position is one of searching to orient itself relative to the unified and rational position that is, in effect, impossible to attain but remains an ideal and a point of orientation. This human desire for unity is at once its exposure, its precariousness and insecurity. Lacan's primary contribution to security thinking is a theory of the subject that sees the subject by virtue of its psychic formation as incessantly and necessarily in search of itself.

By virtue of this precariousness, the subject is inherently normative. The subject tends toward a centre that is inaccessible to it, toward an ideal place that inevitably disappoints it. This is the *pathos* of the subject of security: it holds instinctive 'knowledge' of security, of the secure centre of what escapes it. This 'knowledge', which is, strictly speaking, no knowledge at all since it has no intimate connection with the object it pretends to know, is the fundamental source of its discontent, its precariousness and its normative drive toward something else, somewhere else. This fundamental drive impels the subject, translating the inadequacy or incoherence of its 'present' into the normative inclination, orientating it toward the position of greater value that it, *a priori*, does not hold, aligning itself into a constellation of basic values, structuring its orientation, its priorities and its politics. Starting from a position of displacement, of not being where it 'should' be, the subject seeks that place whose most general identifying property is its security, the absence of the need or want in the broadest sense, the neutralization of the normative impulse. Normativity is, in this fundamental sense, the primary mode of insecurity.

In Lacanian terms, the constellation of relativizing orders and priorities that we call values do not preexist the subject, do not have any essence that would have some form of immanence that precedes the normative drive of desire, instinct or psychic impulse. The object of desire (the 'value') is constructed, projected or channelled as the desire of another, as the impulse that channels desire toward an alignment with impulse of the other, accessing thus a presumed identity with the other. This dependency or secondary-ness does not by any means diminish the fullness, completeness and coherence of the normative imperative that drives the subject toward it. Nor does it weaken in any way the imperative of security that is attached to it. On the contrary, there is evidence that it is the very envisaging of a future state of security in the experience of identification with the other that forms and determines the value set that provides the motivation, passion or, in the case of full-blown politics, legitimacy for taking measures in its name.

Paranoia and insecurity

In everyday language, 'paranoia' is used to refer to suspicion, mistrust, fear and insecurity relative to others. Its psychiatric usage supplements this suite of emotions with the observation that the paranoid's delusional or obsessional qualities most often focus on some idea of persecution. The variance between the two understandings is remarkable and instructive. The conceptual map of paranoia in its everyday sense provides a template for many aspects of a psychoanalytic model. As the derisive joke has it: 'just because you are paranoid does not mean that nobody is out to get you'. On the one hand, following the spirit of the joke, there is a cloaking or deceptive function to paranoia. That fact of being preoccupied with some complex of imagined, 'unreal' dangers doesn't actually have consequences for what 'real' threats may lie in waiting. On the contrary, one is arguably in a situation of greater insecurity by the reassurance of the 'non-reality' of the paranoiac delusions. Imagined insecurity caused by paranoia, the derided state of false insecurity, has its part in *real* insecurity. Indeed, it actually generates real insecurity, leaves the subject actually less secure because it is less concerned with real threats. On the other hand, self-conscious paranoia has the function of actually providing security for the one suffering from it by providing an alternative truth or explanation about the insecurity caused by the paranoid anxiety. The experience of insecurity may be caused by objective threats, but given the paranoid condition, these must be considered as only one of many causes of the anxiety, thus relatizised on the overall threat–anxiety axis.

Many philosophers and theoreticians theorize the strange experience of psychic life as an experience of insecurity, some of which we address in this book. In Lacan's work, this experience is problematized and studied at the deepest levels of psychic life, and subjectivity becomes a chessboard of securities and insecurities woven, around and against one another. Here the very concept of insecurity as we have studied it so far must be re-tooled in order to continue our mapping onto Lacan's thought. For Lacan is in agreement on the basic postulate of our hypothesis concerning the split, contentious and thus ethical subject of security. Yet for Lacan the contention relocates again, this time to the disposition of exposure that makes the subject position a fundamental component of *personality*.

Lacan was trained as a doctor and subsequently specialized in psychiatry, taking a special interest in the problem of paranoia. His 1937 doctoral thesis *On Paranoid Psychosis in its Relations with the Personality* is situated at an extra-ordinary meeting place between psychiatry and psychoanalysis.[2] In the course of his psychiatric studies, Lacan became interested in the writings of Freud, himself eventually undergoing psychoanalysis. A long and complex history of psychiatry will have to be bracketed in order to summarize the central elements of the thesis. It is, in essence, a critique of the concept of *personality* in psychiatry. His objections to the dominant understandings and clinical practices are essentially two. He objects both to the current *definition* of personality and to the way it is *used* in explaining psychosis.

'Psychosis', a global designation for mental illness, was, in the 19th century, before the discovery of psychoanalysis, explained through primarily 'organic' or 'functional' causes and treated through a variety of medical means. Clinical psychiatry typically resorts to a deterministic or functional approach to psychosis, while the psychoanalytic approach focuses on dysfunction in the way the mind experiences the world. The key innovation of Lacan's thesis is directed toward the current understandings of the relationship between what was called 'personality' and mental illness occurring in relationship to it. The canonical view explains paranoid psychosis according to a 'causal topology', that is according to some cause essentially external to the otherwise healthy core personality, destabilizing it and causing illness. The cause of psychosis in the traditional view can either be 'organic', congenital or due to a problem of perception or memory, or brought on by some kind of shock in the life of the patient.

Psychosis is, according to Lacan, a dysfunction of personality itself, and not, as was common psychiatric wisdom in the 1930s, a sickness that affected a well-established and healthy personality. Lacan's hypothesis builds upon three primary characteristic elements of a revised understanding of 'personality': (1) the biographical development of the patient, (2) the understanding the patient has of him- or herself and (3) tensions in the social relations (Lacan, 1975: 42–3). Lacan's thesis is inspired by his discovery of Freud's few writings on paranoid psychosis, not ordinarily considered as part of the scientific corpus of psychiatry. Lacan essentially reverses the accepted causality of personality. In his analysis, personality is the production of a certain synthesis of psychic elements, including the 'conflictual' elements that ordinarily would be described as some sort of mutation of personality. In short, the problem of the psychotic paranoid is a problem of the *ego* in the Freudian sense. The structure of ego is, according to Lacan, itself paranoid in the sense described above.

After completing his thesis, Lacan spent several years in psychoanalytic training and medical practice, returning in 1946 to the problems raised in his 1936 thesis. The primary thrust of his work is to decouple paranoia from psychosis, generalizing the latter instead as a general characteristic of the ego and of knowledge itself. Lacan begins to describe the critique of the subject as a critique of the evidence-based model of psychic disorder oriented on the Cartesian subject. The hypothesis of a simple cause-and-effect, or 'instrumental' model of paranoia, is inadequate for Lacan because it fails to recognize that the ego itself is structured in a paranoid way (Lacan, 1966c: 153–4). The 'paranoid model' sees the personality itself as caused by the search for adequate knowledge (ibid.: 187).

By asking the question of the origin of the paranoid condition, Lacan runs headlong into a paradox. In the course of its development the child becomes interested in, even fascinated by, its objective environment, projecting and spatializing its desire *before* it knows or understands what it is that it is desiring. The desire of the child is both directed and has no finality. Thus the Cartesian paradigm of a clear distinction between the subject and the object, the self and the other, is not in place at the moment of the entry into 'subjectivity'. By extension, what we could call the Cartesian security paradigm, opposing the threatened and the threat, is also not in place at the origin of the 'subjectivity' of threat. The child desires without desiring something particular, is fascinated with knowing itself, and the desire is then enhanced in it and returned to itself by a world of 'objects' that do not yet register as objects.

In terms of our study of the subject of security, we can summarize by noting that in the development of subjectivity, the object and subject are co-determinate, the existence of the subject does not precede the existence of the objects it desires or is fascinated by (or threatened by). This implies that the subject of security, the primary position from which threat is cognized and assessed, can precede the 'fascination' with or even the desire for the object that threatens. This fascination with or desire for the object of threat will prove to be an essential reading of the ethical meaning of the Lacanian *real*, and the start of an explanation of our generation's fascination with security and danger.

A psychic site of struggle in the 'mirror stage'

It is worth reiterating that the originality of Lacan's re-reading of Freud begins with the essential observation that the *subject* is not identical to the *ego*. The theoretical position from which objective knowledge of the world is established and assessed, assertions made and judgements accorded (essentially the Cartesian subject) is misaligned with the personality, 'identity' or 'self' of the individual. Or, to put it in more Lacanian terms, the subject of speech is not the same as the subject of the unconscious. Things we say (or do) are not, in any simple or straightforward way, the expressions of a self-present, self-knowing, autonomous, free rational subject. On the contrary, supposing such a pure or idealized Cartesian subject actually existed, it would be processed and transformed before becoming what we call the 'self', the ego, the personal reference for who we are, the position from which we speak or act. The ego, that self we identify with – our self-image – as well as that which others identify with us, is not a rarefied essence but the product of processes. The process begins in what Lacan famously calls the 'mirror stage' (Lacan, 1966b, 1937). Lacan holds on to the notion of the Cartesian subject to designate the subject of the unconscious, a kind of idealized position without substance that nonetheless structures the processes there (Lacan, 1988b: 126). The subject is, in a sense, only known in fragments, never fully present.

In Lacan's teaching, the emergence of the subject takes place simultaneously with the emergence of the ego at the moment of the *mirror stage* and together with what Lacan calls the *imaginary, symbolic* and *real* orders. Both the meaning of these three concepts and the emphasis Lacan places on them develop significantly over the course of his teaching. The first phase of this post-thesis theoretical development, beginning with his teaching on the mirror phase, revolves first and foremost around the role of the image for the formation and function of the subject, closely linked to the relation of the subject to the symbolic order. Entry into the symbolic order then implies the need for the concept of the real. We will attempt to summarize these three components of the Lacanian subject in as much as they are relevant for our theory of the subject of security.

The *mirror stage* is the scene of our first experience of our own bodies and the complex universe of needs, drives, desires, satisfactions and dissatisfactions that result from it. As it is the first step in our relationship to our bodies it is also the first shape given to our identity, our knowledge of ourselves and our knowledge of others. These experiences of self will be necessarily frustrated in ways that are formative for our general experience of ourselves and the world. Before the mirror stage, the child does not experience his or her body as something unified. There is, in effect, no primordial distinction between interior and exterior, between self and other. Thus, in Lacan's thinking there is no self at all in the Cartesian sense. In the moment the child perceives another body, the projection or specular image it forms determines its relation to the objective world and what we usually think of as 'objective' knowledge about the world.

The *imaginary* is the set of fundamental events and experiences related to the *images* that are projected first by the child in the mirror stage, then continuously through life. It is, strictly speaking, the process through which the subject *identifies* with the image of something outside of itself. The mirror stage for the child is the structured process by which the child identifies with something that is foreign to it. This contradiction will form the dialectical basis for all experience:

> It suffices to understand the mirror stage in this context *as an identifi-cation*, in the full sense analysis gives to the term: namely the transformation that takes place in the subject when he assumes an image – an image that is seemingly predestined to have an effect at this phase, as witnessed by the use in analytic theory of antiquity's term, 'imago'.
>
> (Lacan, 1999: 76)

In this sense our identity stems from something different from us. We model ourselves on something we cannot be, we value the thing that is unattainable. Complete knowledge of our self is unattainable because that self is always an other. In this first moment of subjective experience the subject identifies with the image of the other, either literally by catching a gaze of itself in a mirror or other reflective surface, or by seeing another body as the 'reflection' of itself. Yet where as adult we would speak of 'identifying' with another at the level of the ego, that is taking the other's qualities as model for our own, in Lacan's mirror stage this identification is literal. The subject forms an identity with the other: the other is, in the experience of the subject, *itself*. This is the origin of the ego, the origin of the self-understanding or self-image.

As we will discuss in Chapter 6 on 'Intolerable insecurity', this dialectic of identity, in the Lacanian conceptualization of identification, stands as a kind of template for the tension in the security subject. On the one hand, to be threatened is to possess knowledge of the threat, the potential consequences it can bring, its scope and breadth. Yet on the other hand, in as much as the insecurity is based on a threat that is not yet reality, it cannot be adequately known, cannot be entirely planned for. A structurally similar dialectic of identity and difference can be developed on an anthropological plane, as discussed in Chapter 5, 'Identity, community, security' – whereby group identity provides a kind of security against the threats of what is different, without entirely possessing knowledge of the difference, resorting instead to the project of an *image* – in the Lacanian sense, of what one's self is relative to the unknown other.

In constituting the origin of the ego, the mirror stage is at the same time instituting the split between the subject and the ego, a split that will never again be mended.

> But the important point is that this form situates the agency known as the ego, prior to its social determination, in a fictional direction that will forever remain irreducible for any single individual or, rather, that will only asymptotically approach the subject's becoming, no matter how successful the dialectical syntheses by which he must resolve, as *I*, his discordance with his own reality.
>
> (Lacan, 1999: 76)

The subject constitutes itself through an image, a pure form or *gestalt*. This form, this image, becomes the basis for the subject's formation, its self-understanding.

The insight that the ego is somehow shaped in relation to perceptions or impressions from the outside world is, in the 1930s, at the time when Lacan first formulated the concept of the mirror phase, already under discussion in the field of ego psychology, in particular in a widely circulated article by Wallon entitled 'How the notion of the child's own body develops' (Wallon, 1931). However, Lacan's approach reverses the notion that the ego, something possessed in essence in the human from birth, is awakened or develops through its experience of otherness. For Lacan, there is no subject that somehow precedes an experience of and fascination with objects outside of itself.

> Through these two aspects of its appearance, this gestalt – whose power should be considered linked to the species, though its motor style is as yet unrecognizable – symbolizes the *I*'s mental permanence, at the same time as it prefigures its alienating destination.
>
> (Lacan, 1999: 76)

The 'exterior' is, in effect, not at all exterior but rather already interior to the subject. The 'other' is already the subject itself. There is no exteriority or any possible experience of exteriority before the subject acquires the capacity to experience any real exteriority (cf. Ogilvie, 2005: 105–6). From the basically Freudian position of the 'second topology' in *The Ego and the Id*, that the ego is interior and develops through exterior stimulus, Lacan goes so far as to suggest that the ego itself is exterior to the subject, not independent, but by no means implicit or inherent.

This basic, even primordial, structure of disjunction, of splitting of the subject between the logical position of the ego (or ideal ego, as Freud would say), marks the evolution of human experience as one of incompleteness, precariousness and defence.

> The mirror stage is a drama whose internal pressure pushes precipitously from insufficiency to anticipation – and, for the subject caught up in the lure of spatial identification, turns out fantasies that proceed from a fragmented image of the body to what I will call an 'orthopaedic' form of its totality – and to the finally donned armour of an alienating identify that will mark his entire mental development with its rigid structure.
>
> (Lacan, 1999: 78)

The consequence of this reasoning is that, in Lacan's model, the subject and the ego will never be unified. Its experience of itself, the basic structure of subjectivity, is one of alienation, and thus one of defence, struggle and insecurity. This is the logic of identification inspired by Kojève's reading of Hegel's dialectic: identification is a double (dialectical) movement of both being narcissistically drawn to the other as to one's self and repulsed by the other as different. The struggle or logic of security and insecurity lies at this level of subjectivity. The force of desire pushes the subject to identify with the other (other person, other group, other body or, ultimately, the otherness of its ideal self, which it is not) producing the insight that this identity is not quite identical, thus a kind of ruse or deception, a mistaking of what is actually different for oneself. On the political plan we can observe this structure distinctly in the narcissisum of western Europe towards the United States, which we analyze in Chapter 8. Discord, disharmony or misprision is the primary source of aggressiveness in the human psyche (Lacan, 1966a).

The order of the *imaginary* can, in this sense, be seen as one of the organizational elements of what today is called risk analysis and management. The lack that it aspires to fulfil is the complete, unified and fully constituted certainty about the dangers faced by the subject of security. The *imaginary* is the field of analysis and action in the attempt to establish, or reestablish, objective security, the *imaginary* unity of safety and protection.

The frustrated security of the *symbolic* order

The image of the subject just described develops in what Lacan calls the *symbolic* order. As the child grows, the specific limitations of the image in the mirror phase are replaced by a general set of limitations, codes and laws of the kind that characterize the rules and dictates of society. The experience of accepting the defeat of not being identical to the thing with which we identify becomes the general experience of the symbolic function. Just as the infant looks to the object to recognize it as what it is, a request that is impossible to fulfil, we look to society, social codes and language as the place of recognition and for a link to other members of society. The symbolic order is both a reassurance and a kind of reminder that complete security is at odds with the very essence of the self.

> But we know that, in the absence of such recognition, analytic action can only be experienced as aggressive at the level at which it is situated; and that, in the absence of the social 'resistances' which the psychoanalytic group used to find reassuring, the limits of its tolerance toward its own activity – 'accepted,' if not actually approved of – no longer depend upon anything but the numerical percentage by which its presence in society is measured.
>
> (Lacan, 2009: 203–4)

This structure of the *imaginary*, the *symbolic* (and the *real*, to which we will turn shortly) is also the site for playing out the fundamental insecurity of psychic life:

> The principles suffice to separate out the symbolic, imaginary, and real
> conditions that determine the defences we can recognize in the doctrine
> – isolation, undoing what has been done, denial, and in general,
> misrecognition.
>
> (ibid.: 204)

A structure of conflict thus plays itself out in the formation of the self and
continues on the level of interpersonal reactions and social relations,
exemplified by language and all forms of symbolic communication that
depend on a universal intelligibility, validity and recognition of their status
as code. What the individual seeks from the other, from an interior other, an
other of the institution of social life as constituted by the language and
norms of the collectivity, can never be requited by virtue of the very structure
of otherness.

Because of the particular process of evolution of the subject, from infancy,
through childhood and on, the subject is characterized by a fundamental
lack. In a number of contexts, Lacan refers to this lack as a 'lack of being',
both as a fundamental incompleteness or lack of unity, in the subject and its
relation to the world, but also as the presumption or logical prerequisite of
lack, of a prior or potential unity. This lack of unity is, however, not simply
contingent; it is constitutive of the subject. The subject is precisely that which
lives the experience of lack. This fact and this experience are what make the
subject what it is. This potential and yet impossible unity is the meaning of
the word *imaginary*. The 'order of the *imaginary*' is the field in which the
subject struggles to reestablish its lost unity. In this sense it is a normative
space, the of a subject striving to carry out what is impossible for. It is
therefore a profoundly ethical moment.

The *symbolic* is the set of rules, be they grammatical, social or culture, that
limit and channel human expressions in the world. The finite set of
possibilities for thinking and acting in the world. What are the recognizable,
thinkable and conceptualizable parameters that contribute to forming the
dangers, insecurities and risks in our experience of life? These rules, unlike
the *real*, to which we will return in a moment, are to some extent available to
us, though they cannot be altered consciously. Our possibilities for grasping
security, that is for understanding it and formulating ways to approach and
deal with it are thus limited by the symbolic order. The fantasy of obtaining
objective security in the world is closely linked to our dependence on this
order of framing limitations. Nonetheless, the *objective security* that is the aim
of security analysis and thus all thinking about security is only partly related
to these limitations. The source of fear and fascination also precedes and
transcends the framing of socially based rules. It is predetermined by another
order of reality, the reality of that catastrophe that penetrates even the most
robust sense of security. This is the order that Lacan calls the *real*.

The unthinkable threat of the *real*

The *real* in Lacanian theory passes through a number of phases in the course of Lacan's teaching. In his earliest writings, the *real* is simply and directly opposed to the 'image' (Lacan, 1966b: 75). Beginning in the 1950s he uses the term in a sense inspired by the Hegelian edict that 'what is rational is real and what is real is rational' (Hegel, 2008: xix), integrating it into his theory of the three 'orders', together with the *symbolic* and the *imaginary* (Lacan, 1988a). The primary characteristic of the *real* in these writings is that, in opposition to the symbolic order distinguished by a finite though changeable social, cultural, linguistic code, it is perfectly undifferentiated. The *real* can be neither spoken nor written. It is outside language and inaccessible to signification or representation. The *real* is both unknowable and, in a certain sense, rationality itself. Yet the *real* reaches beyond the simple epistemological quandary of Kant's *thing-in-itself* and metaphysical premises of Hegel's notion of *Absolute Knowledge* (Zupancic, 2000). The *real* is the experience of our insecurities becoming reality, an experience, by definition, unknowable and, to a large degree, unthinkable. Should the worst of our insecurities actually become reality, they would no longer be insecurities, but rather truth in its most disastrous form.

Insecurity is the certainty of an uncertainty, the expression of the degree to which we know that the unknowable is the case, and that this unknowable is an inescapable condition of our existence. The *real* is the unavoidable thought and somatic experience of that uncertainty, the unattainable fulfilment of the desire to know it and the experience of that uncertainty through partial erasure or foreclosure of it, a weighted certainty of uncertainty. It is the experience of the unrealized catastrophe by projection, a reality we, at times, dedicate considerable resources to.

This is the paradoxical logic of security, that it cannot be entirely knowable, analyzable, cognizabe or masterable in pure terms of security and insecurity. Security, as we have underscored, presupposes the impossibility of adequate knowing. Our status in Lacanian psychoanalytic terms is measured by the degree to which we know we do not know it, our experience of the knowledge of the unknowable, and this knowledge, combined with some paradoxical – or more likely, self-contradictory – rationalization of the knowledge of the unknowable. If security-knowledge, if the strategy or method for knowing it, the logic of its knowability, were fully available, it would not be security at all, but rather a matter of everyday safety.

Security and insecurity circulate as a relationship to the desire for knowledge of the catastrophe, without the inconvenience of having to live through the catastrophe itself. From a pragmatic perspective this is quite sensible. From a phenomenological point of view it is equally uncontroversial. For were the catastrophe to actually become reality, it would not be a possible object of experience. By definition, catastrophe is an event that obliterates the possibility of experience. In effect, no experience of catastrophe is possible.

Were the catastrophe to happen, we would not know it, for we would not exist in a condition in which experience were possible. For this reason, in terms of security, the experience of the Lacanian real, an imagined and projected experience of the catastrophe, is far more real than a 'real' one and, as Taleb points out, has far more social, political and economic consequences (Taleb, 2007). It is the fulfilment of security, security in a fully unfolded reality. It is the playing out of the fantasy of possible certainty. This certainty is the desire for security. It is what creates and nourishes both the trepidation that security politics incorporates as part of its normal function and the objective security that is the false backdrop for it.

The Lacanian 'lack of being' constitutive of the subject of security is essential to the lack of objective security. This lack can be reduced, minimalized, and this would be the aim of security analysis. But the very existence and nature of the subject of security, according to this Lacanian interpretation, is not reducible in any comprehensive way to objective security. This is because the order of the *symbolic* cannot be entirely assimilated to the subject. It is always otherly, always foreign, never masterable or instrumentalizable. In terms of security, the *symbolic*, analytic or linguistic tools we possess in order to externalize insecurity, to seize it in the process of security politics and thereby systematize and rationalize it, are never adequate to it. An irreducible part of security still remains unconscious in the subject of security. As individuals and collectively we can never entirely grasp the social or symbolic totality that constitutes the sum of our security universe. On the other hand, this totality structures the subject of security. This is the fundamental asymmetry of security politics in its broadest sense.

The *real*, then, is always necessarily beyond the reach of the subject. The fundamental lack in the subject is caused by its inability to adequately access the symbolic order, to give full expression to the unconscious or, in terms of the subject of security, to fully articulate an understanding of the scope and meaning of the threat, its connection to the values of culture and society, its potential consequences and its relation to fear, hope and aspiration. This lack itself is what Lacan calls the *object petit-a*. It corresponds to the lack in our ability to express and systematize security in a way that adequately corresponds to our inner desire to do so. It is the source of the necessary illusion that we can indeed reestablish the rational unity necessary to fully bring objective security. The *object petit-a* is the perceived *objective insecurity* caused by risk or danger. It produces both the desire to seek the adequate analysis of insecurity and its causes in order to render them transparent, and assures that such adequation will not take place.

The name Lacan gives to the place where the subject is in identity with the order of the symbolic and where it would have access to the *real* is *fantasy*. It is the function of *fantasy* to give the subject the means to sustain the illusion of unity, of the fullness of the *real* and of full objective security.

Insecurity as desire

The mobilization of the concept of security is, generally speaking, a response to our desire to know about and understand the future. Security threats resist our efforts to plan for them, to make their factual reality fully present and their consequences fully tangible. To make a security threat plausible, as securitization theory teaches, has a transformational function, making liveable danger that is otherwise intolerable, either in a strong existential sense or according to an instrumental cost–benefit logic. Complete knowledge about what will happen in the future corresponds to society's apparently inexhaustible need for security. This need is increasingly construed as *predictability* and grows out of the early modern assumption that such knowledge is indeed entirely possible. The original function of the concept of security is to satisfy modernity's fantasy of total knowledge. In some ways unexpectedly, security serves as an analytic tool that provides a kind of epistemological balm, artificial security for a body politic cramped with insecurity.

Security mediates between the human life-world (in the Luhmanian sense) and nature. It is a continuous and variable index of the humanity of nature and the nature of humanity. On the one hand, it refers to the degree of humanness in nature, the degree to which human values are projected on to nature, in order to de-limit the non-human and identify it as a threat to humans. On the other hand it is the continuous reminder of the nature in us. In short, that the danger, the threat to us is in some sense already here, that the otherness of nature is not to be found *out there* but, rather, is already part of us.

If there exists anything like 'pure nature', then it is clearly exhausted by security analysis, entirely encapsulated in the calculus of security thinking. Supposing that 'purely' natural dangers do indeed exist, they are transformed by security thinking into a measurable and acceptable cost, internalized and assimilated into the governance of human activity. In other words, 'purely natural' security is not security at all. It is always already transformed into the logic of human contingency.

Thus 'authentic' danger (which may indeed not exist, but whose conceptualization we cannot avoid here) is that which cannot be assimilated, cannot be entirely internalized into the conventional calculus of security. It is danger in purgatory, danger that is not instrumentalizable through the calculus of security. However, the subject of security cannot entirely grasp this danger, cannot know where it starts and where it ends. Attempts to govern take the form of a struggle to distinguish the 'natural facts' from the human ones, to quantify or instrumentalize the subjective side of security and objectify it to the greatest extent possible. Objective objectifiable security, governable, as we said, dissolves from the security horizon. The insecurity that remains is the insecurity that resists this process, insecurity that cannot be assimilated or governed, cannot be objectified, cannot become an object in any simple sense of the word.

The objective security, which is the ostensible aim of security policy, does not in this sense belong to a simply epistemological order. Though it must be construed in epistemological terms as certainty, it lies in a field or constellation of fears, desires, fantasies, impressions, suspicions and suppositions. The challenge both for understanding security and for managing it is to articulate a concept that comprehends these heterogeneous elements. The Lacanian grid of *symbolic, imaginary* and *real* serves this aim, at least in part, and makes a considerable step toward pulling together the otherwise incommensurate elements of security.

In his 1964 discussion of the subject of the unconscious in Freud's *Interpretation of Dreams*, Lacan turns to Freud's interest for the dynamics of the forgetting of dreams, their distortion and the particular way they are transmitted by the subject. 'The major term in Freud's analysis', he asserts, 'is not "truth", but rather "certitude" or "certainty" (*certitude/Gewissheit*))'. Freud's project is Cartesian, Lacan continues,

> in the sense that it builds upon the subject of certainty. It concerns that about which one can be certain. To this end, the first thing to do is to overcome what connotes anything about the unconscious, especially when it has to do with making it merge from the dream experience, to surmount what floats about ubiquitously, what punctuates, what blurs, what blotches the text of any dream communication: I am not sure, I doubt.
>
> (Lacan, 1973: 36)

The complex drives of human subjectivity have in common with the notion of security the fact that they relay the uncertain, the unclear, the partially articulated, the distorted, the indistinct, the undecided. These 'epistemological' categories, while relating to the most common daily experiences, resist or derail the analyses of conventional epistemology. They are the essence of security and yet they are not 'real' knowledge. They occupy an in-between place, between what we know, what we do not know, what we wish to know and what we struggle to know. Conventional epistemology can, at best, stretch itself to cover what we *cannot* know. It fails however to make the unavoidable link between a certain unknown knowledge and the ambition and struggle to know it. The unknown, in the grid of security-experience, is never purely unknown. It is tainted and conditioned by the knowledge of the unknown, and thus by an impulse to uncover the knowledge that by some pre-knowledge or para-knowledge we know or suspect lies in wait. Security-knowledge is a kind of contract, a promise of 'real' knowledge, a reward for those who would seek, a compensation for curiosity, courage, audacity, tenacity, etc. Who or what is the subject of this promise? Lacan's philosophy of the subject proposes the beginning of an answer.

Notes

1 The entire talk can be accessed at http://www.londonsociety-nls.org.uk/ (accessed 6 January 2011).
2 An excellent review of the thorny history of psychoanalysis in France may be found in (Roudinesco, 1990).

4   Butler, or the precarious subject

Any number of accounts of western modernity will place a distinct notion of the *subject* as its *alpha* and *omega*. This tacit notion of the subject structuring the very idea of rationality, anchoring politics and setting the premise for moral reflexion, grows out of a Cartesian philosophical universe that has thrived for centuries. The critical re-readings of Marx, Freud and Nietzsche at the close of the 19th century, followed by many others, began to expose and analyze the assumptions of this distinctly Cartesian subject: it is rational, autonomous, sovereign, self-conscious, self-present, unified, stable and, above all, free. More recent research in gender studies, critical anthropology and subaltern studies has added awareness that the subject passed on through the Cartesian heritage is also male, Eurocentric and northern. By extension, a wide range of critical accounts of the modern subject have, in the last decades, emphasized the historical situation of the subject, its social and cultural setting, its politics and its inscription in a field of power.

The subject of gender identity

Butler's starting point in her early and widely read book *Gender Trouble* is a critique of the feminism and, in particular, a critique of the essentially political postulate that 'woman' can and should be the subject of feminism. Starting with Simone de Beauvoir's well-travelled insight that 'one is not born a woman, but becomes one', and passing by Irigaray, Wittig, Foucault, Lacan, Lévi-Strauss and others, she develops a detailed critique of the heterocentrism of the subject of feminism. This analysis of *Gender Trouble*, however, leads much further and has implications, in its widest reach, for the very notion of identity in its relation to the status of the subject of gender identity. It will lead us to a better understanding of the fundamental insecurity of the subject.

Butler's critique of feminism leads to a critique of the subject of gender, opening for a critique of the very notion of identity and what she regards as its 'subversion of identity' (1990: 185). The critique begins with an assessment of the premises of feminist theory. 'For the most part,' says Butler at the outset of *Gender Trouble* (1990),

> Feminist theory has assumed that there is some existing identity, under-
> stood through the category of women, who not only initiates feminist
> interests and goals with discourse, but constitutes the subject for whom
> political representation is pursued.
>
> (ibid.: 3)

Feminism in its mainstream form is built upon a certain conception of
woman. This conception of woman, according to traditional feminist
thinking, has not had equal standing in the Enlightenment discourse of
autonomy, liberty, individual and collective rights, etc. This concept of
woman has been denied standing by a range of explicit and implicit
political, social and cultural forces that it is the task of the feminist
political project to confront and reverse through politically motivated
critique. Woman, in this traditional optic, is a coherent, unified political
subject under duress and denied the full political realization of this core
essence.

Butler's approach to feminism is a critique of the tacit assumptions in
feminist theory about the status of the subject of feminism. Having noted
this political discourse of feminism in *Gender Trouble*, Butler assumes a critical
posture toward it, joining what she describes as a growing number of critical
voices who challenge the conception of woman implicit in the feminist
discourse. The general point of objection of this challenge is the very
understanding of woman as the subject of feminism. According to Butler,
'the very subject of women is no longer understood in stable and abiding
terms' (ibid.: 4). The subject of woman, the hinge to the coherence of the
feminist project, is contested.

This contestation has, on the one hand, a pragmatic ground, stemming
from the very contentiousness of the category of woman from a variety of
standpoints: psychological, biological, moral, social, cultural, etc. More
crucial, on the other hand, is the problem of the unity of the subject *writ
large*. The discourse of feminism has, according to Butler, tended to begin
with a cohesive subject – 'woman' – only to build a political project around
its liberation in simple political terms.

> The domains of public and political 'representation' set out in advance
> the criterion by which the subjects themselves are formed with the result
> that the representation is extended only to what can be acknowledged
> as a subject.
>
> (ibid.: 4)

The discourse of feminism, in Butler's reading, places itself unwittingly
outside of the discourse of identity put there to enact its politics. In other
words, the question of the identity, indeed the gender identity of the subject
of feminism is not posed outside of feminism. As a consequence, the
'woman' that is defined as the central focus of feminist politics is defined

aside from the politics of identity, the sexual contention that provides the force of the feminist project to start with.

> Rather than a stable signifier that commands the assent of those whom it purports to describe and represent, *women*, even in the plural, has become a troublesome term, a site of contest, a cause for anxiety.
>
> (ibid.: 6)

In doing so, it places itself outside of the discourse of the subject it postulates, to pretend in some sense to precede the formation of the subject of gender or to be universally identical to it. In effect, it is feminism that defines woman through its politics of identity, not the contrary.

On the one hand, Butler wants to warn against the 'foundationalist fictions' that support the notion of the Cartesian subject of politics. On the other hand, she is aware that the political thrust of feminism requires a common political subject around which the feminist political project can gravitate. The premise for collective political action is, according to common wisdom, the assumption of universal values in play. Collective political action presupposes not only unified political agency but also collective political experience, in this case, a certain experience of male domination through gender institutions, both formal and informal.

And yet, argues Butler, mobilizing feminist politics according to the conceptual framework may do more harm than good. Feminism, in its traditional 20th-century political form, yields to a political requirement of universality, a politics of universality that reaches beyond the experience of gender. The feminist subject remains ensconced as a Cartesian subject, characterized by stable and unified representation: if feminism does not represent women, it is not feminism. Yet what is the status of 'women'? What is the effect of a unified political subject – feminism – on an irregular, non-universal, culturally, politically and socially determined experience of gender?

The political assumption that there must be a universal basis for feminism, one which must be found in an identity assumed to exist cross-culturally, often accompanies the notion that the oppression of women has some singular form discernible in the universal or hegemonic structure of patriarchy or masculine domination (ibid.: 6).

'Women', in particular, but gender itself, in more general terms, is not unified. Gender identity is not singular, cohesive, non-contextual, eternal, etc. On the contrary,

> By conforming to a requirement of representational politics that feminism articulate a stable subject, feminism thus opens itself to charges of gross misrepresentation.
>
> (ibid.: 8)

The subject of women and the subject of gender in general should not be taken as given. According to Butler they are produced:

> The identity of the feminist subject ought not to be the foundation of feminist politics, if the formation of the subject takes place within a field of power regularly buried through the assertion of that foundation. Perhaps, paradoxically, 'representation' will be shown to make sense for feminism only when the subject of 'women' is nowhere presumed.
>
> (ibid.: 9)

By most accounts of feminism, or any 'isms' – that is of coherently defined, stable, *secure* conceptual positions from which to exercise social and political engagement – Butler is not a feminist.

In gender politics writ large, gender identity is thus taken for granted. The crucial question for Butler and a generation of readers of *Gender Trouble* is: How is gender identity itself generated and regulated by the politics of gender?

We need not look far to see how gender identity is transformed through the politics of gender. The transformation can be tracked in any number of public social debates (gay and lesbian rights, adoption, family and marriage, sexuality in the clergy, gays in the military, etc.). If there was ever some clearly de-limited 'origin' of gender identity 'about which' such a debate could possibly take place, it is most clearly erased and deformed, reconstituted and reconfigured through the politics itself.

The politics of gender is the condition for the formation and articulation of gender identity. To be capable of saying what my gender 'is', one must specify what experiences have relevance as empirical evidence of gender, what values play a role in giving legitimacy any sense of what one's gender is, what cultural references have significance, what social frameworks link to it or even enrich it. All these indices flow from a politics of engaging the subject of identity and the subject of gender.

The subject of gender is exposed, dependent upon the variegations of the politics of gender, and these are indeed among the least predictable we know. Security, certainly, and invulnerability flow from a foundation. The deconstruction of identity operated by Butler exposes the dependency, insecurity and vulnerability of the gendered subject.

Paradoxically, the most authentic subject is the one that is inauthentic, derived, secondary, generated through the political turmoil of its own formation, self-formation in one discourse of the subject or another (reason, emancipation, progress, social wellbeing, etc.). The closer we can approach the vulnerability of the subject, the closer we come to gaining insight into its authentic way of being.

> If identities were no longer fixed as the premises of a political syllogism, and politics no longer understood as a set of practices derived from the alleged interests that belong to a set of ready-made subjects, a new

configuration of politics would surely emerge from the ruins of the old.
(ibid.: 189–90)

If the gendered subject were actually foundational, as much of feminist politics presupposes, it would have a contrary effect to what it seeks. It would restrict, restrain and contain instead of emancipate. (Indeed, a parallel critique of the metaphysics of liberty would likely reveal a generalized conceptual foreclosure to the subject of emancipation.)

The analysis of the discourse of feminism, of woman and of gender identity in the early phase of work, moves far beyond the liberation of the subject from a standpoint feminism where it was held hostage. It is, in other words, not to be understood as a liberation project that opposes the liberated to the unliberated, one in which a more authentic orientation toward gender in general and woman in particular would result in the satisfaction of a certain set of abiding political demands. As we will see, Butler's later work generalizes this effect over and beyond gender determinations.

According to the canonical view, feminism is the name of an analytic place where something has gone wrong. Yet in the name of overturning a practice of political oppression, feminism has instituted – and institutionalized – an essentialized, 'unnatural' concept of gender identity, presumed instilled as the subject of gender. *Gender Trouble* shows that gendered identity is undecided. It shows the politics of feminism less as a project of liberating a gender identity from a masculine mould than of assigning identity. More importantly, the book suggests the necessity of openness, and exposure to the need for self-articulation of actual self-creation.

The ambivalent subject of gender identity is bound to seek itself on a path that is not created but given to it, a path toward a horizon without the comfort of closure that would insert it into any discourse of political mobilization. Gender identity is the experience of this vulnerability.

Performativity: the subject of injurious speech

Where *Gender Trouble* unpacks the interplay between the constitution of the subject and the formation of identity, *Excitable Speech* (1997) examines the subject in the field of language, its formation and mutation in and through speech.

Here, the concerns move closer to what we would commonly see as matters of security. How is threat created, maintained and resolved in language? In what way is language bodily? How does the possibility of bodily injury link to speech itself? How are we threatened or injured by speech?

Taking Austin's (1955) *How to Do Things with Words* (1975 [1955]) as her point of departure, Butler develops an analysis of what it can mean to do violence with words. 'Injurious speech', in its most elementary form a social-legal analysis of the notion of libel, is unpacked in order to reveal the conditions under which a speaking subject is able to produce damage by use of speech and what meaning injury caused by speech can possibly have.

Austin, as we know, turned the mid-20th century world of linguistics on its ear by arguing what might seem a commonplace, namely that language possesses functions other than stating facts. Utterances, Austin could reveal to us, produce not only *illocutionary*, but also *perlocutionary* effects. They not only say things, but also in saying things *do* things as well. Speech is often, indeed most often, *performative*.

An attentive reader of Austin, Butler develops, in the pages of *Excitable Speech*, a multi-level interpretation of *performativity*. Though it is Butler's reflexions on injurious speech that are most relevant for our concern with the vulnerability of the subject, it is certainly her theory of *gender performativity* that has garnered most attention. The theory, first developed in *Gender Trouble* (Butler, 1990: 171–90), then in a range of other texts (Butler, 1988, 1991; Butler et al., 2000; Butler, 2003) reads gender as an enactment of a pre-assigned subject position, a repetition according to scripts, creating the effect of a 'stable identity locus' or 'ground' (Butler, 1990: 179).

In *Excitable Speech*, Butler turns her attention to the question of what kind of violence speech can be said to constitute, what violence can be produced through speech, under what conditions and with what form of agency it can be transmitted through language.

> When we claim to be injured by language, what kind of claim do we make? We ascribe an agency to language, a power to injure, and position ourselves as the objects of its injurious trajectory. We claim that language acts, and acts against us, and the claim we make is a further instance of language, one which seeks to arrest the force of the prior instance. Thus, we exercise the force of language even as we seek to counter its force, caught up in a bind that no act of censorship can undo.
>
> (ibid.: 1)

We are less interested in re-analyzing Butler's understanding of the structure of injurious language than in understanding what are the characteristics of the subject that make possible this injury. In what sense is the subject exposed to a kind of insecurity, even fundamental insecurity?

What is the characteristic proper to the subject that permits language to do harm? How does language harm? In what sense does it come from a place of insecurity and in what sense is it destined to occupy a place of insecurity.

We may, by way of example, establish threshold conditions for injury through speech. Assuming that injury is not a kind of necessity (this presumption may be a poor one), what are the minimum conditions for successful (or 'felicitous', to use Austin's term) injury. Some level of indifference, ignorance or misunderstanding would adequately shelter from injury. And yet complete withdrawl from risk and insecurity would not only be a withdrawal from subjectivity, but also from being itself. The 'survival' of any subject, 'linguistic survival', as Butler calls it, takes place within language (Butler, 1997a: 4).

According to the logic of the Enlightenment subject, the speaking subject is the seat and source of speech. It is not only the singular material originator of the speech itself, but also the origin of the *meaning* of the annunciation. The Enlightenment subject presumed to sustain a self-conscious, coherent intention, couched in the will.

By the same token, does injurious speech touch the body? Butler's theory of the performativity of injurious speech is not a phenomenology in any simple sense. As in the theories of the subject advanced by Nietzsche, Foucault or Lacan, the *phenomenon* does not remain ordered in a constellation of pure consciousness. The phenomenology of injurious speech never remains phenomenological. It exceeds the aims and limits of pure study of the structures of consciousness as in the Husserlian tradition (Stein, Heidegger, Scheler, Hartmann, Merleau-Ponty, Sartre, Schültz, Ricoeur, even Levinas).

Commonsense would tell us that the body is the house of language. That the body, the materiality of vocal tools, the mechanics of breath or the technologies of writing are, at first glance, what support and sustain language as a material means of transmission of something non-material, intellectual or spiritual. Yet among the most significant contributions of newer gender theory is to re-valorize the body, to re-situate the body in the flow of the social, cultural and political. Supported but not exhausted by the theory of biopolitics, consciousness becomes the support of the body. Thus Butler explains:

> Certain words or certain forms of address not only operate as threat to one's physical well-being, but there is a strong sense in which the body is alternately sustained and threatened through modes of address. [...]
> Language sustains the body not by bringing it into being or feeding it in a literal way; rather, it is by being interpellated within the terms of language that a certain social existence of the body first becomes possible.
> (ibid.: 5)

Language as social fabric is not secondary to a bodily voice that emits it. On the contrary, it is speech that inserts the body into the social, situates it relative to others, to material limitations, possible paths and channels, resistance and limitations. It is through, or on to the body, that we are isolated, identified and fixed. A speech, understood as a certain symbolic order or representation is imposed upon us. And yet it is always incomplete, frustrated and frustrating. In both its benevolent and malicious incarnations, speech cannot cover us entirely, cannot exhaust or completely represent us. A body is also a sign, a reminder of what cannot be signified. The body, mine or yours, is not a simple material thing among others. It is, as Butler says, 'the blindspot of speech, that which acts in excess of what is said, but which also acts in and through what is said' (ibid.: 11).

> We might be tempted to think that attributing agency to language is not quite right, that only subjects do things with language, and that agency has its origins in the subject. But is the agency of language the same as the agency of the subject? Is there a way to distinguish between the two?
>
> (ibid.: 7)

What can we use speech for? And when we use it, to what degree do we control it? If we were to, in a sovereign and autonomous way, control others with it and express our will through it, in some determined aim, what power or influence, damage or injury, could be expressed? In Austin's system of locutionary and perlocutionary utterances, communication takes place, *when* it takes place, according to pre-given conventions and codes. Some sort of unified and solitary subject is thought to speak. This subject, according to the traditional model, has an intention, puts that intention into language, then addresses it to another. In Austin's system the difference between the illocutionary and the perlocutionary lies essentially at this point. The 'doing' of the language happens at the moment of intentionality. Others, such as Derrida (1982), have shown how this distinction does not entirely lie within the control of the speaker. The same can be said, in Butler's vision, of the power that is, intentionally or unintentionally, explicitly or implicitly, placed in language and transmitted to another.

Two moments of insecurity of the subject appear here. One is the abandon with which the user of speech must send forth the message, the uncertainty or insecurity of the prospects for felicitous communication. The sender cannot be sure, and the degree of this uncertainty will vary with the gravity of the message to be transmitted. The other moment of insecurity corresponds to the insecurity of the receiver for whom the impossibility of entirely 'receiving' what has been 'sent' is constant.

Now, if the agency of speech in question is of an injurious kind, if the sender's intention is malevolent and the receivers intention in some sense benign, then the consequences of insecurity can be desirable in their ambiguity. And yet this ambiguity lies so deeply in our experience of language that it codes and structures the subject of communications from its very foundation. The 'primary dependency on language', as Butler calls it (Butler, 1997a: 26) goes hand in hand, or even precedes our recognition of ourselves (by ourselves and, as a consequence, by others), of our existence. 'Thus', says Butler 'we sometimes cling to the terms that pain us because, at a minimum, they offer us some form of social and discursive existence. The address that inaugurates the possibility of agency, in a single stroke, forecloses the possibility of radical autonomy' (ibid.: 26).

The ethical issues opened by the vulnerability of the subject are complex. It must in any case start at the fundamental unity between the subject and language? What is the ethical and political nature of this dependency on language. When a political actor in a public sphere expresses its agency, takes political action, as a sovereign entity, individual, group or state, what do the conditions of dependency (on language) imply, engage and oblige?

> Who are 'we' such that without language we cannot be, and what does it mean 'to be' within language? How is it that injurious language strikes at this very condition of possibility, of linguistic persistence and survival? If the subject who speaks is also constituted by the language that she or he speaks, then language is the condition of possibility for the speaking subject, and not merely its instrument of expression. This means that the subject has its own 'existence' implicated in a language that precedes and exceeds the subject, a language whose historicity includes a past and future that exceeds that of the subject who speaks. And yet, this 'excess' is what makes possible the speech of the subject.
>
> (ibid.: 28)

Any sovereign subject is exceeded by the language in which it is forced to mobilize its sovereignty. If we understand political authority to be the concentration in the sovereign of recognized political power, then this power must be considered to be dependent or secondary, depended on language. Authority is in its essence, if we can call it essence, insecure. Dependent upon the otherness, not simply in a dialectical fashion that was the object of the Hegelian master and slave, but dependent on the medium that assures the reflexivity of recognition. The sovereign voice is:

> …implicated in a notion of sovereign power, power figured as emanating from a subject, activated in a voice, whose effects appear to be the magical effects of that voice.
>
> (ibid.: 33)

For this reason, the very power of the speaking subject is derivative, cannot have its source 'within the speaking subject' (ibid.: 33). The sovereign subject speaks, for this is the only way to assert sovereignty, to be sovereign, to be *a* sovereign and to assert sovereignty. And yet the sovereign is not sovereign over itself. The very condition of sovereignty is the threat against it, the insecurity of sovereignty: 'Although the subject surely speaks, and there is no speaking without the subject, the subject does not exercise sovereign power over what it says' (ibid.: 25).

The degree to which a subject can be injured by speech is a measure of its vulnerability. According to what terms does this vulnerability vary? By what means might it be protected? Is it avoidable? Accordingly to Butler,

> The subject is called a name, but 'who' the subject is depends as much on the names that he or she is never called: the possibilities for linguistic life are both inaugurated and foreclosed through the name. [. . .] Thus language constitutes the subject in part through foreclosure, a kind of

unofficial censorship or primary restriction in speech that constitutes the possibility of agency in speech.

(Butler, 1997a: 40)

The subject of speech, of sovereignty, is disarmed, disabled ('undone', as Butler will develop later in *Undoing Gender*) by its own necessary self-assertion as subject.

The subject of precariousness

The shift in political temperament and the framing of political events after 11 September 2001 prompt a reflexion on subjectivity and vulnerability. This is the starting point for two of Judith Butler's recent books, *Precarious Life* (2004) and *Frames of War* (2009). In simple psychological terms, few would contest that the attacks on the US together with the political mobilization they so quickly and seamlessly opened, were due to a wake-up call of Americans to a kind of *vulnerability*. The too general and often too hasty conclusions about the meaning and political implications of the events of 9/11 give a sense that something crucial had been lost, a sense that something of the self had been weakened and that a certain invincibility had been disrupted.

Clearly, however, the disruption of the sovereign self-sufficiency of the American geopolitical subject has by no means disabled or precluded political action. On the contrary, we can observe that it is the very disruption or displacement of the political subject that directly or indirectly *generates* action. Countless political analyses of 9/11 take exactly this kind of reaction, or even reactivity, as the point of departure for understanding a new chapter in geopolitics, based, more or less, on political and ethical business as usual. In these analyses, the injury, the damage, the insult are taken as simple indices of future threats, inserted into a finite political formula or calculation based on a realist mechanics of geopolitical force. Butler's theory of the precarious subject takes issue with this approach.

Bulter's ninth book, *Precarious LIfe*, is about injury, damage and loss, of the kind that was produced, in an exemplary sort of way, by the shared experience of 9/11. It is precisely this shared experience, this shared-ness, and not the question of objective or physical threat or damage, that is the starting point for Butler's analysis of the events. What is more, she does not take the injury performed under the attacks itself as the object of the analysis, but rather examines the *conditions* of its possibility, the 'injurability' of the political and moral subject in general, asking what kind of subject lets itself be injured by such an attack. And if such a subject is not directly, physically implicated in the death and destruction brought about by this or any other violence, what is, in general, our relationship to that violence? She answers:

> One insight that injury affords is that there are others out there on whom my life depends, people I do not know and may never know. This fundamental dependency on anonymous others is not a condition I can will away. No security measure will foreclose this dependency; no violent act of sovereignty will rid the world of this fact. [...]
>
> (Butler, 2004: xii)

What does our awareness of these others imply for our own self-security?

The violence of the attacks of 9/11 takes hold of the political and ethical subject, or perhaps most prominently the geopolitical subject, in several ways. *Firstly*, it is most evidently the materialization of concrete or determinate exposure to a certain kind of danger, material danger becoming material damage. *Secondly*, this materialization enacts a certain fantasy of threat, focuses it, intensifies it and, in certain ways, disappoints it. The liveable, empirical, material damage plays a psychic role in exhausting violence. The fantasy of complete material destruction satisfies a drive for completion or totality, a need to complete, totalize and encapsulate suffering as discharged, the work of mourning as finished. Yet while material calamity projects, it does not entirely satisfy a cataclysmic need for completing suffering by suffering completely. *Thirdly*, material damage opens the spectre of danger to the *reality* of others, to the experience of violence as done by others, by imagined or real persons, with concrete aims, material means and with more or less malicious intent. *Finally*, and in the same movement of thought or self-insight, it *re-cloaks* these others, establishes them as occult, configures them through the stealth of their nefarious aims, the invisibility and incomprehensibility of their lives for us.

It is, in part, this secrecy, this anonymity of the other, the impossibility of knowing for sure who or what it is, the otherness of the other, which stands at the centre of Butler's analysis. It is our incapacity to entirely share the experience, the experience of being forced to only imagine it, and the need, in ethical terms, to project it, to fantasize, to live the ethical life of the attack, as a kind of extension of our own ethical universe. Not only is it impossible to know this other, to authentically understand the life and ambitions, fears, wants, needs, hopes, anger, frustration and desperation of someone who would do great harm, but it is also the very impossibility of knowing, the lack of access to shared experience around the event, to an understanding of what others have experienced of it, and of why and how this has led them to find ethical meaning in their actions based on that experience. It is the inadequacy or inability of our attempts to seize this, together, of course, with the shock of physical destruction and loss, that lies at the heart of our injurability (Butler, 2005: 3–40).

This is, in a sense, the ethical logic of security in general. Security can be conceptualized in many ways. Among these, it is an ethical or axiological concept, that is, a discourse of values. Security is a way of organizing or structuring values around facts, expectations, fears and experiences. It is a kind of orientation relative to what is important and not important to us. Most commonly, security organizes a link between the tacit values of a given cultural or social setting and the political and technological measures marshalled to sustain it.

The way that security measures itself is shaped, informed *speculation* about dangers that could materialize. Such speculations are by nature inadequately grounded in knowledge. A security measure based on adequate knowledge would erase before the fact both insecurity itself and the need and meaningfulness of a security measure. Our injurability is in this sense a consequence of the structural inadequacy of the security knowledge.

This other, or others, to which we relate in our injurability exist and operate, like the discourse of security in general, in a regime of the unknown, a place of uncertainty, risk and fantasy. It is not the concrete or determinate other that threats or brings about our injury – *knowing* the other would cancel the injury – it is rather the experience of the unknown part of the other, the projection, fantasy or speculation that makes injury possible. When the presence of the other is evoked through media-nourished, xenophobic images of the wild-eyed, Arabic-speaking religious fanatic, this figure is simply a place-holder, a marker, playing a kind of role in the theatre of our collective security.

In a perhaps more complex way, our injurability is also linked to the injurability of the physical *other* who would do us harm. Here it seems that the only cure for our pain is the negation of the other human who authored it. (This is the work of grief in reverse.) But, for better or worse, we are required, in order to understand events, to react to the reality and to the situated-ness of the perpetrator of violence, to accept or understand, even through a demonizing denial, their own injurability, fragility or precariousness.

This moment has a double effect: On the one hand there is a radicalization of the individuality of the perpetrator, singularizing him or her or them as absolute unique originator of violence borne upon infinite personal accountability. On the other hand, there is a force of erasing the injurability of the perpetrator's exposure to danger, threat, risk and fear, precisely those moral emotions that we would mobilize from our own experience in order to condemn others.

The phenomenology of mourning

In *Precarious Life*, Butler develops a kind of phenomenology of mourning, an analysis of vulnerability understood as potential loss, as the presence, in potential mourning, of the death of those close to us, those ostensibly distant from us or estranged, and even ourselves, in the guise of a vision of our own deaths. This phenomenological horizon of loss invokes what Butler calls the 'human':

> ...I propose to start, and to end, with the question of the human (as if there were any other way for us to start or end!). We start here not because there is a human condition that is universally shared. This is surely not yet the case. The question that preoccupies me in the light of recent global violence is, who counts as human? Whose lives count as lives? And, finally, what *makes for grievable life?*
>
> (Butler, 2004: 20)

The horizon of grief is the invocation of the 'human' at a level adequately general to invoke the 'we' that unites us. This 'we' constitutes, then, the basis for a basic ethics of recognition, a recognition of the humanity of the human. This humanity is, in the time of the global war on terror, visibly not generalized. The empirical starting point of Butler's reflexion, which accompanies this theoretical opening is that the value of life has become qualitatively differentiated. The universal value of life writ large has been disrupted in the name of assuring security, itself only possible by drawing sharp religious, moral, cultural, social, even ethnic lines between good and bad, friend and foe.

> Despite our differences in location and history, my guess is that it is possible to appeal to a 'we,' for all of us have some notion of what it is to have lost somebody. [...] This means that each of us is constituted politically in part by virtue of the social vulnerability of our bodies – as a site of desire and physical vulnerability, as a site of publicity at once assertive and exposed. Loss and vulnerability seem to follow from our being socially constituted bodies, attached to others, at risk of losing those attachments, exposed to others, at risk of violence by virtue of that exposure.
>
> (ibid.: 20)

The subject-foundation of the universal position from which to engage this critique is not the shared canonical Enlightenment values of the western subject, autonomous, sovereign, self-knowing, self-understanding, but rather our shared vulnerability. Shared vulnerability provides the foundation for a political community and for shared ethical reflexion on the meaning of political action. The expression or embodiment of this shared vulnerability is *grief*.

> Many people think that grief is privatizing, that it returns us to a solitary situation and is, in that sense, depoliticizing. But I think it furnishes a sense of political community of a complex order, and it does this first of all by bringing to the fore the relational ties that have implications for theorizing fundamental dependency and ethical responsibility.
>
> (ibid.: 23)

Grief signals a dependency, it is true. But let us be careful not to construe this dependency as a kind anthropological economy of power, opposing the one who possesses the thing that the other needs or wants, able and willing to negotiate a clear exchange against another need or want. Grief does not integrate into this oppositional logic. Grief reflects both a loss and thereby some need to replace, reconstitute or reiterate what is gone. It also works through a need for the need, a need for the loss. Grief is the work of generalizing lack, generalizing a need for the other, for unity, for belonging or completeness. Grief is the work of letting go, of releasing what is gone. But it is also the work of reconstructing a new whole, and the realization of the need for this completeness. It is working through our relation to others in our new cosmos, without or beyond what was lost.

> What grief displays, in contrast, is the thrall in which our relations with others hold us, in ways that we cannot always recount or explain, in ways that often interrupt the self-conscious account of ourselves we might try to provide, in ways that challenge the very notion of ourselves as autonomous and in control. I might try to tell a story here about what I am feeling, but it would have to be a story in which the very 'I' who seeks to tell the story is stopped in the midst of the telling; the very 'I' is called into question by its relation.
>
> (Butler, 2004a: 23)

Such a story, what Butler elsewhere calls 'an account of oneself' (Butler, 2004), is a kind of derivative self-consciousness, or even self-knowledge. It is a way of relating to one's self about one's place in the world.

Grief, is not merely the loss of the object. It is, to a certain degree, the loss of the words to describe the loss of the object, to describe that empty hole in our capacity to make reference, our capacity to referentiality itself. What grief 'expresses', if we can call it that, is the empty spot between me and the object, the unrepresentable link between the other and me, akin to what Butler elsewhere describes as 'ethical violence', the suspension of the demand for 'self-identity' (Butler, 2005: 41–5). Grief is expressed in the gaping mouth, the silent sob. It is the referent of the words that will not come, the breath caught in the lungs. Because grief represents nothing, or perhaps, rather, it is the representation of not representing anything, representality that does not represent, it calls into question conventional notions of representation. In some sense, grief is a representation not outward, but inward, and expression to one's self. We grieve by talking to ourselves, but not through silent meditation. Grief is a talking to one's self in and through the body, talking through the physical instruments of voice, breath, vocal chords, etc. to oneself, in effect a physical impossibility.

Through grief I see that not only am I *not* autonomous – for I needed and need the other that is now lost – but I am also not even master of the relationship between myself and the object that is lost. This double-loss of the object is, as Butler puts it,

> . . . a relation that does not precisely reduce me to speechlessness, but does nevertheless clutter my speech with signs of its undoing. I tell a story about the relations I choose, only to expose, somewhere along the way, the way I am gripped and undone by these very relations. My narrative falters, as it must.
>
> (ibid.: 23)

As in the analysis of *Excitable Speech* (1997a), Butler focuses on language and representation as the link to materiality and the body. Clearly, language is the conduit to public discussion and debate, the material link to other interlocutors. But it is more. By the relation to loss, to death of the other, the work of grief as a kind of expression is also a relation to death itself:

> The body implies mortality, vulnerability, agency: the skin and the flesh expose us to the gaze of others, but also to touch, and to violence, and bodies put us at risk of becoming the agency and instrument of all these as well. Although we struggle for rights over our own bodies, the very bodies for which we struggle are not quite ever only our own.
>
> (ibid.: 28)

It is most remarkable to note that vulnerability, in Butler's reasoning, is not a contingent property of human beings, not a simple characteristic of humanness, which can be added or subtracted from the equation of the human. It cannot be a question of being human with being vulnerable. Vulnerability is the given, the baseline, the foundation itself.

> We cannot, however, will away this vulnerability. We must attend to it, even abide by it, as we begin to think about what politics might be implied by staying with the thought of corporeal vulnerability itself, a situation in which we can be vanquished or lose others. Is there something to be learned about the geopolitical distribution of corporeal vulnerability from our own brief and devastating exposure to this condition?
>
> (ibid.: 29)

This observation might at first glance seem self-evident. If it is, then we must also explain why conventional conceptualizations of security lift us out and away from such a view. The security discourse that dominates our lives, carrying immense consequences for our wellbeing is organized into a kind of teleology of vulnerability quite foreign to Butler's. It is a teleology where the *alpha*, the original, authentic or baseline 'human', and the *omega* of security, its goal or finality, are both some non-vulnerable state. It is as though the natural form of human life, should such a thing exist, were the invulnerable. This is, according to Butler, unthinkable, not for some empirical reason, but rather because vulnerability lies at the core of the subject of security.

Vulnerability as insecurity

The subject of security understood as 'in' security, or 'possessing' a thing called security, is in its kernel impossible. Subjectivity is the fundamental experience of insecurity, and insecurity that is generalizable across a wide domain. For this reason we cannot recover the 'source of this invulnerability' in order to somehow counter it or erase it, thus recovering or reinstating, an aboriginal, invulnerable subject. We cannot make ourselves invulnerable, as is the argument, implicit or explicit, made by many entrepreneurs of security and the political class alike. The coherence of the ethical, political subject of security is its inherent vulnerability: '... it precedes the formation of "I". This is a condition, a condition of being laid bare from the start and with which we cannot argue' (ibid.: 31).

Butler means, instead, to refer to a more general concept of vulnerability and thus a more general concept of violence, differentiated from any kind of structural or systemic violence. It is a kind of primeval violence, as she says, one in which we are:

> ... from the start, given over to the other, one in which we are, from the start, even prior to individuation itself and by virtue of bodily requirements, given over to some set of primary others.
>
> (ibid.: 31)

This vulnerability, she points out, must somehow precede judgement, precede the predication of knowledge and precede the notion of physical existence as contingent, precede the primary distinction between our lives and the material support we require for the sustenance for our lives (ibid.: 31). To the degree that we can talk about a stable, solid, rigid, i.e. invulnerable, foundation of the subject of security, it is *vulnerability*. This fundamental vulnerability or precariousness resists predication, resists conceptualization, but above all, resists subjectivization.

In *Frames of War* (2009), Butler explains:

> To say that a life is precarious requires not only that a life be apprehended as a life, but also that precariousness be an aspect of what is apprehended in what is living.
>
> (Butler, 2009: 11)

Clearly, precariousness is a form of dependency. It should, however, not be reduced to a simple metaphysics of dependency, to a logic of have and have not, to satisfiable need, or satiable want. Precariousness that can be stabilized, un-precarious, removed from threat or danger, is not precariousness, but rather a finite risk calculation.

> Precariousness implies living socially, that is, the fact that one's life is always in some sense in the hands of the other. It implies exposure both to those we know and to those we do not know; a dependency on people we know, or barely know, or know not at all. Reciprocally, it implies being impinged upon by the exposure and dependency of others, most of whom remain anonymous.
>
> (ibid.: 13)

In this sense, the theory of the precarious subject founds an ethics of sociality. It poses the subject, the self, in a position that would be meaningless without others, both visible and invisible. Subjectivity is buoyed by obligation.

The same goes for the political and ethical subject of security. The subjectivity of security is opened by its own vulnerability. The position from which securitization takes places, from which security is invoked, or from which the exception is declared, is already necessarily fragile.

The subject of security is thus the place from which security is both mobilized and lived, embodies at least three discourses, three modes of being. The *first* is a social or anthropological mode. According to a logic or metaphysics of threat versus threatened, the subject that invokes security is already under duress, already under threat. It is this threat that obliges the security measure. *Second,* from an epistemological point of view, the subject of security is also at a loss for knowledge, the force of its position in whatever human or technological chain of command is always deficient, always behind the ball, as they say. Insecurity emerges not from knowledge, but from the absence of knowledge. Security is mobilization for an unknown future. *Finally,* the vulnerability of the subject, its precariousness in the face of the injury of others, of potential types of injuries to others, envelops the security subject as the subject of vulnerability and, as such, signals an ethics of security as an ethics of sociality.

Part II
Holding together

5 Identity, community and security

Among the most marked characteristics of our late modern society is the emergence of a vast range of multicultural communities. Yet what marks this phenomenon is less the actual existence of these new communities or the enhanced meaning of community as such, but rather the experience, the phenomenology of their emergence. A powerful discourse of recognition and legitimization has come into play, linking identity and community on a number of levels, generating rights and privileges founded upon an experience of belonging that itself builds upon individual and group self-understanding as much as it does on the transformational politics of category: on who belongs to what, in the name of whom and in the service of what (Fiore and Nelson, 2003; Fraser, 2001; Haacke, 2005; Honneth, 1995b; Taylor et al., 1994).

Ethnic, cultural, sexual, professional, aesthetic, religious identities, to name a few, generate legitimacy effects by the force of collective rights and the logic of recognition. In late modern, liberal societies, minority communities find rights and privileges that even seem to defy principles of liberal individuality. To be a minority in a large number of cultural contexts is to enjoy a kind of status, an appreciation, an acknowledgement, a home and security. From the moment a selective community achieves conceptual standing based on a shared identity, it becomes the object of a certain kind of securitization. Its very existence sets in motion a dialectic of recognition, threat and defence.

Identity is enabled through a logic, not of identity but of difference. The 'we' invoked by any assertion of identity draws not only its meaning and meaningfulness, but also its stability, strength, longevity and security from its opposition to, or even negation of, the other. The affirmation of the identity of a group is not only a categorical one, setting out the rules and terms under which something or someone belongs or does not belong to a group. It is also an assertion of the durability or temporality of that group or the collection and, by consequence, avowal of the possibility of its disappearance, the very source of its insecurity. From Hegel onward, a long line of canonical texts develops the dialectical counterparts of identity and difference, the unity of the self-understanding as inseparable from the opposition to the other.

As a consequence, identity, collectively recognized in community, generates a special set of security issues. In the field of political philosophy, it concerns the long-standing debate between liberals and communitarians. In sociology, it joins discussions within social theory on the nature of collective identity. In political science it builds upon advances within the theory of international relations, both through its indebtedness to the advances made by the Copenhagen School and in solidarity with advances in political theory. This chapter seeks to dialogue with some of the main issues of concern in current debates, drawing out some of the political and ethical consequences of identity and community for the general concept of security (Mattern, 2001; Qizilbash, 2009; Von Busekist, 2004).

Identity

By identity we understand the discourse of the self, both individual and collective, that is operative in the organization of social and political theory. We intentionally model the concept of identity in this way in order, among other things, to underscore the notion that although social and political theory are clearly based on a certain conception of individual identity they do not exhaust it. Today's widely used concept of identity grows out of the articulation of the individual self across virtually all fields of scientific study (Taylor, 1989). The discussions within the social sciences around the concept of identity reveal a general critique of modern philosophy of the subject and a reconsideration of the basic principles of the *self* in the western tradition. As has been well documented, such a critique of Enlightenment rationality is more or less as old as the Enlightenment itself.

A number of strands of social theory of the last three decades has problematized the notion of the centred, autonomous subject as a basis for social cohesion (Beck, 1992; Giddens, 1990, 1991; Beck et al., 1994; Delanty, 1999; Joas, 1998; Harré, 1998; Melluci, 1996; Honneth, 1996, 1995a; Gouldner, 1970). These critiques put into question such ideas as the basis of Cartesian subjectivity, the discourse of origin and absolute reference, the monopoly of universal reason and universal ethics, the critique of freedom and the centricity of the subject, among many other themes that most mainstream political theory shows only minor awareness or interest in.

Ever since Descartes, in his *Metaphysical Meditations* (Descartes, 1996), posited the individual subject as firmly situated in the spirit, opposed to matter and endowed with the capacity of autonomous rational thought, the modern *individual* took on a new meaning. Following Descartes, Locke, in *Essay on Human Understanding* (1690), recast the individual as 'sameness of rational being', that is, as the self-identical and invariable rationality of the subject (Locke, 1967). According to the modern paradigm, the individual is thus 'indivivisible': *in-dividium*. It is integrally itself, unified and centred, even if it inhabits a culturally decentred world (Delanty, 2000).

My identity is who I am or what I am. This simple characterization is a satisfactory first cut, but ultimately inadequate. For according to whom, according to what *subject,* am I who I am, or what I am?[1] In other words, identity, like any human property cannot be objectively characterized. Understanding identity must pass through a hermeneutic of the self, encompassing dialectic of objective certitude and subjective projection. Identity is simultaneously the object of cognition – my own and that of others – and the subject from the point of view of which identity is determined. Identity is the object of cognition and the condition of cognition.[2]

Identity is not merely what we understand ourselves to be; it is also what others think we are. It is, in other words, both subjective and objective. It is subjective in the sense that it is a representation of the way a certain individual or group understands itself. It is objective in the sense that it is a representation of how others see the group. Clearly, these two sides are co-determinate. In other words, an individual or group identity is, in part, formed by how it or its member sees itself, and in part by who others see it. In the case of groups, individual identity is also determined by how the individual members of the group see one another.

In this sense, identity of an individual or a group is always connected to an *other*. It is always associated with a someone or something that is *not* the individual or the group. I am never entirely the author of my own identity. I am who I am only as far as others see me and recognize me. The others can be another group, another individual or – and here is the difficult part of the structure of identity – the other can be myself. One always has some idea of one's self. But when we look at ourselves, when we look in the mirror, when we ask what our own identity is, what do we see? Do we see an object, a thing, that is other and foreign to us, a thing that we can conceive with objectivity? Or do we see something that is identical to us, something which is the same, has the same experience of being itself (Ricœur, 1990). The thing we see in the mirror is *both* us and other, both an object that is seen and a subject that sees. In order to be ourselves we require the other who perceives us, even if that other is ourselves (Kristeva, 1988).

Thus, identity is the incidence of both subject and object. It is simultaneously the experience of seeing and being seen, hearing and being heard, recognizing and being recognized. In order to understand ourselves as ourselves, be it on the individual or group level, we require the other who is different from us. The other can be other individuals or other groups (or the other in ourselves).

In other words, *difference* is an essential trait of identity. The experience of one's identity – individual or group – is intimately bound together with the experience of being different from others. Indeed, our *difference* from other identities is *part* of our identity. As we will argue in Chapter 6, 'Intolerable insecurity', our opposition to other groups, or differences with respect to other identities, are fundamental to the formation and evolution of our own. The consequence of this conclusion is clear and direct: the very survival of our group identity is *not* assured by asserting its predominance over others, or in the extreme by erasing others. On the contrary, the survival of our identity is *based upon* our tolerance of others.

A first articulation of individual identity is thus a differential one. The ideal type of the perfect self-present, self-sufficient identity is arguably the unconscious fantasy of the high-modern individuality at the moment of its internal breakdown and differentiation into the postmodern conception of identity to self-identity.

Identity is henceforth the *act* of conceiving one's self as a self. My identity is not this subject that is speaking, articulating my identity, it is the object of reference of me talking about my identity. And yet this identity precedes the talking, the conceptualization, and most certainly the conception. My identity is something else, somewhere else. Indeed, this otherness is what permits me to make it an object of my thought, and of my speech. My identity is never completely my own. It is only a proper object when it is the object of another, when another observes it, observes me.

My identity is always first a relation to the conceptions of my identity that others might have. Just as I am not the best judge of the objectivity of my own thoughts, I cannot be the objective observer of my own self. The meaning of myself is only available to me through the mediation of another. Our individual identity is invisible to us, like a tattoo on our mid-lower backs: intimately a part of us yet forever invisible to us. Identity is an experience of the other, through the gaze of the other, as Lacanian psychoanalysis or Levinasian phenomenology (Levinas, 1972) would express it. It is through the *other* that our identity is constituted.

The commonplace conception of collective identity is, to some degree, a projection of the notion of the individual self on to collective experience (be they ethnic, cultural, sexual, political, professional), which are singular with respect to the broader context in which they are situated. Collective identity is the generalization of the logical of singularity-plurality.

It is difficult to imagine a sure and stable foundation for the formation of a group's collective common identity reposing on anything other than a certain notion of the self-identical person. However, the paradox that characterizes the concept of identity in our era can be traced to the fact that the new emphasis on individual identity, its valorization as a foundation of legitimacy, goes hand-in-hand with the discovery of the *hybrid* nature of that identity. If social and political modernity is characterized by the emergence of identity, this emergence must be inseparable from our conscience of the explosion of identities, of the general identity crisis that unites all of society's sub-groups (Bauman, 2001). At the same time, what we call today *identity* in the field of social sciences appears necessarily in a certain phase of social and political modernity. Only after World War II did the term *identity* become detached from the its *philosophical* conceptual network in order to be associated with the social sciences, first and foremost in the Anglo-Saxon academic world (Niethammer, 2000).

Community

The rise of the discourse of identity has breathed new life into a number of forms of social studies and laid the foundations for a new generation of social politics. It has also, to a large degree, revitalized social philosophy by reformulating the question of community and its ethical consequences. Perhaps more persistently than other social developments, the multiplication and penetration of identities accompanied a mutation in the study of the social sciences. To a large degree, the discourse of identity appears as a stage in the evolution of the notion of individuality (ibid., 2000). From turn-of-the-century personal psychology arises the concept of individual personality, which in turn joins that of the unity of the member of a group whose cohesion is derived from shared personal values or characteristics (Mauss, 1989). The post WW II period sees the social sciences conceptualizing an increasing number of identity-based discourses, the notions of racial, sexual, political and cultural identity are thereby transferred to the collective groups that share them. The notion of moral personality and legal personality is transferred to the group, permitting the development of concepts of rights associated with communities sharing a given collective identity.[3]

The analysis of individual identity in relation to community has become one of the central themes of the analysis of modernity. This has led to the full integration of the discourse of identity in the social sciences, and the exuberant appearance of new cottage industries in the study and differentiation of forms of self-understanding. On the one hand, the social sciences enjoy a raised consciousness of the diversity and heterogeneity of the global anthropological landscape. New methodologies and empirical studies have broadened and deepen the study and understanding of the cultural diversity of our globe. On the other hand, new de-limitations within social sciences live out the consequences of raised consciousness of the multiplication of the components of individual identity. With growing sophistication, gender studies, cross-cultural studies, racial studies, etc. paint an increasingly complex picture of the overlapping and criss-crossing make-up of social relations. In this way the rise of the study of identity has thus gone hand-in-hand with 'discovery' of new communities, both in the complexity of a more self-aware global community and in the raised awareness of the diversity of interconnected and overlapping communities in which we already live. No individual belongs to one community alone. Identity is understood as composite. All individuals exist in a network of criss-crossing identities, organizing the way they understand themselves and others.

The hybrid and composite nature of identity has the result that the communities to which we multifariously belong are necessarily porous. Like the categorical labels that identify them, communities do not have hard, impenetrable borders. The characteristics and values proper to any given community coexist. None is absolutely constricted with respect to the other.

Among the complex and composite ways in which modernity has evolved, the development of community is among the most pervasive within social theory (Wagner, 1994). The theorists of high modernity – Tönnies, Weber, Spencer, Durkheim and others – characterize modernity itself as the loss of a certain kind of community. 'Community', especially as it is formulated by Ferdinand Tönnies' 1867 classic, *Community and Society*, is the organic, complex, cohesive bonds that connect the individual to a tradition of value and meaning (Delanty, 2000; Tönnies, 2002). Tönnies opposes this notion of community against the modern notion of society. The modern form of social cohesion is based on a set of artificial, constructed, pragmatic bonds. As Delanty points out, the notion of community is thus associated with a sense of place, proximity and totality, while society is associated with fragmentation, alienation and distance (2000: 116). Boundaries are not disappearing, but rather appearing on every street corner (Friedman, 1999; Bauman, 2001). A need to recreate an invisible origin to the identity is often expressed. It must not be lived as arbitrary, but rather as necessity itself. As Bauman puts it, 'Identity sprouts on the graveyard of communities, but flourishes thanks to the promise of a resurrection of the dead' (ibid.: 16).

This opposition is recurrent in social theory from the close of the 19th century until well into the postwar era. It promotes a general conservative logic according to which the requirements of interpersonal relations are interpreted as best served by the foundational cohesion of community. According to Bauman, modern society, with advanced capitalism in the lead, attempts to replace the 'feeling' of organic cohesion through artificially designed and coercively imposed routines, accompanied by an extraordinary capacity to replace the sense of origin from which 'society' is supposed to be detached (Bauman, 2001).

With the near mythological privileging of community, the eternal lost origin of collective organization, modernization as mourning process or separation anxiety is fully empowered. A series of canonical culprits can be underscored under the sign of the evil's instrumental rationality: capitalism and scientism are the main theatres of reproach. In the complexity of their sociological contributions, Marx, Weber and Simmel are in agreement that a cultural substrate to human organization is under repression through the scientific and economic systems of our time. Yet perhaps a stronger explanation for the transformation from community to society was not included in the theoretization of Weber, Marx or Simmel. According to Bauman, the fundamental rupture in the fabric of community was the advent of *telecommunication*.

> Precisely such a breach in the protective walls of community became a foregone conclusion with the appearance of mechanical means of transportation; carriers of alternative information (or people who very strangeness was information distinct from, and clashing with, the knowledge internally available) could now in principle travel as quickly

or faster than the word-of-mouth messages originating and circulated within the circumference of 'natural' human mobility. Distance, once the most formidable among the communal defences, lost much of its significance. The mortal blow to the 'naturalness' of communal understanding was delivered, however, by the advent of informatics: the emancipation of the flow of information from the transport of bodies. Once information could travel independently of its carriers, and with a speed far beyond the capacity of even the most advanced means of transportation (as in the kind of society we nowadays inhabit), the boundary between 'inside' and 'outside' could no longer be drawn, let alone sustained.

(ibid.: 13–14)

Through the question of community, globalization unites identity and ethics. The most powerful heritage of the political and social modernity in the 20th century is the notion that the finality of humanity is a universal community. This utopian vision is based on a simple proposition: that a certain set of essential roots and social needs are common to all. Modern ethical theory presupposes, either explicitly or implicitly, the global generality of this notion. The challenge arises with the realization that the national movements that mark the 18th and 19th centuries, based on the notion of a national community of values, has reached a point of exhaustion. The rise of the discourse of the post-national marks the end of the equivalence between community values and national values.

From the point of view of philosophical ethics, this situation leads to two fundamental questions: firstly, can we envisage a global community that reflects social relations on a global level? Secondly, can we conceptualize systems of universal values applicable to the particular conditions of multiple overlapping communities? The tools and categories of classical philosophy are poorly suited to understand and analyze the effects of the global revolution. First and foremost, the universalist narratives of social ethics lose some of their legitimacy while traditional concepts like 'society' and 'nationality' become increasingly problematic. Community values exceed national borders and traditional community categories.

The 'communitarian' debate

Since the 1970s ethical philosophy has experienced a particularly productive rejuvenation through debates, on several levels and along several lines, between communitarians and liberals. The centre of gravity of these debates is the question of 'distributitive justice', which opposes defenders of the 'liberal egalitarianism' (Rawls and Dworkin) against 'libertarians' (Nozick and Buchman) and 'utilitarians' (Mill, Sigwick, Harsanyi, Goodin, Hare). The utilitarian condition continues the classical conception of utilitarianism: a just distribution of social goods is that which maximizes the general satisfaction of the community. The liberal position of Rawls (and others) is based on the 'principle of difference': the equal distribution of goods is desirable except if an unequal distribution of the same goods is advantageous to the most disadvantaged (Rawls, 1971).

The novelty of Rawls' theory is its explicit presupposition that inequality is social and not based on objective measures of merit. Rawls rejects the notion of substantial or essential value of action. Justice and injustice are determined based on social givens themselves derived from communal relations. *Natural* value – the cornerstone of Enlightenment ethics of social organization – cannot be adduced within the formula of justice. Rawls' theory of justice thus distances itself from conventional utilitarianism, which measures value based on the good brought to the community in general. According to that, the existence of disadvantages, even the privation of certain individuals, can in principle contribute to the the welfare of the community. Rawls' liberal point of view is to insist on the separation of individuals: the liberty of an individual cannot be violated to the advantage of others.

The communitarianism response to this reasoning (MacIntyre, Snadel, Taylor, Walzer) is in conformity with more or less classical utilitarianism. Put simply, instead of basing moral claims on a conception of the individual, communitarians base claims on the value of community. Accordingly, it is considered an error to embrace a voluntarist theory of subject, which supposedly exists prior to the aims it engages in. On the contrary, it is impossible to detach the individual from the ends it assumes. Individual identity is dependent upon the acts of the individual. Action, according to communitarians, has meaning only when contextualized.

Despite the considerable opposition between these two philosophical positions, they remain common in the sense that the concepts upon which they are founded are, in the one case, date, and in the other, impossibly inflexible.

The liberalism of Rawls and Dworkin is essentially based on a conception of the individual, which has not evolved since the 18th century Enlightenment framework. The liberal (Rawlsian) subject is more or less identical to the Cartesian subject, in other words, autonomous, rational, master of its own will, etc. Moreover, the liberal model presupposes the very liberty it intends to assure 'A person is acting autonomously when the principles of his action are chosen by him as the most adequate possible expression of his nature as a free and equal rational being' (Rawls, 1971). Through its various forms, ethical liberalism presupposes this stable and unequivocal conception of the individual. The aim of this philosophical strategy is to proscribe the social and political structures most likely to give free course to this autonomous subject, without actually problematizing the subject. The implicit subjective liberty is thus conjectured internally. The only problem that thus remains is to find the framework in which this ready-made subject can realize its own implicit liberty. From the standpoint of the subject, liberalism does not consider relevant the multiples axes of variance of either liberty or individual identity, such as psychic, sexual, economic or other dimensions. From the standpoint of the social and the political, the state is considered neutral and transparent, a meeting-place in which communication, exchange, ethical substance, etc. are not already saturated with power, a state that is indifferent to ethics, disinterested by its own relation to the values that might organize its operation. According to the liberal model, autonomy can only be realized within a cultural of ethnic collectivity. The basis of cultural identity – individual autonomy – is forcibly limited to the context of the group.

At first glance, communitarianism seems more susceptible to tackle the ethical challenges of globalization. It is based on an idea of community that is not necessarily identical to the political and social frameworks furnished by the nation-state. Communitarianism thus also possesses a neoliberal dimension. Individualism is not implicit to the extent that individual identity is articulated as a function of the situation of the community. The critique of communitarianism also takes its point of departure from this position: the choices made by the communitarian actor are, in some sense, already made for him or her, already foreseen in the ethical system, already given by the community that transcends him or her. Communitarianism is not tenable if one does not first establish both the meaning and thereby the destiny of the community.

From the liberal standpoint, the difference in identity is negotiated in terms of individual choices, based on the principle of free (individual) choice. Identity is the result of one choice in relation to other possible choices. According to the liberal theory, this choice is external to the individual. The individual is sovereign, complete, self-present. S/he makes choices with regard to alternatives that are objectively external (Bauman, 1997). For communitarians the difference in identity is negotiated in terms of *internal* differences within the collectivity. The identities of the individual and of the collectivity are produced through an internal dialogue with the various resources of the group. This identity, as we have seen, is not only fluctuating, it is multiple.

Consequentially, the free choice presupposed by liberal theory is not a precondition of identity. It is derived from it. True enough, it is the result of a free choice, but not in the manner understood by liberalism. Identity is not chosen directly, it is the product of the paradoxically impossible experience of choice. On the other hand, the collective construction of identity presumed by communitarians is fluctuating. While it is true that individual identity is produced in dialogue with the collective identity of the group involved, the fluctuating available identities are never identical to the multiple identities of the community. On the contrary, they transcend it.

The constitutive identities available for the construction of collective or individual identity precede and transcend any instrumental thought of identity formation. Communitarians suppose that identity is chosen *avant la lettre,* as the moment of the constitution of the collectivity. Liberals suppose that identity is contingent, the simple object of choice. Neither recognizes that freedom of choice is indeed a *constraint* in a reality made up of multiple identities.

Community and security

The status and liberty of the subject of community and of identity will have significant consequences for the constitution of any given community, be it social, cultural, political, academic, sexual, etc. Such communities presuppose a set of borders, predominantly but not exclusively invisible, the object of a subject whose status is either invisible, ambiguous or simply not coherent. Such borders are in some cases the material borders that mark the traditional conception of the nation-state; political boundaries, physical de-limitations, spaces of restriction, passages, etc. In the age of multiculturalism, however, borders are increasingly conceptual, categorical or imaginary.

Community is, among other things, the organization of individuals with respect to a concept or principle. The concept defines the rules and parameters of admission (Burgess, 2001a). These rules and parameters function primarily to de-limit individuals – those who belong and those who do not belong to the collective categories. It contains a force of inclusion and a force of exclusion. It responds to the will of applicants with denial or permission. Such rules take as the object, primarily, but not exclusively, individuals. A community possesses a kind of sovereignty foreign to the conventional study of international politics. A community possesses conceptual sovereignty, maintains conceptual borders, setting up conceptual border guards. Community is thus also a mechanism of surveillance, control and discipline, sanction and reward (Foucault, 1975).

Any community is also a security problem. Yet among the most relevant communities of our time are those *not* enshrined in concrete institutions, and thus those that can be subjected to material risks. The threats to which such communities are exposed are threats to the identities that constitute them. Indeed, the very existence of community creates or institutes its own threat. In the atmosphere of multiculturalism in which communities overlap, redoubling and competing with one another, as Bauman formulates it, 'Community of common understanding is fragile':

> Security is the necessary condition of dialogue between cultures. [...] The security in question is, however, a wider problem than most advocates of multiculturalism, in tacit (or inadvertent) collusion with the preachers of communal separation, are willing to admit. Narrowing the issue of endemic insecurity to genuine or putative threats to communally sustained uniqueness is a mistake which draws attention away from its true sources. Nowadays, community is sought as a shelter from the gathering

tides of global turbulence – tides originating as a rule in faraway places which no locality can control on its own. The sources of the overwhelming feeling of insecurity are sunk deep in the widening gap between the condition of 'individuality *de jure*' and the task of acquiring 'individuality *de facto*'. The construction of walled-up communities does nothing to close that gap, but everything to make closing it more difficult – nay impossible. Instead of aiming at the sources of insecurity, it channels attention and energy away from them. None of the adversaries in the ongong 'us versus them' war gain in security from it; all, however, are made easier targets, indeed 'sitting ducks', for the globalizing forces – the only forces likely to benefit from suspending the search for common humanity and joint control over the human condition.

(Bauman, 2001: 142–3)

A *political* community can be defined as a group of individuals sharing the same political identity. That political identity is concentrated in the notion of sovereignty. A long and powerful tradition of international studies, from Thomas Hobbes onward, understands this sovereignty in conformity with the understanding of the *self* presented above. The sovereign subject of political identity is understood to be the singular, self-centred concentration of will and authority from which the political community represents itself to the world.[4] In modern political theory, the political community is assumed to be identical to the state. International politics, according to this view, is the relation between the political identity of one sovereign state in relation to the chaos of all others.

A number of thoughtful re-readings of this tradition have questioned the implicit premises on which it is based (Weber, 1995). In his wide-ranging critique of the premises of realist thought in international relations, R.B.J. Walker problematizes the idea of sovereignty as a spatially determined and a-historical category (Walker, 1993). In other words, he calls into question the two foundations of common wisdom on sovereignty: first, that the state sovereignty constitutes a clearly de-limited political community within its discrete geographical boundaries. And second, that once the state is constituted by whatever political means may be applicable, the nature of that sovereignty is unchanging in time. The 'security debate' is already set *hors-débat* by the presuppositions of the 'debate'. The security debate is already completed before it is opened. In this sense, the 'debate' adheres to a well-documented structure of discursive power. The discourse of security studies controls the concepts and ideas, and empirical data that are admissible to the debate.

The dominant notion of political identity in international relations essentially falls back upon the early modern conception of collective identity, which we have critiqued above. As Walker explains, this way of conceiving identity hides the same pitfalls as the general sociological conception:

Claims about some common identity convey a great deal about our capacity to imagine particular identities, for a common identity is precisely what we do not have, at least in any politically meaningful sense. Modern political identities are fractured and dispersed among a multiplicity of sites, a condition sometimes attributed to a specifically postmodern experience but one that has been a familiar, though selectively forgotten, characteristic of modern political life for several centuries. This specifically modern proliferation of spatially delimited identities has had sharp limits. The presumed anarchy among state has been an anarchy of the select few. But it is this proliferation, affirmed by accounts of the modern state as institution, container of all cultural meaning, and site of sovereign jurisdiction over territory, property and abstract space, and consequently over history, possibility and abstract time, that still shapes our capacity to affirm both particular and collective identities. It does so despite all the dislocations, accelerations and contingencies of a world less and less able to recognize itself in the cracked mirror of Cartesian coordinates.

(Walker, 1993: 161–2)

Identity cannot be understood as geographical. While there are political identities and communities that nominally adhere to geographical categories and boundaries, the networks of their self-understandings, the movement of their influence and dependency, is not identical with them.

It is impossible to understand the changing political landscape of globalized communities without an identity toolkit that retrospectively understands the formation and evolution of conventional political identity. According to Walker, a critique is needed of the origins of the traditional conception of political identity as sovereignty. That tradition tends to associate the origin of sovereignty with a singular moment when sovereign power was consolidated. By critiquing the notion of singular origin, one begins to understand the degree to which the *principle* of sovereignty is neither permanent nor unambiguous (Walker, 1993: 163). Sovereignty, like the security to which it lays claim, is under constant mutation, changing with the ebb and flow of global power, but also with the changes in intra-state political identities (Linklater, 1998; Mattern, 2001; Nathan, 2006; Purvis and Hunt, 1999; Weber, 1995; Hansen and Stepputat, 2005).

Security is thus the fluctuation of the experience of insecurity/security. In this sense the only true 'security studies' would be a *phenomenology* of security. Phenomenology is a mode of analysis which, instead of focusing on the empirical facts of security – geographical, institutional, demographic and technological dimensions – would seek to uncover the implicit and otherwise invisible structures that make possible and organize the connection of the different empirical facts and concepts. A phenomenology of security would seek to uncover the registers in which the insecurity/security nexus is regarded as a structuring function of the experience of being.

The imperative of security, of self-protection implicit in the notion of community, in this way opens toward an ethical imperative. The other, which we found to be constitutive of the self, is far from ethically neutral. Security is a need implicit in community. This need is the pathos of community. Implicit in the phenomenology of community is its constant state of siege, not only by some contingent, concrete other, be it the military enemy, the economic competitor, the environmental menace or the social incertitude. The pathos of community is *phenomenal*; it belongs to the structural make of community itself. Connolly brilliantly describes this structural tic as 'the paradox of evil':

> The definition of difference is a requirement built into the logic of identity, and the construction of otherness is a temptation that readily insinuates itself into that logic – and more than a temptation: a temptation because it is constantly at work and because there may be political ways to fend it off or reduce its power; more than a temptation because it typically moves below the threshold of conscious reflection and because every attempt to come to terms with it encounters stubborn obstacles built into the logic of identity and the structural imperatives of social organization. To come to terms with one's implication in these strategies, one needs to examine established tactics of self-identity, not so much by engaging in self-inquiry into one's deep interior as by exploring the means by which one has become constituted as what one is, by probing the structures that maintain the plausibility of those configurations, and by analyzing from a perspective that problematizes the certainty of one's self-identity the effects these structures and tactics have on others. These same tactics apply when *we* encounter the problem of evil in *our* identity.
>
> (Connolly, 1991: 9)

Notes

1   The only ultimately 'adequate' formulation of identity is the definition of adequacy itself: A = A, 'I am I'. Yet even this type of adequacy begs the question of identity by failing to provide a meaningful response to the question according to which subject the formula is adequate (Burgess, 2001c).
2   'Cognition' will ultimately be too restrictive. Work in progress will problematize the autonomy of the cognizant subject, seeking to inscribe it in a framework of phenomenological ethics of the kind developed by Levinas (1961; 1974; 1998).
3   It is important to underscore that the very notion of social science issues from approximately the same period as the alleged transformation in collective norms. The *Geisteswissenschaften* first formulated by Rickert and Dilthey and already embodied in the work of Weber, Simmel, Scheler, Marx and others responds directly to the need for a new type of analysis of the radical change in social organization brought about by the mechanisms of high modernity.

4   In the classic Cold-War work *Political Community and the North Atlantic Area*, Karl Deutsch (1957a) launched a new concept, which responds both to the sociological longing for a community-based cohesion and to the Cold-War induced mechanical or procedural policy: security as game theory (cf. also Williams and Neumann, 2000; Adler and Barnett, 1998; Adler, 2008).

6   Intolerable insecurity

Although tolerance is the primary ethical inheritance of the Enlightenment it was hardly the preferred solution through the long and bloody history of religious-based violence in Europe. Nonetheless, with the increasing fragmentation of the religious 'superpowers' after the Thirty Years War, the notion of religious tolerance became a more common means of coping, both philosophically and politically, with religious difference (Outram, 1995; Gay, 1977). The concept of tolerance is alive and well today in the field of philosophical ethics, safely inserted into debates between liberalism, cosmopolitanism and communitarianism. In these debates, however, it is assimilated to the traditional question of *liberty*. (What liberties are just and affordable in a society where not all can be free?) Yet while canonical ethical debates about tolerance take the identity of the individual or group as a starting point for reflexion about the nature of tolerance to be ascribed to them or claimed by them, we will in this chapter try to better understand the insecurity of our time by posing the question of tolerance as one at the heart of identity itself, and look for a response to the question of the modern-day relation between tolerance and security.

The concept of tolerance is structured around a curious double logic, based on a more or less contradictory relation to a directive, law, convention, custom, norm or ethical principle. Tolerance is the subject position from which one adopts or, at least recognizes the law or convention, and then simultaneously enacts a rule or principle by which breaking the convention is both sanctioned and regulated: 'The teaching language in US classrooms is English; however, the use of Spanish will be *tolerated*.'

According to the logic of tolerance, the rule is asserted, presented under the sign of a certain kind of recognition and validity at the same time as the principles of its violation. The rule is established, as are the mode and limits of its implicit or explicit violability. These limits vary considerably. The *measure* of tolerance corresponds to the variance between the convention and its violation, either in terms of the *frequency* of its violation or the *degree* of its violation. For Hegel, the course of history of universal reason requires a certain form of tolerance, a spiritual 'patience' to undertake the 'enormous labour of the world's history' with the non-alignment of the *Weltgeist* with knowledge of the imperfect world it is meant to be a model for (Hegel, 1977: 17).

Identity and difference

In what sense does tolerance approach a logic of threat? What is threatened when our tolerance is tested? What is the relation between threat and tolerance? Which insecurities are at play? Which defences are mobilized against the intolerable, and in the name of what? Clearly, our own identity, its self-consciousness, self-presence, self-sufficiency, capability, etc. plays a role in our relation to the identity we tolerate.

In Chapter 5 we conceptualized identity in terms of the insecurity of the community, extending the analysis; in Chapter 10 we will link it to the community of values. In order to understand tolerance as a function of identity, we will in this chapter examine more closely the dialectic of identity in difference, of self and other, that structures on a fundamental level the notion of tolerance.

Identity is who we are or what we are, whether we are referring to a person or a group. All those who understand themselves – as German or Italian, Muslim or Hindu, gay or straight, cricketer or birdwatcher – are, in so doing, referring implicitly to an identity. They are referring to an implicit or explicit principle, articulated or unconscious, understood by all those who share the notion of belonging to the particular group. If we call ourselves French it is because we attach to the word 'French' a signification that extends well beyond a simple kind of state or national category. It extends beyond the simple fact that we carry a certain passport instead of another. We refer to another category, to a kind of community, a community that is far more complex and far more rich, but also far more ambiguous. Herein lies the conceptual challenge: if we have, at a given moment, an identity – national, cultural, religious, sexual or otherwise – then it is this *ambiguous* but somehow imagined community that is the source and the determining force of that identity. It is what makes us what, or who, we are. That community is our identifier for ourselves and for others. It is what permits others to identify us. What is fascinating, however, is that this cultural community that identifies us for others identifies us also for ourselves, shapes who we are, determines our self-understanding. It functions itself as if it were an other, as if it were a kind of external authority, an authority or agency that directs and determines our identity, our cultural identity. Even if I am German by *right*, I am obliged to understand that German-ness (in relation to the criterion for German-ness), which does not belong to me, is external to me, in effect belongs to someone else. This other, as we discovered in Lacan's theory of the mirror stage in Chapter 3, is not only formative for who we are in terms of personality, but also of what structure of logic of self and otherness is available to us. So when we go to ask the question, 'What is a

Norwegian?' the first question that imposes itself is, 'To whom do we pose the question?' To ourselves? To someone else? And if we pose it to ourselves, what is the sense? Don't we already know? If we pose it to another, what is the sense? Does that other know us?

All this being said, it is obvious that the question of cultural identity imposes itself more today than at any other time in recent history. It is to be numbered among the great ethical imperatives of our time. Never since World War II has the notion of Europe and of the cultural identity of Europe in its totality been more incessantly interrogated than today.

The urgency of the question of the threat against Europe and the role played by tolerance manifests itself by the confluence of two particular phenomena: on the one hand, we are living in a Europe of *unification*, a Europe that has organized itself, both in its way of thinking and in its political forums, in concert with a number of unifying forces, centralizing forces, which are doubtless nourished by economic interests, but also determined by a real will for unity and cultural homogenization. This movement of unification is clearly seen in the question of the European Union, in the question of the future form of the eastward expansion, of the possible entry of new member states into the Union, of the general geopolitical changes in Europe. On the other hand, we are living a Europe of *disintegration*, in the historical shadow of the decomposition of the Soviet Union, of Czechoslovakia, of Yugoslavia, the Greco-Macedonian conflicts, Hispano-Basque and Anglo-Irish identity-based conflicts and the secessionist dispute in Georgia. They testify to the gravity of the internal crisis of national identities.

Identity can be differentiated along two axes, vertical and horizontal. On the *vertical* axis, identity refers to a hierarchy of generality: we speak of personal identity, family identity, institutional identity, national identity, global identity, etc. In this way identity is understood as a set of concentric circles, one identity encircling the other in a rising order of generality. One type of identity is more general than the next. On the *horizontal* axis, identity also refers to a range of complexity. We speak of sexual identity, moral identity, professional identity, political identity, racial identity, etc. In this sense identities overlap, supplement and, at times, compete with one another, as well as with the vertical axis of identity.

This understanding of identity can now be further developed. Identity is not merely what we think we are; it is also what others think we are. It has, in other words, both subjective and objective aspects. It is subjective in the sense that it is a representation of the way a certain individual or group understands itself. It is objective in the sense that it is a representation of how others see the group. Clearly, these two sides are co-determinate. In other words, an individual or group identity is, in part, formed by how it or its members see itself, and in part by how others see it. In the case of groups, individual identity is also determined by how the individual members of the group see one another.

In this sense, identity of an individual or a group is always connected to an *other*. It is always associated with a someone or something that is *not* the individual or the group. I am never entirely the author of my own identity. I am who I am only as far as others see me and recognize me. The others can be another group, another individual or – and here is the difficult part of the structure of identity – the other can be myself. The other can be my *past* or my imagined future. One always has some idea of one's self. But when we look at ourselves, when we look in the mirror, when we ask what our own identity is, what do we see? Do we see another – an object, a thing that is other and foreign to us, a thing that we can conceive of with objectivity? Or do we see something that is identical to us, something that is the same, has the same experience of being itself? This is the distinction made by Ricœur between identity understood as *ipse* and identity understood as *idem* (Ricœur, 1990: 11–15). The thing we see in the mirror is *both* us and other, both an object that is seen and a subject that sees. In order to be ourselves we require the other who perceives us, even if that other is ourselves (Kristeva, 1988: 283–4; 1990). This is the fundamental paradox of self-consciousness.

Thus, identity is the incidence of both subject and object. It is simultaneously the experience of seeing and being seen, hearing and being heard, recognizing and being recognized. In order to understand ourselves as ourselves, be it on the individual or group level, we require the other who is different from us. The other can be other individuals or other groups (or the other in ourselves).

In other words, *difference* is an essential trait of identity. The experience of one's identity – individual or group – is intimately bound together with the experience of being different from others. Indeed, our *difference* from other identities is *part* of our identity. Our opposition to other groups, or differences with respect to other identities, are fundamental to the formation and evolution of our own. Identity is always identity in relation to other identity. Unless there is an other, any other, or perhaps many others, there is no self. If all humans were Norwegians, the concept of the Norwegian would be incomprehensible. Understanding one's self in relation to others is the tolerance of others, the experience of difference from others as a *part* of us, of what we are.

This is where our reflexion upon the nature of identity rejoins the notion of tolerance. In short, the assurance of our own identity, both individual and group, is based upon our tolerance of others. The very survival of our group identity is *not* assured by asserting its predominance over others or, in the extreme, by erasing others. On the contrary, the survival of our identity is *based upon* our tolerance of other.

Self and tolerance of the other

Tolerance is the action of allowing something that in essence is not allowed, that is discredited, devalued, frowned upon. Tolerance is allowing the un-allowable. In other words, tolerance (like identity) contains a double, self-contradicting movement. On the one hand, it represents recognition of a norm, a rule, a structure, a value or set of values, a person, a group, institution, etc. On the other hand, it takes exception to that which it recognizes. It resists the person, group, norm, value, etc. It disputes the validity of the thing recognized while at the same time recognizing it.

Clearly, tolerance is a response to difference. It is a response to something that is not me, not us, not this, something that is implicitly in opposition – possibly in open conflict – with my identity. This opposition can range from a simple perception of difference to an existential conflict. Difference is a strange thing. It is a kind of reference to the empty space between two things. Like tolerance, it is a substance, but it has no content. It lies between the two things in opposition. It is neither the one nor the other. Tolerance is tolerance of difference. Tolerance is not just the experience of the religion I find insulting, the ethnic songs that I find offensive to my people, the attitude I find reprehensible, the pair of shoes I find ugly. Rather, it is the experience of the difference between my religion and the other, my music and the other, my shoes and the other.

The burden of tolerance is the recognition of the validity of religions, songs and shoes, *and* the rejection of *that* religion. In order to reject a religion (or a folksong, or a pair of shoes), we must, in our case, believe in the general value of religion. We must believe in the religiosity of religion. We must have respect – indeed a very pronounced respect – for the religiosity of the religion, the musicality of the music and the shoe-ness of the shoes, and at the same time a negative experience of the way the concepts are treated by others. I cannot *not* be offended by, nor be required to tolerate, a phenomenon that has no counterpart in my identity.

In this way, tolerance always lies in a strange, perhaps impossible, place between full recognition of the other and full rejection. It gives life and meaning to both that which we oppose and our opposition. Tolerance is both an expression of the right of something other to exist and the assertion of the right of opposition to that other. It is the place in between. Tolerance says 'yes, because no'.

Tolerance takes place on many levels, from the individual to the global. The precondition and guarantee of tolerance is simple: the existence of another *subject* (alterity). On the personal level, I can experience tolerance of my brother, who has dreadful taste in music. At university, I, or a group of students, can experience tolerance in our attitude toward the curriculum. In any given community, certain political interests and desires must coexist with others. In religious settings – the historical origin of the very concept of tolerance – certain sub-groups must tolerate others. Ethnic groups coexist in different settings. The examples can be multiplied.

What is the other of a culture? What is the foreigner with respect to cultural identity? How should we understand the relation between a culture and that which it excludes? If, as I have already suggested, identity is always, by its very nature, in question, then the relation between a group and that which it excludes, must be extremely problematic. Because in posing the question of cultural identity, we must necessarily admit that identity is open and impure, that it is far from obvious or self-evident. If, for example, European culture were absolutely pure and homogeneous, it would be impossible to pose the question of the foreigner, of the other. Living in a homogeneous and absolutely pure culture, we would have absolutely no knowledge of foreigners, we would be surrounded by the purity of one unique culture. There would be no other, no exterior, no alternative.

Every European society knows ethnic and religious minorities, refugees, legal and illegal migrant workers. The very fact that discussion about the immigration even takes place, the fact that there are debates, sometimes even strenuous debates, concerning the presence of foreigners within a given culture, is just one more indication of the state of overture of any and all cultures. If a cultural identity were completely sovereign, if it were present unto itself, unified, pure and sure, there would be no discussion. The foreigner would not represent any threat to the substance of a culture. The physical presence of the foreigner in a country wouldn't have any role to play and certainly nothing to say concerning the foreigner. Physical and cultural presence would be clearly separated.

As we all know, the reality is otherwise. On the one hand, it's clear that the richness of any European culture will have a long way to go before it recognizes its debt to 'foreign' cultures. On the other hand, the notion of 'original cultural purity' – quite widespread in certain quarters – can be easily overturned by the anthropological observation that absolutely all cultures are themselves originally derived from others.

It is clear that every society has always tended to confuse 'its' own culture with culture in general, going as far as to cast out of humanity those human beings who simply belong to another culture. The Greeks called 'barbarians' those men and women who were foreign to their institutions. Linguistics suggests that the word 'barbarian' refers to the confusion and the inarticulation of the songs of birds, which is opposed to the signifying value of human speech. Thus what creates the foreign-ness of 'barbarians' is actually the foreign-ness of their language. The word 'savage' means 'from the forest', evoking the same kind of animal desire to describe that which is simply unknown, that which does not belong to the 'human' culture. In the two cases, there is a clear refusal to admit the notion of cultural diversity. It seems always preferable to reject outside the culture (and into the nature) everything which does not immediately conform to the culture's norm.

Another example of the same is the asymmetrical treatment of the Spanish and the Native Americans at the time of the so-called 'discovery' of America. It is said that the Spanish designated religious commissions in order to determine whether or not the Indians had souls. In other words, whether or not they were authentically men. But the exclusion doesn't end there; the Indians too had their own brand of exclusion. They observed carefully the cadavers of their enemies, the Spanish, in order to verify whether or not they would be subject to putrefaction like the cadavers of real men.

Thus it seems that the first movement of any society that is put into contact with individuals of another is to reject it, to cast it out of the boundaries of the culture and thus out of the boundaries of humanity.

The other side of this logic of exclusion is a logic of inclusion. What happens when we openly attempt to exclude the other, the foreigner from our group? In the very act of excluding we cannot avoid assimilating. At the very moment when a group questions the validity of another culture within its borders it cannot avoid incorporating that culture. This is neither a mere effect of chance nor a simple choice. It is a logical necessity, for it is obvious that we cannot judge a foreign group without knowing it, without having first approached an understanding of it, without first comparing it with our own. But if the foreign culture can be compared, if we can think of the foreigner according to our way of thinking, if we can think the other alongside our own group, that group has already become a child of our own. A Norwegian who knows his way around the Pakistani milieu in Oslo, a Norwegian who can sufficiently open his spirit to this other in order to observe it, to judge it as non-Norwegian, foreign, in other words, in order to exclude it, renders it, at least in part, his own. Norwegian cultural identity is already partially Pakistani, if only by virtue of its attempts to exclude it. French cultural identity is already partially Mahgreb, if only because it refuses to assimilate it. In order to reject, it is necessary to know and understand. In order to know and understand, it is necessary to assimilate intellectually, spiritually, even personally. Any rejection of foreign-ness is a partially rejection of one's self and any affirmation of one's self is in part an assimilation of the other, the foreigner.

Thus if it were not possible to ask the question of the other, the foreigner, to consider the presence of the foreign group, it wouldn't even be possible to talk about a group. The unity of any group identity presupposes that the group be oriented with respect to other groups. Group identity has thus both a positive and a negative function. It affirms itself by excluding what it is not. It affirms itself by expressing its rules of membership. The rules and codes that define it define also what it is not, what it is necessary to exclude in order to retain its sovereignty. Culture depends on the very culture it excludes in order to create itself.

Finally, if tolerance is the essence of identity, what is intolerance? What is intolerable? We can distinguish between two types of intolerable (Ricœur, 1991: 307). The first is simple intolerance, the expression of the enthusiasm and the violence of our convictions with respect to alternatives. The other meaning of the 'intolerable' goes to the extreme of what can be recognized. It defies recognition because it does not recognize us, does not recognize others. However, the consequence of this discussion is that the identity that defies tolerance is not an identity.

The intolerable is the refusal of identity, of subjectivity, of humanity. The intolerable is not only the refusal of the other, it is the refusal of one's self, a particular kind of insecurity in which the object of security, external by all accounts, has an internal life as well.

There is in this respect no identity without a certain threat to that identity, an opposition or oppositionality that puts into question, on an existential basis, the universal validity that must be assumed to be one's self. Unless I am everywhere and always myself, then I am not myself. The need for recognition by the other, made famous in Hegel's dialectic of master and servant, makes my identity, its ubiquity and timelessness, a matter of dependence. The very condition for being something, for having an identity, either individual or group, is the same as the precondition for conflict. It can never be a question of learning to have a 'good' identity, which is not opposed to others. And we should not seek non-conflicting identities.

The other side of the dialectical coin is that all culturally, ethnically or religiously based insecurity shares a certain kind of tolerance. Identity is only threatened when there is common ground, common interests, common goals, commons desires despite the differences. In other words, conflict reposes upon the notion that two parties in conflict are unified in their reciprocal menace. Regardless of what other shared values might incidentally be involved, tolerance itself is always a shared value. It is what permits two identities to coexist. No identity conflict is so absolute that it does not require tolerance on one level or another in order to continue to be an identity conflict.

If there were something that could be called the 'intolerable', it would thus mean the loss of identity. If a threat to our security were so great that it could not be managed in some form or by some means, there will not be any self-understanding, no culture, no identity. The absence of recognition for the other deprives one of the recognition of the other and the loss of identity. At the same time, tolerance is never the same as indifference. Two parties brought together by conflict always share a minimum of tolerance. This does not mean they are indifferent to the identities' differences that they are capable of tolerating. If there is tolerance, there is never indifference.

7 Justice in political, legal and moral community

This chapter investigates the hypothesis of a correlation between two distinct crises in the human and social sciences. The one involves recent rich and vigorous attempts to articulate the set of conditions adequate and necessary to the constitution of a *just society*; the other attempts to account for the rise and expansion of the notion of *community*. We will argue that the evolution of these two discourses has always been intertwined, if not co-determinate, and that attention to this interrelation will cast light on our particular understanding of justice.

The literature on rivalling theories of *justice* has, for the past 25 years, sought to give an account of which principles best organize political and legal institutions relative to given social settings. The most schematic expression of this attempt is the so-called liberal-communitarian debate, reawakened in the aftermath of the publication of John Rawls' *A Theory of Justice* in 1971. This terrain is well covered, and I will do no more here than sketch the contours of the controversy. In a nutshell, where liberals (the most conspicuous examples being Rawls and Dworkin), libertarians and utilitarians give the notion of individual rights a pre-eminent role in the foundation and legitimation of the notion of justice, communitarians (Taylor, Sandel, MacIntyre, Walzer) tend to reaffirm the common good as the essential foundation of the just society.

It is clear that communities emerge, multiply and overlap. They produce criss-crossing identities and loyalties. By the same token, the predicates that determine communities are not stable and the political bodies that represent them to both community members and non-members are not fixed. This sense of crisis, which emerges from variability of political community, corresponds to the rise of the idea of 'multiculturalism' and the notion of a multi-layered amalgamation of cultural and social identities known as 'glocalization'. By virtue of a variety of global factors, cultural identity becomes more intermingled, making community boundaries more porous. Global awareness has given force to local legitimacy and cultural sovereignty. The local is legitimated against a wider global awareness by virtue of it being local.

To what extent does this flourish in the question of community correspond to the ascent of debate over the question of justice? In order to reconstruct the relationship between *community* and *justice*, we begin by brief analyses of three sub-discourses of community: *political, legal* and *moral*. We will then turn to the recent debate around the concept of justice in order map its relation to the concept of community.

Political community

By 'political community' we mean the community referred to by the political philosophy of communitarianism. Unfortunately, defining community according to the logic of this debate does not reduce, but rather multiplies, problems. This is the case for at least two reasons. First, a central aim of the political philosophy of communitarianism is to problematize the very concept of community, to give it a new scope and to open its social dimensions to normative claims. Second, as we know, communitarianism itself is not an uncontested concept. It is thus senseless to speak of communitarianism in the singular. Rather, one must speak of the 'communitarian debate'. I take it as uncontroversial to claim, however, that a central axis of the debate surrounds the question of what constitutes the foundation of a polity. It is along this axis that we will interpret the notion of justice relative to the political community.

The notion of communitarianism has received its greatest impetus and, by and large, evolved out of learned opposition to the theory of liberalism first developed nearly 30 years ago in Rawls' *A Theory of Justice* (1971), developed and nuanced in the essays collected as *Political Liberalism* in 1996 and given an international scope in *Law of Peoples* in 1999. The publication of *A Theory of Justice* inaugurated a momentous debate, engaging political philosophers from all persuasions, bringing to light numerous positions. Opposing positions have been also *legio*, advancing to the extent that the debate among communitarians has become as fruitful as that which opposed communitarians and liberals. For this schematic consideration, the main positions revolve around the work of Walzer (1983), MacIntyre (1988, 1984), Selznick (1992) and Taylor (1989).

From a sociological perspective, communitarians seek to articulate the difference between small-scale traditional societies and the civic community of polity (Delanty, 2003: 73–4). From a philosophical perspective, the communitarian conception of community is not distinct from what we later describe as moral community. Rather, it is, by and large, an attempt to deny the notion of moral autonomy of the individual, turning instead toward raising the moral substrate to the sphere of the community.

The liberal-communitarian debate is often reduced to the opposition of individual and community. This has a limited, though perhaps heuristic, value. The liberal position commonly argues that the values of the individual should take priority in the formulation of rights; the communitarian position argues that shared values should be the basis for claims of rights and justice. This is, naturally, an egregious simplification. Among the many interventions that complicate this picture is the question of what the sources of rights and justice are, their independence from or dependence upon the individual, as well as the question of a universal good, all following from more or less contested readings of the Kantian tradition of moral philosophy.

One dominant and classically communitarian definition of 'community' is formulated in Selznick's *The Moral Commonwealth* from 1992 as the synthesis of seven primary elements: *historicity* ('the bonds of community are strongest when they are fashioned from strands of shared history and culture'); *identity* ('a shared history tends to produce a sense of community, and this sense is manifested in loyalty, piety and a distinctive identity'); *mutuality* ('community begins with, and is largely supported by, the experience of interdependence and reciprocity'); *plurality* ('community draws much of its vitality from 'intermediate associations' [...] the health differentiation of institutions and of personal, family, ethnic, locality and occupational groups [...] within a framework of legitimacy'); *autonomy* ('the assumption that individual wellbeing corresponds with a framework of legitimacy, and without fracturing or fragmenting the social order'); *participation* ('personal autonomy can be achieved only in and through social participation'); and *integration* ('the supportive institutions, norms and beliefs, and practices' that 'sustain the foundations of a common life') (Selznick, 1992: 361–3).

'Community', in this complete communitarian view, is thus constituted by 'fellowship and moral wellbeing', by a kind of fundamental or 'core' participation in moral consensus, which implicates the notion of an individual self; 'the primacy of the particular in moral experience', 'authority as a function of the quality of consent', the 'transition from management to governance; institutional integrity, responsiveness and responsibility' (ibid.: 357).

By contrast, in his discussion of 'the idea of social union', Rawls perhaps comes closest to formulating the notion of community when he speaks of a collection of pre-figured and pre-constituted individuals who share final ends:

> Now the shared end of a social union is clearly not merely a common desire for the same particular thing. Grant and Lee were one in their desire to hold Richmond but this desire did not establish community between them. Persons generally want similar sort of things, liberty and opportunity, shelter and nourishment, yet these wants may put them at odds. Whether individuals have a shared end depends upon the more detailed features of the activity to which their interests incline them as these are regulated by principles of justice. There must be an agreed scheme of conduct in which the excellences and enjoyments of each are complementary to the good of all. Each can then take pleasure in the actions of the others as they jointly execute a plan acceptable to everyone.
>
> (Rawls, 1971: 526)

This is what Sandel, in his critique of Rawls, describes as a 'sentimental account' of community (Sandel, 1982: 150). It is based on a set of individuals whose shared interests are occasional or contingent, and not on a synthetic sense of moral commonality. According to Sandel, community in the strong, constitutive sense required by both Rawls and, not least, Dworkin, cannot be accounted for by a conception that is individualistic, even in Rawls' sense of the term.

Legal community

By *legal community* we understand the scope of a given legal system. In terms of our general definition of *community*, the common predicate that constitutes it is the codified adherence to its rules and procedures. The first cut at understanding legal community must seek to articulate and work out its distinction from the political community. At first approach, the legality of the legal community is inseparable from the rights and obligations associated with state sovereignty, the classical paradigm of the monopoly on violence, and exclusivity of courts and systems of adjudication and review.[1]

This way of conceptualizing legal community must be situated in the essential and abiding tension in legal philosophy between natural law theories and theories of legal positivism. In its classical version legal positivism opposes natural law as understood as grounded in a transcendental notion of justice and common good, and legal positivism's emphasis on authority. In its more modern incarnation, embodied by the opposition between Grotius and Hobbes, it acquires the characteristics of an opposition between Grotius' view of law as the set of principles defining individual rights, and Hobbes' view of law as an empirical necessity for social order, distinct from rights.

Legal positivism, in its high modern form, is articulated in John Austin's 1885 *Lectures on Jurisprudence* in terms of the positivist 'social fact thesis' central to legal positivism as it is understood today: 'A rule is legally valid (i.e. is a law) in a given society if and only if the rule is commanded by the sovereign in the society and is backed up with the threat of a sanction' (Austin, 2002). The relevant social fact that confers validity, in Austin's view, is promulgation by a sovereign willing to impose a sanction for non-compliance. Many critiques and variations on the social fact thesis have been proposed. It is enough for our concerns here that the validity of a law is identical to its status within a functioning sovereign state.

The strictly positivist view of legal community developed, among others, by H.L.A. Hart in *The Concept of Law*, is essentially an ideal type open to critique from a number of angles. Its most persistent weakness lies in its more or less one-to-one correspondence with the state ideal type. The political community that surrounds and provides a basis for the state is porous (Hart, 1997). A legal community is, in this view, inseparable from the sovereignty that constitutes it. The exchange between the sovereign state and its legal system is among the primary characteristics of the modern state.

For our purposes we adopt the position of Hartian positivism for the sole reason that its meta-legal orientation responds to the needs of this analysis. It is relevant to our demonstration for the sole reason that it is discrete from what we wish to call moral community. For legal positivism in Hart's terms involves claims about the *concept* of law, not about any particular instances of law, either normative or factual. While Hart would allow the fact that *some* legal systems may make moral values relevant to legal validity, he would insist that, where this is so, it is in virtue of the particular conventional criteria accepted within that system (Simmonds, 2002).

To sum up this cursory constellation of concepts, political, legal and moral community are understood as ideal unities defined on three different shared characteristics. Schematically speaking, these are (1) a common set of social codes and norms, (2) a common set of legal rules and procedures, and (3) a common set of moral values.

Moral community

By *moral* community we understand a community whose belonging is determined by a shared set of values. This plays out differently relative to the two axes of community mentioned earlier: community as a set of predicates and community as a body. A community is a set of predicates. The predicates of a moral community are *values*. The catalogue of shared values becomes distinct in relation to other communities that do not possess the same values, or which possess a different composition of values. Thus, values are relative to the Other, to the non-community member, to the immigrant, to the other religion, the other culture, etc. No community of values is based on one value alone. Predicates are always multiple. The interplay of values forms the unique character of the community as body: the composition of the community has a value in itself on a par with the constitutive values.

A community of values is also a thing in itself, actively implicated and involved in the formation and mutation of values. The community itself has a certain value, both to members and non-members of the community. The community is inherently conservative, regardless of the actual values involved in its constitution. Any community, including a community of value, tends toward its own self-preservation.

By *value* we understand an abstract notion whose concrete realization is estimated, by common consensus, relative difference or absolute authority, as being of significant worth. Without endorsing a *politically* relative view of value, it must be admitted that no value has absolute worth. Something is *a* value from the moment it has more worth than something else. Whether the source of this worth is implicit or not, does not change the relative nature of its value-ness. The *source* of values of communities is inevitably occult. This fact contributes to preserving its relativity, by assuring that any absolute reference, historical or otherwise, is also situated in a context.

These basic ideas and definitions open on to the first paradox of the community of values: values are both universal from the point of view of the community, and particular and situational from the point of view of moral communities. As abstract concepts, values are only meaningful to the degree that they are considered universally valid. If a value is not everywhere and always a value for the members of the community, then it is not a value at all.

The community as a whole is defined by its values as against other entities, other groups, individuals and communities, which do not possess its values. In this sense, the universal nature of the given values depends upon their particularity, on the opposition to the situations where they are not valid. Supposed universality makes visible *internal* divergence or particularity. The value principles upon whose consensus the community is formed do not guarantee their concrete universality, their universality in effect. Indeed, the very presence of the universal principle is a reminder that the reality to which it refers is not yet universal.

The moral community is always disjointed with respect to its own boundaries. Moreover, it is both lesser than and greater than its boundaries. Any moral community is characterized by internal heterogeneity, strife, disagreement, political friction, etc. On the other hand, moral community always exceeds the political boundaries of which it is constitutive. Any moral community constitutes itself by relating to others. It thereby lies partially beyond its own conceived borders. In other words, the existence of the moral community depends upon the negative relation to its other.

Based on its supposed universality, the moral community aims at the other as an object of action. It must relate to the other individual, the other community, the other moral ideal, even though it is foreign to him/her. It is the essence of a moral community to fail to be a moral community. Moral community is the movement of non-correspondence between the conceptual: that is, the level of ideas, and the empirical.

A moral community is therefore one that is constantly self-interrogating, constantly forming a new idea of itself based on the ever-changing empirical landscape of that which it seeks to encompass. The movement is dialectical, swinging from the articulation of moral or norms to the identification of the empirical reality of existing, valid values.

Justice

The notion of justice in the English language is inseparable from a fundamental ambivalence between, on the one hand, 'the substantive quality of being just' and on the other, 'the judicial administration of law or equity' (OED, 1971). Justice is thus associated with righteousness, uprightness or equity. And yet this moral, substantive sense of the word 'justice' remains inseparable from its instrumentality. It is an act of application of a rule, statute, law or tenet. Justice refers to the quality of being just, but typically in terms of the observation of some higher-order, divine or transcendental law. Justice is seldom a moral virtue in itself; it is, rather, the application of virtue, a means to an end. That end is not necessarily just.

The substantive notion of justice is associated with an external or transcendental reference, be it one of the cardinal virtues, the observance of divine law or divine righteousness, or conformity to one form or another of moral right or reason, propriety or truth. The instrumental notion of justice is associated with the exercise of authority of power in maintenance of right, with vindication of right by assignment of reward or punishment. It refers to the *administration* of law, or the forms and processes attending it, to judicial proceedings, legal proceedings, etc. It is the infliction of punishment, legal vengeance, on an offender.

Both axes of the notion of justice are historically determined. In particular, the social, moral and political mutations we commonly associate with modernization have important consequences for both the substantial and the instrumental dimensions of justice. Processes of modernization have brought fundamental changes to both axes of this concept of justice.

In terms of semantic or symbolic structure, a community is not only a social praxis, it is also a system of meaning (Cohen, 1985; Anderson, 1991). Both access to community and access to understanding a community are determined by codes of conduct and semantics of the community's actions. The primary hypothesis here is that justice is fundamentally connected to the cohesion of community.

Justice in the political community

The concept of justice in the political philosophy of communitarianism was originally, and continues to be, articulated as a critique of liberal philosophical positions, both egalitarian and libertarian. Throughout its evolution, in the last 25 years, it has become nothing if not complex and interwoven. Yet its primary attribute remains more or less stable: it disavows the notion that justice can be articulated and arranged as a function of the rights of individual atomistic members of society.

For Sandel, for example, this means that the response to the questions of whether a community is *just* can never be answered by reference to the sentiments and desires of individual members alone (Sandel, 1998). Justice is, in this sense, *constitutive* of a community. It is not a matter of the community existing *a priori*, and possessing, or not, the predicate *justice*. Rather, it is justice that renders a certain kind of community.

> As a person's values and ends are always attributes and never constituents of the self, so a sense of community is only an attribute and never a constituent of a well-ordered society. As the self is prior to the aims it

affirms, so a well-ordered society, defined by justice, is prior to the aims – communitarian or otherwise – its members may profess. This is the sense, both moral and epistemological, in which justice is the first virtue of social institutions.

(Sandel, 1982: 64)

Similarly, in MacIntyre's analysis of Aristotle, the notion of justice 'articulates the claims of one particular type of practice-based community' (MacIntyre, 1988). Thus Macintyre's critique of the notion of justice by those who do not see it as socially constituent and constituted is, in effect, an argument against the autonomy of philosophical thinking in general. MacIntyre's communitarianism, if it can be called that, is a meta-theory of ethical knowledge base on a notion of community embeddedness.

As many have pointed out, the overwhelming presupposition of the liberal position relative to the question of justice is the atomist nature of the individual (Taylor, 1995: 74; 1989: 193). Liberal justice is incompatible with the contemporary notion of *identity* in as much as it is situated in a dialectic with *community*.

According to the communitarian perspective, it is senseless to predicate conclusions about just human association from the standpoint of rootless beings, entering into contracts or dealing with one another on the basis of arbitrary sentiments. Positing a moral individual without community, claim opponents of this conception, downplays or disregards entirely those moral roles that *only* exist in community settings (Harris, 2003). This critique is compelling, even though Rawls has subsequently argued that his claims in *A Theory of Justice* and elsewhere have no metaphysical ambition, only political interest, an assertion based on a relatively dubious opposition between the metaphysical and the political (Rawls, 1996).

By the same token, in Walzer's terms, 'justice is relative to social meaning'. There is not a transcendental notion of justice that precedes the constitution of a community, social or otherwise. Community and justice are co-determinate, and the distribution of membership is not 'pervasively subject to the constraints of justice' (Walzer, 1983: 61–2).

Finally, it is the natural law tradition that is most accommodating to the notion of tradition. According to Selznick, it is this tradition of legal thinking that has the most important contribution to the 'affirmation of community':

> The doctrine presumes that every legal order has an implicit consti-
> tution. Beyond the specifics of positive law are the *premises* of the legal
> order, to which appeal can be made in the name of justice and com-
> munity. The premises create legitimate authority; they are the source of
> civic obligation. The duty of officials and citizens to obey the law is
> grounded on the implicit constitution, which in turn presumes com-
> munity membership. At bottom, fidelity to law is fidelity to community.
>
> (Selznick, 1992: 445)

Justice in the legal community

The interpretive moment in legal application takes place at two moments. First, in cases that require the intervention of judgement, law is explicitly interpreted, both in terms of its applicability and in terms of the scope of its application. To varying degrees, a judge must evaluate the standards of applicability of a statue, based on his or her reading of both the statute and the narrative of events in question. Second, in cases where the intervention of learned judgement is not required, application of law does, nonetheless, require the discretionary choice of a valid authority. Law does not deploy itself. Law that did not require discretionary application would simply not be law, but rather some kind of implicit social substance or structure. The appropriateness of a given law to a given situation, the scope of its application, the isolation of its object, are all moments in the application of law, which produce the *effect* of justice. Moreover, they are all non-legal moments. They are extra-legal, external to, and prior to, adjudication.

In both cases the 'justice' of the law is a measure of the correct *application* of the legal code. Legal justice is thus formal. However, utterly formal justice would be meaningless. Though a judge may convict one person for murder, the same judgement cannot *automatically* apply to *all* persons who carry out the very same act under identical conditions. Indeed, despite express intention, they are not even guilty of murder in the strict sense. Justice is therefore not done until the facts of the case are brought forth and the person in question is interpolated.

We speak popularly, in my language, of 'bringing a criminal to justice'. Yet what is actually meant is 'to bring an individual to judgement'. Justice is only done when a judgement is carried out according to a correct application of procedures and the law and an authorized agent interprets the case. Nor is the person essentially a criminal before justice has been done.

Yet this is not the same thing as saying that justice is *procedural.* Nor can legal justice be conceived as somehow pure substance. Perfectly formal, procedural justice would imply an automaticity, which would render discretion impossible. Justice, understood as an ideal state, Rawls' 'well-ordered society', is also meaningless in the sense that it denies a standard of applicability. Any ordinary step beyond strictly formal conceptions of justice leads inevitably to the paradox inherent in judgement. The strictly procedural pole of the rule of law contains, in principle, no dimension of interpretation. Law is not just, in and of itself.

Justice lies, paradoxically, between the natural law model and the positive model. It arises from law as a collective culture of agency and application, and law as a set of legal facts, statues, structures and rules of application.

Justice in the moral community

First, perhaps before all else, justice is a discourse of rationality. As Kolm puts it, 'by its very definition, *justice* is *justification*, and hence *rationality* in the normal sense of the term: for a valid reason, or 'justified" (Kolm, 1996: 7). This insight places the entire ethical enterprise of justice in a peculiar light. Normative claims, at least conventionally, oppose reason. This opposition is one of their primary attributes. If morality were reducible to a calculus of values, to a checklist of empirically verifiable predicates, it would be not be ethical. Rather, it would simply be assimilated into the general scope of universal rationality. It would no longer possess a discretionary function, erasing the moral particularity of the moral community. The moral community would evaporate since its particularity would no longer be viable.

The application of justice as justification to the moral community exposes it to a universality that exceeds the limited set of shared values at its core. Rationality rules out moral intuitionism, emotivism and aestheticism, that is, 'opinions based on *a priori* views of the solution, on emotions such as indignation, and on the satisfaction of beauty, although these may all signal the existence of an ethical issue' (ibid.: 8).

If the justice of the moral community cannot be of an instrumental rational kind, then morality cannot be part of the logic of its membership. Its relationship to the principle of its morality must be external to the rationality of the community: it must come from somewhere else, from an extra-rational space. It must be based on one form or another of deontological principle, both preceding, and thus not contingent upon, the community itself, and resisting the instrumentalization of that principle must thus characterize the moral community.

And yet, if the moral principle precedes the existence of the community, then its predication, the act by which the members of the community adopt the moral principle, must forcibly be amoral. The constitution of the moral community cannot itself be a moral moment. It is, rather, an instrumentally rational one. Thus the second aporia of the moral community: its constitution is ultimately amoral or non-moral. The morality of the moral community does not belong to the community, but is exterior to it. It cannot be dependent upon the rational principle of community for its being.

In a moral community, there is always already justice, in the sense of equality of the content of the relevant moral principles.

Justice in the moral community can also be understood, in the practical sense, as the justice of validity of applications or interpretations of the moral principles that constitute the community. Variation among individual claims to validity of application or interpretation of the moral principles can differ without interrupting the basic cohesion of the community. Here justice-as-equality is shifted from the level of the community as integrated unity to the level of the community as constituted by a set of individuals. Such variation can depend on any number of variables not susceptible to evaluation in terms of the moral values that bind the community: from differing interpretative horizons to experiential differences, and capacities for application, etc. The split into two levels is a typically dialectical one. The unity of community on one level is folded into the *necessary* diversity of the other. The *commonality*, equality or *justesse* at the level of the moral community bears a *determinate* connection to the diversity of practice on the secondary level. The disunity of the otherwise unified moral community becomes necessary in term of this analysis. The essence of a moral community lies in the contestation of the interpretation of its moral principles. *Antagonism* becomes the fundamental meta-unifier of the moral community otherwise unified by common values. Justice in the sphere of the moral community must be about justice of competing claims to the identical values.[2]

Conclusion

A central generalization that can be made, based on this complex correlation of justice and community, is therefore that justice is never essential or implicit. Justice is always derivative, a secondary element in a network of reference. It emerges only from a process of interpretation, an act of fixing an otherwise mobile production of juridical meaning. Justice is only attained in some pragmatic procedure, never as ideal type. Furthermore, we have seen that justice is an *effect* of *contention*. It is inseparable from one or several *conflicts* of interpretations. It is in this sense the meeting-place of interpretative communities.

The rule of law is thus *both* the repetition of a positive law, the assertion of its applicability in multiple settings *and* the novelty of its *original* application in a unique setting. Each case is different, each application of the rule of law must necessarily be unique. At the same time, each case must communicate with a general principle of law; it must surpass its setting, and make implicit reference to the possibility of other settings (Derrida, 1992a). This dialectic between universal type and particular culture meaning assures not only the vitality of legal institutions but also the possibility of their meaningfulness. It is the imbrication of the discourses of justice that support the discourses of moral, social and political communities that makes justice a meaningful term.

Notes

1 In this context, perhaps the most salient *exception* to this definition is the legal system associated with European Union law. As current debate in European circles testifies, the *sui generis* nature of the European legal landscape is troubling and innovative for all classical models. It builds upon a porous notion of a state-based model of jurisprudence.
2 Thus Sandel's central claim in his interpretation of Rawls' liberalism, that community is constitutive of justice, has an application here (Sandel, 1982).

8 Psychoanalysis of the national *thing*

The countless constellations of war and peace, past and present, and the wide variety of conceivable ethical approaches to them, resist discrete summary. And yet it should at once be underscored that both the 'ethics' in question and the 'war' (and peace) to which they aspire to take recourse are of a special brand and breed, belonging to a very specific historical moment, to a unique politics and to a constellation of tacitly shared values whose origin and finality exceed the frame of the war room. The transformation of the notions of both ethics and of war and peace have accelerated in the course of what Hobsbawm called 'the short 20th century' in unforeseeable ways. Ethics – the systematic mapping of rights and obligations, premises and conditions of conduct – has veered from its classical roots and is no longer merely understood as the systematic search for a singular response to the question of the 'Good Life'.[1] 'War and peace', a constantly evolving pair, have made a leap from the perfunctory character of violence in something like Herodotus' *Histories* to the desperate theses of Baudrillard's *The Gulf War Did not Take Place* (Baudrillard, 1995). Today, questions of war and peace are more frequently rediscovered in intra-state relations, in experiments with new weapon technologies, opening new questions of modalities, aims and means, collateral consequences, circumstances and scope, objects and actors.

The paradox of the nation-state's *ethical* universality was clear from the start, that is, already in the first Enlightenment philosophies of state, people and rule of law. It was famously dramatized by Kant's thinking on the nature of a cosmopolitan world republic, the natural consequence of the universal principles of the nation-state in his well-known 1784 essay 'The Idea of a Universal History with a Cosmopolitan Intent,' and his 1795 essay 'On Perpetual Peace' (Kant, 1983b; 1983c). In the currently expanding debate on post-nationalism and the limits of nationality, Kant's concept of cosmopolitanism has been repeatedly revisited, both in the debate on the nature of globalization (Höffe, 1999: 64–7; Delanty, 2000; Bauman, 1998), and on the possible forms of a European superstate (Schultz, 1994; Segers and Viehoff, 1996; Ferry, 2000; Habermas, 1998b; Pogge, 1992). Much of the discussion concerns the modifications and clarifications necessary in order to bring Kant's conception of a cosmopolitan world order to a contemporary coherence in general or to make it applicable to a possible European federal state in particular.

The contemporary historical determination of these debates revolves around the geopolitical changes in the wake of the fall of the Berlin wall. Most of these arguments would have been impossible before the *Wende*, the more or less peaceful collapse of the Soviet-steered Eastern Bloc beginning with the dramatic events in October 1989. Before then, the Cold War and the ideological borders frozen along the lines of European national borders completely overshadowed the prospects of any sort of philosophical cosmopolitanism. Although globalization was far from a reality, principled questions about the nature of a universal order based on political or ethical doctrine were as good as unthinkable.

The less thoroughly scrutinized reality of the *Wende* is that it marks the birth of a new brand of nationalism, inevitably proceeding, explicitly or implicitly, from the assumption of a certain kind of national core or kernel. By 'kernel' I mean an essence or substance that is essential to the nation, but which is neither equivalent to it nor reducible to it. A great deal of available scholarship highlights and explores the ethical nature of the nation-state by looking at its ethical presuppositions and consequences. It examines the relationships between various actors and concrete situations and interprets them in terms of a network of ethical meaning linked to the nation-state. Nations are ultimately defined by power and, when necessary, they are created and defended by force. The kernel is a hard one: on the one hand, the nation-state is the original form of the political and ethical principles of self-determination and non-intervention. On the other, the nation-state can still not be dissociated from the violence carried out in its name.

Psychoanalysis of the national self

The Slovenian theorist, Slavoj Žižek, makes a radical attempt at penetrating this national core by means of a re-reading of the post-*Wende* nationalist crises through the optic of Lacanian psychoanalysis and Hegelian dialectical theory. Žižek sets aside the traditional discourses of political science and ethics in order to examine the pre-philosophical basis of both. The novelty of his approach is that he deploys psychoanalytic concepts completely foreign to the discourse of political philosophy in an attempt to gain insight into its tacit presuppositions. In this way he brings Hegelian dialectics and Lacanian psychoanalysis to bear on contemporary political situations. With illustrations from post-colonial Europe, the Europe of immigration, globalization and multiculturalism, his project is a kind of psychoanalysis of western political self-understanding: European nationalism on the couch.

Eastern Europe is, of course, also part of Europe. It is, in many ways, also a kind of Enlightenment-inspired geopolitical self-image of Western Europe.

Western Europe has a long tradition of projecting itself, its values and experiences on the relatively exotic world of the East (Walters, 1987; Wolff, 1994). Thus the 'liberation' of the Eastern Bloc in the wake the fall of the Berlin wall has more than a passive importance for Western Europeans. To witness the rebirth of the East is to enjoy the projected rebirth of the West. Thus the East is simultaneously intimately known and yet unknown: *unheimlich,* as Freud would put. The West is fascinated by the collapse and rebirth of its eastern other. According to Žižek, this fascination is based precisely on this paradoxical experience. Western European witnesses its own rebirth. The rebirth of the East in the image of the West is, in effect, the nostalgic rebirth of the West. In eastern Europe, 'the West seeks for its own lost origins, its own lost original experience of 'democratic invention' (Žižek, 1993: 200).

In psychoanalytic terms, the West sees the East as a happy image of itself, the pure, innocent, idealized and likeable past, the birth of ourselves, something both identical to us and different. Without doubt, the reality is otherwise. The situation in the Balkans, as in the other emerging democracies of Eastern Europe, is far from idyllic, far from the Enlightenment model of democracy and well-organized free markets. Just as rapidly as the imagined model of democratic spirit motivated the 'soft revolution' of the East, the liberal democratic tendency evaporated in the face of the emergence of corporate national populism and its attendant evils, xenophobia and anti-Semitism in the new east European democracies (ibid.: 200).

Yet while geopolitical changes have been taking place in eastern Europe, the identity crisis that consciousness of these events creates seems to plague far more the West. Late 20th-century western national identification, Žižek claims, is an exemplary case of *external* borders being reflected into *internal* borders. The identity of a nation has two phases or levels. On the one hand, the nation is defined against its *external* other, through differences relative to all, in ways in which it is not to other nations, peoples and groups. But the nation is also, on the other hand, an interior demarcation of the endogenous members of the nation against each other. Even a superficial empirical assessment of any national community shows that no member is completely *proper.* Evoking the example of the English, Žižek underscores: 'the final answer is of course that *nobody* is fully English, that every empirical Englishman contains something "non-English" – Englishness thus becomes an 'internal limit', an unattainable point that prevents empirical Englishmen from achieving full identity with themselves' (Žižek, 1991: 110). The national identity of the exemplary Englishman is shaken by consciousness of the radical changes in the East. That new consciousness has a double-effect. The *external* changes observed in the East are empirically new, but they also affect his way of seeing one's self in his own immediate situation. In the jargon of psychoanalysis, the sameness of the other underscores the otherness of the same.

Modernity's neurosis: capitalism and liberal democracy

According to Žižek, the post-*Wende* growth of eastern European nationalism is characterized by two specific dimensions: (1) its eruption from an ideologically saturated socialist system into a late capitalist system of values and cultural relations, and (2) the promises of formal democracy. Capitalism is not just a set of values; it is also a striving for the universalization of those values. A critical feature of capitalism, in particular in the Marxian analysis, is the dissolution of particularity – be it ethnic, racial, cultural or other – as hindrances to the universality of the capitalist system. The internally configured need for growth and expansion renders it a missionary project. The creation of surplus value is most fruitful; the marginal gain of investment is greatest precisely where the refined mechanisms of investment and exchange are not yet refined. The other side of the global capitalist coin is that the insatiable thirst for expansion and the creation of ever-new surplus value has, historically, been the very force of technological progress, of the innovation that erases borders, reduces distance and brings on the globalized economic integration. Of course, this process of globalization is a false universalization since, by its very nature, it economically ghettoizes the largest part of the globe and increases the marginalization of the poorest parts of the world. These processes of globalization are the same as those that challenge the viability of the nation-state, of national culture – the same as those into which the new eastern democracies are thrust (Žižek, 1992: 162). At the very moment when national identity is challenged by globalization (and more 'locally' by European construction and eastern expansion), the thirst for a national substance emerges.

According to Žižek, liberal democracy is the other motivation for the crisis of the nation-state. In its ordinary sense, universalization erases particularity. Žižek notes that the universalization of formal democracy can only occur through the abstraction of the individual from all concrete substantial ties. The *ideal* democratic subject has no *particular* ethnic or cultural substance, nothing that can set him/her apart from any other democratic subject. All are equivalent in the eyes of the plebiscite. The person, groups or institutions assigned to the place of power by the result of the plebiscite are *external* to the democratic process, or at least external to the phase of equivalence that marks the plebiscite. This is the very sense of formal democracy: social differences are smoothed over in order to assure the coherence of the political voice. It is the aim of liberal democracy to evacuate both power and the ethical good from any *one* subjective place. Any and all individual subjects of liberal democracy must be, at any given time, closed off from 'the Good and the Powerful' in order to participate in its constitution. Moral law can only be found in a pure form (ibid.: 221). No one person can rule without usurping, without losing purity. That this is the obvious compromise made in any representational democracy does not change its paradoxical structure. Žižek reminds that the place of power, law and justice – the nature of which is decided by a well-functioning democracy – is nonetheless excluded from the democratic moment, from the plebiscite. The place of power and law is occupied by a sovereign who, in precisely the Hobbesian sense, is not an individual political subject, but rather a kind of concentration of all the individual subjectivities of the Commonwealth. Power and law – the sovereign – is not a *part* of democracy, and yet it is inseparable. It is, as Žižek puts it, a 'substantial extra', which must be abstracted in order for democracy to function. It is carried along as both superfluous and necessary: 'the indivisible remainder' (Žižek, 1992: 164; 1993). Nationalism, in Žižek's sense, is the tendency for the 'nation' to usurp this empty space of power left open by democracy, to occupy the necessarily empty or abstract space of justice and power. This 'indivisible remainder', this empty space, is the 'national remainder'.

Both late capitalism and the formal liberal democracy contribute to the persistence of this 'national remainder', this essential part of the national substance, which can neither be institutionalized nor formalized. Žižek associates this paradoxical, irreducible national kernel with what the French philosopher and psychoanalyst Jacques Lacan, following Freud, calls the 'thing' (Lacan, 1992: 25–103). Here Žižek's approach veers considerably from conventional political science, sociology or social anthropology. The notion of an irreducible national Thing permits Žižek to formulate two moments in the psychoanalytic model of understanding nationalism: (1) hatred of the other as hatred of the other's national enjoyment, and (2) hatred of one's own national enjoyment as hatred of the other in one's self.

The other's national enjoyment

Following Lacan, Žižek identifies this irreducible 'national Thing' with the pathological and aesthetic notion of *enjoyment* (*jouissance*). Žižek is fully aware that the analysis of 'enjoyment' rubs the discourse and methodologies of social science and humanities against the grain. Still, one must bear in mind that the intention in his work on nationalism in the Balkans and in Europe at large is to map out the contours of this 'thing'. It is an object that the social sciences and humanities fail to grasp because it is foreign to them.

The heart of the problem for Žižek, the 'place' of the 'national thing', is in the dynamics of national community. The bond linking any community, national or ethnic, is, he claims, not some concept of the community; not, as is canonically claimed, the *idea* of shared memories, traditions and rituals:

> The bond linking together its members always implies a shared relationship toward a Thing, toward Enjoyment incarnated. This relationship toward the Thing, structured by means of fantasies, is what is at stake when we speak of the menace to our 'way of life' presented by the Other: it is what is threatened when, for example, a white Englishman is panicked because of the growing presence of 'aliens'.

What he wants to defend is not reducible to the so-called set of values
that offer support to national identity.

(Žižek, 1993: 201)

If we accept Žižek's category of 'enjoyment' and all that it implies in terms
of the particularity of national, ethnic, cultural or religious character, then
nationalism is to be understood as the moment where enjoyment erupts into
'the social field' (ibid.: 202). Yet he goes further. Nationalism is a *materialization* of national enjoyment. Enjoyment is also an existential element in
the very being of the nation). The very existence of the nation (in the
cultural or ethnic sense of the term) reposes on the network of tensions in
the economy of 'national enjoyment'. 'A nation *exists* only as long as its
specific *enjoyment* continues to be materialized in a set of social practices and
transmitted through national myths that structure these practices.' In this
regard, Žižek distances himself from 'deconstructive' analyses of nationalism
that refuse the biological or trans-historical conception of the nation in
favour of an understanding of the nation as 'discursive or textual practices'
(ibid.: 202).

And yet in common with other deconstructive approaches, there is a
paradox at its centre. For the 'national Thing' is both threatened by the
other and utterly inaccessible to him/her. This opposition between self and
other can be witnessed again and again in the formulation of 'national
identity', 'national character' or 'national interests'. The foreigner threatens
'our' national culture by risking altering it or rendering it impure, *and at the
same time*, his/her otherness can never be reduced to something more like
'us'.

We always impute to the 'other' an excessive enjoyment: he wants to
steal our enjoyment (by ruining our way of life) and/or he has access to
some secret, perverse enjoyment. In short, what really bothers us about
the 'other' is the peculiar way he organizes his enjoyment, precisely the
surplus, the 'excess' that pertains to this way.

(ibid.: 203)

The revulsion toward the foreign other is, therefore, both pathological and
aesthetic. The 'danger' of the foreign other, the threat to my national Thing
is a threat to my emotional and aesthetic experience of my nationality. Once
again, the nation is not reducible to the sum of its members, be they citizens
or members of an ethnic collectivity. It is clearly not reducible to the
political and social institutions that embody the national character, nor is
it reducible to the national principle, to the simple concept of the nation
as a set of allegiances, rights and duties. According to Žižek, whenever we
attempt to sum up the nation – conceptually, ontologically or morally – we
are left with a remainder, which both resists totalization and becomes the
tenacious anchoring pin of national self-organization.

Why does the Other remain Other? What is the cause for our hatred of him, in his very being? It is hatred of the enjoyment in the Other. This would be the most general formula of modern racism: a hatred of the particular way the Other enjoys. The question of tolerance or intolerance is not at all concerned with the subject of science and its human rights. It is located on the level of tolerance or intolerance toward the enjoyment of the Other, the Other as he who essentially steals my own enjoyment (ibid.: 203)

Hatred of one's self as other

The explosion of ethnic conflict in the Balkans, and the diverse conflicts erupting in the new democracies of eastern Europe are clearly perceived as a threat to the West. This threat-perception manifests itself both in the debates on EU enlargement to the east and in the question of the expansion of NATO to include former Eastern Bloc countries or even Russia. The emergence of new capitalist democracies in the East is a glorious opportunity for the West to re-enact its own self-perception, to project its own capitalistic and democratic values on to the *tabula rasa* of the East, to re-experience the validity, and even superiority, of these values reaffirmed like some primal recreation of the Same.

As already noted, in Žižek's analysis, these moves toward integration into western Europe are measured along two axes, the democratic and the capitalistic. Both serve to frustrate the processes of national identitification. Firstly, formal democracy is based on a notion of subjectivity that erases particular difference. Formal democratic validity places a plenum of subjective equivalence that is not in alignment with cultural, ethnic, religious and racial equality. Democracy, like justice, must be blind. That is why it is just. Yet the impartiality presupposed by the blindness of democracy is precisely what threatens the particularity of individual cultural and ethical experience in relation to more global interests, be they those of a federation, union or global society at large. Secondly, capitalism, according to Žižek's analysis, is equally incapable of creating a properly normative cultural or ethical foundation. The basic feature of capitalism is its inherent structural *imbalance* (ibid.: 209). Capitalism (not to be confused with the simple concept of the free market) is based on a logic of crisis and change, on the need for constant innovation, constant reformulation of values, constant expansion, reinvestment, 'the permanent production of excess' (ibid.: 209). As the classical Marxian analysis shows, capitalism produces not only value, innovation, invention and progress; it also produces the *insatiable need* for these. Capitalism is effective at satisfying human needs by simultaneously manufacturing new ones.

In Žižek's view, part of the crisis of eastern European expansion is the spontaneous discovery that the 'revolution' (democratic and capitalistic) is not toward a solidified identity, but rather toward a state of displacement from the former, original sense of self (in formal democracy) and toward a state of cultural-economic displacement. Disappointment is thus inevitable, even structural. Even so, this analysis differs little from classical neoconservative cultural critique: formal democracy and market capitalism allegedly threaten to decouple value systems from their deeper anchoring in tradition. Žižek's conclusion is different. He takes the value-conservative analysis of eastern capitalistic democracies one step further, by insisting on the projection of the western self-understanding onto the East as its other. Formulated in another way: the East is the West's other. At the same time, the West is deeply embedded in it.

In other words, the knife cuts two ways: on the one hand, the East is the good, though empirically imperfect democratic capitalist other of the West; on the other, communism is the 'evil' empirical other of the East, which is inseparable from its past but which must be negated in order to integrate the East in what it already 'truly' is. For Žižek, this paradox is a symptom of liberal society and, not the least, liberal intellectual self-congratulatory self-sufficiency.

This reveals, moreover, a fundamental flaw in liberal democracy, a flaw that is above all interesting because it falls outside the bounds of the human and social sciences. It is *liberal democracy itself* (or rather the 'blind spot' of liberal democracy) that opens the space for nationalist fundamentalism. In the troubled wake of Francis Fukuyama's *The End of History and the Last Man* (Fukuyama, 1992), as much in disrepute as he may be, the only question with which the methodologies of political philosophy are truly confronted is whether liberal democracy is the 'ultimate horizon of our political practice' (ibid.: 221). Once again, the neoconservative reaction is that fundamentalism is a response to the loss of roots brought about by formal democracy and capitalism. Žižek reproaches liberal democratic thinking itself for ignoring this blind spot.

The status of nationalism is ultimately that of the transcendental illusion in the Kantian sense. It is based on the idea that reality is ultimately rational, that there is a kind of transcendental rationality. This transcendental reality of the nation – the 'national thing' – is ultimately inaccessible, even though its function builds upon an illusion of accessibility. This accessibility to the transcendental essence of the nation, the 'national thing', is precisely what formal democracy and capitalism promise. In this sense Žižek's analysis is also a critique of Kantian moral philosophy. Kant construes evil, like good, as a *transcendental* dimension. According to Žižek, Kant is incapable of understanding Evil as 'diabolical', as an ethical attitude (ibid.: 222). From this starting point, the *nation* is only one response to a more deeply human, more pathological and more aesthetic need to fill being with a centre, with a core, to reach toward the transcendental, inaccessible meaning of national belonging. The 'nation thing', which Žižek analyzes, is one formulation, among many others, of the Thing, this insatiable transcendental place, always apparently possible to fill but never completely satisfied. This is where, according to Žižek, both liberal democracy and capitalism, though indispensable, are symptoms of the nation-state's ethical core – its opening and problematization.

Note

1 As illustrated by Foucault, 'most of us no longer believe that ethics is founded in religion, nor do we want a legal system to intervene in our moral, personal, private life. Recent liberation movements suffer from the fact that they cannot find any principle on which to base the elaboration of a new ethics. They need an ethics, but they cannot find any other ethics than an ethics founded on so-called scientific knowledge of what the self is, what desire is, what the unconscious is, and so on' (Foucault, 1997: 255–6, cf. also Yúdice, 1988).

9   Security culture and the new *ethos* of risk

We live in an era of a tidal shift in international relations. We see and feel a need to re-tool our research gaze for wide-ranging changes in political, social and legal research, in particular concerning our way of understanding danger, threat and security. One of these changes involves the rise of the *preemptive impulse*, legitimated and institutionalized by George W. Bush. In presenting the new National Security Strategy one year after 11 September 2001, Bush used the following words.

> If we wait for threats to fully materialize, we will have waited too long. We must take the battle to the enemy, disrupt his plans and confront the worst threats before they emerge In the world we have entered, the only path to safety is the path to action.
>
> (Bush, 2002)

This claim invites a range of moral and political considerations, all originating in a relatively new set of circumstances. First, it arises from a certain acceleration of political action in time. The flow of information, people and things through global channels has increased the need to act *fast*. Second, it flows from a kind of *compression of space*. As a corollary to the acceleration of time, space has become more compact. What is far away is more intensely present. Spatial borders and limitations play less of a role than before. As a result of these two absolutely fundamental changes, the notion of politics itself is put into a different light. The acceleration of time, the compression of space, put a new pressure on politics, a normative pressure, a need to act, to be accountable *now*. It forms what Massumi has called 'potential politics' (Massumi, 2007). And it is the basis for what is sometimes called a new 'security culture'.

Security culture (likes its cousin, strategic culture) has imposed itself as a concept ever since it rumbled forth from Truman's 1947 National Security Strategy. And yet the changing scope and reach of the concept of security, and a distinct evolution in the understanding of the culture that envelopes it, has left us with an inadequately thematized, and thereby frequently abused, concept.

Not all concepts are equal, of course, and 'security' today is, without doubt, a master-concept. 'No other concept in international relations,' observed Der Derian in 1995, 'packs the metaphysical punch, nor commands the disciplinary power of "security"' (1995: 24–5). Security occupies the lexical, semantic, political and ethical centre of any proposition containing it. It is an arch-signifer, a black hole of reference, bending the light rays of all meanings that might pass close to it, absorbing and contorting meeting, and making itself the final referent of all signification. For this reason, 'security culture' is inevitably cast as a certain *kind* of security. 'Culture' is understood as a modifier or determinate variation on the monolithic term 'security'. It is a modality for understanding security and a means or mode of doing security.

However, one might argue that we are experiencing a destablization of 'security culture' that is at once subversive and political, and ethically. In what follows, we will claim that security culture is being changed not only by changes in the *culture of security* but also in a disruption of the *security of culture*. By opening this *double genitive* reading of security, we will situate the question of security in the tension between objective and subjective security. The implicit normative thrust of the argument is then double: let us look to culture to understand security, but also let us look to security and insecurity to understand culture.

We start by clarifying where we stand on the key concepts of this argument: security and culture.

Culture as a concept emerges primarily in the historical conjuncture that produces the scientific field of anthropology (Eriksen and Nielsen, 2001: 7–21; Gupta and Ferguson, 1997). Two important *crises* mark this emergence and evolution of the study of culture. The first involves the early modern explosion into self-awareness of the eschatological world-view of human beings. What remained of the notion of divine design in the mid-19th century was shaken by the multiple subversions of Darwin, Nietzsche and Freud. The empirical given-ness of humans, the determinism of the untouchable, sacrosanct human core, gave way to the viability of evolutionism, psychoanalysis, and the fragility and insecurity of human experience in the form of cultural of civilizational contingency was replaced by the study of the 'essence of man'. The second concerns the rise of the social and human sciences. Anthropology, like many contemporary western academic sub-disciplines of the social and human sciences, is the child of the scientific *ethos* of the dawn of the 20th century. It grew out of the seemingly contradictory and earnest conviction that the study of human beings should build upon an entirely different set of premises than the natural sciences, but that it nonetheless should bear the epistemological status of *science*. What Wilhelm Dilthey had, in 1883, baptised the *Geisteswissenschaften* (human sciences) (Dilthey, 1957, 2002) became the axis of a crisis of all science.

Thus, without doing the necessary detailed analysis, we can take note of the fact that anthropology, to the extent that it is interested in culture and cultures, is a science of borders, of insides and outsides, of inclusions and exclusions. This is the message of Frederik Barth's classic, *Ethnic Groups and Boundaires* (1969). Both in its methodological terms as a historical *Grenzegänger*, and in its substance, the science of cultures is the master discourse of identity crisis, of culture-under-threat from the Other without which it would have no meaning as culture as the experience of threat to culture.

What then of security *per se*? The strange history of *security*, briefer than that of culture is similarly instructive. The notion of security in circulation today is a child of the field of International Relations, itself part of a broader political science discipline with its own particular historical origins and culturally determined evolution. Before the mid-20th century, the term 'security' was never used in connection with international relations issues, or indeed at all in the realm of politics. As late as the end of World War II, the concern for security was effectively non-existent in the terms we use today, a mere whisper compared with the overwhelming role it plays today.

In ancient times, the conception of security was primarily bound to the spirit and to spirituality. It was, in essence, a theological concept. It was perceived as a disposition, a world-view and a spiritual state in both psychological and moral respects. The Greek word *antaraxie* – peace of mind – was used to describe the state of security. In the transition to the Middle Ages, *antaraxie* was translated to the Latin *securitas*. In the moral logic of medieval Christianity, *securitas* thus acquired a *negative* connotation. Security had a distinctly subjective character, signifying a lack of emotional or spiritual problems, interpreted as lack of concern. Security was a personal issue, which had nothing to do with the state, society or any other groups. During the Middle Ages, the terms *ceritudo* and *securitas* went their separate ways. The idea of *certitudo* facilitated the conceptual separation of a more knowledge-oriented branch of security thought from the notion of *securitas*. *Certitudo* means security in knowledge, in thought, in persuasion. *Securitas* remained an idea of security as an individual. This juncture made it possible for the modern conception of security to develop. Security as *securitas* was merely an objective thought, a thought about the dangers out there, not *in* here. It becomes liberated from the subjective aspect of threat, danger and risk, from the moral dimension of security, the relationship to God, the cosmos and to other individuals. Security became objectified. The feudal period sees the discourse of security transformed into an economic system of goods and services. Security could now be bought and sold. The function of the feudal prince was, in some ways, to offer security to those who could pay for it.

When, in 1947, Truman signed the United States' National Security Act, this suddenly changed. The concept of security was entirely overtaken by the notion of *national security*. As a result of the powerful influence of Cold War ideology, the concept was irresistibly and uncritically passed into circulation in the entire world for 40 years, even though before World War II the term 'national security' was virtually unknown. The recognition of a real or imaginary threat against the nation-state during the Cold War contributed to the renaissance of the security concept. Security as a condition without threat, general protection against potential danger, stood in opposition to the notion of defence, which represented a strategy with the objective of potential attack (Buzan and Hansen, 2009: 67).

This concept was further crystallized and institutionalized around the institutionalization of security and strategic studies, understood as national security and strategic studies. When the nuclear threat was added to the security equation, security studies further hardened into an object for the tools of strategic analysis.

The concept of culture in security studies

Culture was not entirely absent from the emergence and evolution of security studies. It followed well-travelled arguments of the realism-liberalism debate, more recently re-tooled as the realism-constructivism debate. The thrust of the debate hardly needs to be rehearsed: is it ideational factors or material power that play the most significant role in explaining 'the way the world works'? In its most mainstream form, the debate revolves around the 'behaviour' of states and the degree to which this is where ideas, on the one hand, and interests on the other, have the most consequential 'impact' on that behaviour.

A first wave of this cultural analysis of security features a host of prominent cultural anthropologists including Geoffrey Bateson, Ruth Benedit, Geoffrey Gorer, Clyde Kluckholn, Alexander Leighton and Margaret Mead. The researchers contributed to what might be called 'national character' analyses (Desch, 1998b: 145). It focused on correlating national culture with the behaviour of states in World War II. Popular versions of this cultural theory of war played an important role in public discourse in the 1950s (Dower, 1986). To the degree that it made cultural 'sense' of national difference, providing a scientific legitimacy for judgement of national differences, it played an important role in working through the past, toward drawing a traumatized world back to its imagined civilization moorings. This cultural movement receded with the rise of the nuclear threat when technology and strategy became the *lingua franca* of international conflict (Trachtenberg, 1991).

A more recent wave of 'culture and security' has taken place within IR theory, most prominently in 1995–96 in the pages of *International Security*. The positions taken in this debate are, by and large, attempts to account for the movement toward a general revision of the concept of security that we observe throughout the 1990s. Attempts made to widen and broaden 'security' and culture seem to be a natural object to include in a broader concept of security. Here 'culture' is more or less equated with the idea side of the equation and evaluated as to whether it plays a role in influencing the power that states operationalize on the playing-field of international relations. In his well-turned critical review of 'Ideas in Security Studies', Desch acknowledges the cultural debate of the 1990s before focusing on four strands of 'cultural theorizing' of international relations in operation today, most of them prolongations of the cultural critique of the 1990s (Desch, 1998b: 142–4). These strands are 'organizational culture' (Desch, 1998b; Kier, 1995, 1997), 'political culture', 'strategic culture' (Kier, 1995) and 'global culture' (Berger, 1996; Price and Tannenwald, 1996). All of these positions essentially surround Peter Katzenstein's 1996 *Culture of National Security* (cf. Buzan and Hansen, 2009: 195–6; Katzenstein, 1996).

Judgements like Desch's of the value of culture in IR rest on a set of criteria of 'explanatory power' formed in terms of scientific variation and predictability. How apt, he asks, are theories of culture in explaining the behaviour of states. The problems of cultural analysis are, according to Desch, threefold: first, cultural variables are difficult to define and operationalize; second, the claim that cultural variables are *sui generis*, thus in effect not variable, corrupts their universal validity; and third, cultural theory is not unified, it is, rather, a movement. Cultural theory is culturalism. Desch's conclusion, not unexpectedly, is that the 'new culturalism' does not provide much explanatory power beyond existing theories (Desch, 1998a: 150–8).

A more directly anthropological turn can be found in the work of other authors such as Dueck, who defines 'culture' in this regard as 'any set of interlocking values, beliefs and assumptions that are held collectively by a given group and passed on through socialization' (Dueck, 2006: 15). The assumption of this experiment is thus that (and we will return to this) material power, interests, the state and indeed the very notion of 'behaviour', not to mention the entire input–output logic of this analysis are somehow free from implicit cultural determinations. Culture, then, is an external force that impacts upon them, bringing discrete consequences.

Thus one critical conclusion from a review of this literature is not that culture 'matters' (or doesn't 'matter') but rather that a central precondition of the debate is a certain exclusion of culture. Security studies is implicitly or explicitly defined as the instrumentalization of ideas. Culture precedes, or is exogenous to, this function. Or one might go even further by suggesting that security studies can be defined as a certain ghettoizing of culture, the function of putting aside or marginalizing.

Culture of uncertainty and the rise of the discourse of risk

Security, whether we regard it in a long or short, broad or narrow perspective, is a certain ordering of danger, threat, shelter, wellbeing, etc. It is a structuring of the relationship between *this* sheltered place and *that* vulnerable place. It frames the relationship between us and them, between wellbeing and menace, danger, threat.

Contrary to what the security literature in a variety of forms tells us, security is never simply a *state-of-affairs* or *situation*. Through a kind of dialectical logic, security is the absence of insecurity, which is nonetheless present in its absence. Security is only possible through the thought of insecurity, through the preparation for what is not yet the case, but rather for what *could* be the case. All security contains the trace, the thought of insecurity, and a thought is all it takes to give life to insecurity. Only an absurdly absolute enunciation, 'You are secure', can truly assure security. Any grain of objective reference ('You are secure from the 7300 nuclear warheads in eastern Europe') begs the issue. It is indeed a source of insecurity. Security has far less to do with what is *known* than with what is *unknown*.

Security is increasingly understood and lived as a way of dealing with this unknown, a means of taking action in the face of unknown danger, in the face of the unknown as danger itself, and even of danger as the unknown. In this sense security can be construed as a kind of *epistemology*, a kind of system for dealing with knowledge – or rather non-knowledge, that is incomplete or inadequate knowledge – of dangers. In this sense, security is a virtual knowledge, a basis for how to act if adequate knowledge had been present. In this sense it represents a continuation of the classic opposition, from the Theory of Just War, between prevention (defensive action against demonstrable aggression) and preemption (defensive action against *likely* aggression).

As we have seen in several theoretical contexts, security exploits a number of different alliances with *knowledge*. This is its culture. Security is a kind of knowledge, and yet insecurity does not adequately break down within the scope of the epistemology of security studies or international relations. This is because security knowledge is the axis of production of a number of pathologies of insecurity, in other words, a number of ways that insecurity is lived by us (Dillon, 1996: 17). The search for security generates a self-replicating need for security and thereby for knowledge in the aim of security.

We cannot be secure in our knowledge unless it is total and global. More knowledge brings with it knowledge of the limits of knowledge, which, in turn, produces more insecurity. The more *transparent* we render our lives in the name of security, the more border controls, bag checks and metal detectors we confront, the less secure we *feel*, and, pragmatically, the less secure society *is* in pragmatic turns. What seems clear from the analysis so far is that the *experience* of security and insecurity has outgrown the *concept* of security. There is a misfit between concept and experience. This misfit can be linked to the rise in the concept of *risk*. Current security thinking, already a kind of mutation from the more or less defunct concept of *strategy* seems to be morphing again in conjunction with the rise of the concept of *risk*.

This extraordinary hybrid concept, risk – in its most current usage – plots a complex constellation of empirical facts, ideas and values. It is a hub between past, present and future, and, as an analytical concept, it links three entirely different epistemologies. As a filter and interpreter of the *past*, it applies a *historiographical* logic, mobilizing the hermeneutical activity that contributes to rendering the past present as a basis for making judgements about the future. As a criterion for assembling facts about the *present*, in view of prognosis about the future, it mobilizes social-scientific principles touching upon questions of scope and depth, salience, operationalizability, etc. Finally, as a *future-oriented, prognostic* concept, it links assessments of likelihood and relevance with judgements of socially, politically and culturally based value. Risk, in this sense, is the new culture of security. What can this mean?

Risk reflects our experience of the past, our perception of the present and our aspirations for the future. It draws upon our own individual experience as well as the experience of others. It reflects what we know and necessarily delves into the unknown. It paradoxically conceptualizes the certainty of uncertainty at the very frontier between faith and reason. In this sense, risk is profoundly involved in the metaphysics of the unknown, in concern for the other-worldly.

Moreover, risk is inseparable from a certain question of power, of mastery and submission. The sciences of risk, from the frivolity of the premodern science, to the challenge of probability and statistical uncertainty, to the new sciences of risk management, all conceptualize risk as something to tame but not to eliminate. Indeed, risk is the very backbone of the financial system that today faces such great challenges. Risk is, in this sense, an indispensable component of capitalism.

Through its brief but rapid evolution, risk analysis has stood firmly on the shoulders of scientific knowledge, and the rapid evolution in risk studies has been driven by advances in science, technology and, not least, actuarial sciences. The dependency of risk studies on science and technology is both odd and disquieting. For the epistemology of the natural sciences, its *alpha* and *omega*, is the bounded field of the known or the immediately-to-be-known. Risk is directly defined out of this field. Risk concerns precisely what we do not know. As soon as the unknown becomes known it ceases to be risk. To better understand this shift in discourse, we need a refocus of the analysis to the human aspects, to culture, to the value side and to the ethical dimensions of risk assessment. On this view, the fundamental, and fundamentally neglected, characteristic of risk is its *ethos*. By the *ethos* of risk we mean its function as a meeting-place for the expression, incorporation and negotiation of human values.

The culture of security begins not with knowledge, but where knowledge ends. When insurance companies carry out assessments based on statistical profiles, likelihoods and probably backgrounds, they are already eliminating the risk, not because the car will not crash, the chain-smoker will not contract emphysema, but rather the *value* of the danger, should it obtain, is henceforth reduced to zero. In the sense of determining the way it will affect human lives, the consequences have already taken place, the accident has already happened, (human) value assessments are already made, actions are already taken, etc.

The portion of risk that is not assimilatable to the value calculus of risk analysis is what we might call *radical* risk. It is the unknown unknown, the part that *counts* in our lives, precisely because it *doesn't count* in the scientific calculus. It cannot be reduced to nil through analysis and planning. It cannot be pulverized. This indestructible radical risk is important precisely *because* it is unforeseeable and it is precisely this *eventuality* that forms the only available basis for judging how we should lead our lives. Radical risk is therefore the site of a *decision* about what we value in human terms, and therefore it is a decision about our own identity, about who we are and what we want, what is dispensable and what is indispensable.

The discourse of risk teaches us that knowledge is security and that security is therefore laden with human, cultural values. As we noted above, Butler teaches us that that culture is the subject's experience of itself as contingent, and therefore as vulnerable, fragile. As cited in Chapter 4, 'Each of us is constituted politically, in part by virtue of the social vulnerability of our bodies, as a site of desire and physical vulnerability, as a site of a publicity at once assertive and exposed'. Loss and vulnerability seem to follow from our being socially constituted bodies, attached to others, at risk of losing those attachments, exposed to others, at risk of violence by virtue of that exposure (Butler, 2004b: 20; Burgess, 2007a).

Security and insecurity are implicitly connected to what we value, an expression of a value constellation that expresses a certain perspective on life, of individual and collective anxieties and aspirations, of expectations about what to sacrifice and what is worth preserving. Security is often associated with the material aspects of life because, in our time, they have a tendency to incorporate, if not replace, human values. But these technical and material values should not be confused with life itself. Security does not involve only *things*. It involves *people* who value things and who need certain things as a means to survive. Security is, in the end, reflexive. It is as much about those who live the threat as it is about the threat itself.

Part III

Geopolitical rationalities of Europe

10 Insecurity of the European community of values

Among the multiple ways in which the European Union seeks to constitute itself as a quasi-sovereign political body endowed with the legitimacy necessary to execute monetary policy, enact law and deploy a unified foreign policy, is through a reference to a discourse of value: the EU is construed as a community of values whose necessity, cohesion and self-evidence is implicit. A wide range of the principles and practices of the EU make reference, directly or sub-jacently, to a set of fundamental values whose origin and homogeneity is seldom put into question. One quite natural consequence of this reference to values is a certain kind of *securitization* of values. If the European Union faces a security challenge, it is related, in one way or another, to its security as a community of values. Yet what does it mean for a community of values to be insecurity, to be the object of security. This chapter argues that while values themselves, and the communities that hold them as there foundation, are indestructible, it is their forms of institutionalization that come under threat. By the very nature of the relation between institutions and values, this insecurity is structurally unavoidable.

Values in the European self-understanding

What are the values that constitute the European community of values? In the pages of the Treaty of the European Union we can recognize at least six types of linkages between values, supposed to be European, and the institutional activities carried out in their name: foundation, general purpose, unity, membership, rights and security (Treaty of the EU, 2008).

Values as foundation

Immediately following the 'Establishment of the Union' in Article 2 of the Treaty is the pronouncement of its values that form the foundation of the European project:

> The Union is founded on the values of respect for human dignity, freedom, democracy, equality, the rule of law and respect for human

rights, including the rights of persons belonging to minorities. These values are common to the Member States in a society in which pluralism, non-discrimination, tolerance, justice, solidarity and equality between women and men prevail.

The foundational European values are not only attributes that can be held or not held, adopted or not adopted, but also the basis on which the rest is built. In this architectural metaphor, the European values form the indispensable groundwork upon which the rest builds. The European values, according to the logic of this metaphor, cannot be chosen away for the European superstructure that is dependent upon them. It is the foundational aspect that assures the commonality of the values. By virtue of depending on them as a foundation, all of Europe shares them.

The Preamble to the Treaty, a page earlier, describes similar values as a source of 'inspiration' for the European project:

> Drawing inspiration from the cultural, religious and humanist inheritance of Europe, from which have developed the universal values of the inviolable and inalienable rights of the human person, freedom, democracy, equality and the rule of law.

Not only is the European house built upon a platform of common values, these values inspire, drive on, ennoble and empower the building project. The values are in this sense less the basis than the ideals to which European construction aspires. They are, in the logical of idealism, virtual, not yet realized; they belong to the future, to the potential logic of what Europe could be if it stays the course, holds on to the possibility of its unrealized promise (Derrida, 1992b; Burgess, 1997).

Values as aim

This idealism of European values, at odds, to a certain degree, with their foundationalism, gives added force to the *objective aims* of the European Union as formulated in Article 3. Values are luxuriatiating principles; they are objectives. These objectives are specified, among other things as the promotion of

> ...peace, its values and the well-being of its peoples.
> [...]
> In its relations with the wider world, the Union shall uphold and promote its values and interests.

The mere fact the European Union constitutes itself around a set of objective aims – that is as a project, political, social, cultural, human or other – strengthens claims that it is an institution *sui generis*. Whereas most nation-state constitutions of basic laws would pronounce their existence as a self-evidence and thereby their purpose as, in effect, that existence, the EU constitutes itself to a large degree as a set of unrealized aims.

Values as intergovernmental unity

Like the overall project of the European Union, the workings of the European Council are to be guided by the promotion of shared values in Articles 32 and 42:

> Member States shall ensure, through the convergence of their actions, that the Union is able to assert its interests and values on the international scene.
> [...]
> ...the Council may entrust the execution of a task, within the Union framework, to a group of Member States in order to protect the Union's values and serve its interests.

More precisely, the Member States, through the tools and mechanisms of the European Council, have a higher-order set of responsibilities, namely to ensure the assertion of interests and values. The Council is in this sense a facilitator of values that precede it and whose finality surpass it.

Values as gatekeeper

European values also serve as the shibboleth or gatekeeper for entry into the European Union. Article 1 of the treaty preserves Article I-1 of the previous treaty, which describes the conditions for membership in the EU:

> The Union shall be open to all European States which respect the values referred to in Article I-2, and are committed to promoting them together.

It also specifies the grounds upon which *exclusion* may take place:

> ...the Council may adopt a European decision determining that there is a clear risk of a serious breach by a Member State of the values referred to in Article 2.

Values as basis for rights

Perhaps most naturally, the European values are closely associated with its charter of rights. The annex to the Treaty of Lisbon containing the entirety of the Charter of Fundamental Rights of the Union describes at length the prescribed European rights, based on a common set of values:

The peoples of Europe, in creating an ever closer union among them, are resolved to share a peaceful future based on common values.
[...]
Conscious of its spiritual and moral heritage, the Union is founded on the indivisible, universal values of human dignity, freedom, equality and solidarity; it is based on the principles of democracy and the rule of law, It places the individual at the heart of its activities, by establishing the citizenship of the Union and by creating and area of freedom, security and justice.
[...]
The Union contributes to the preservation and development of these common values while respecting the diversity of the cultures and traditions of the peoples of Europe as well as the national identities of the Member states and the organization of their public authorities at national, regional and local levels.

Values and security

Finally, the notion of values is associated, in the *Treaty*, with the enterprise of European *external* security, formulated as foreign policy. In the first lines of Article 21 on the EU's External Action.

The Union shall define and pursue common policies and actions, and shall work for a high degree of cooperation in all fields of international relations, in order to [among other things] safeguard its values, fundamental interests, security, independence and integrity.

Finally, the safeguarding of values is set as a priority, in the *Treaty*, of European *external* security, formulated as foreign policy. In the first lines of Article 21 on the EU's External Action.

The Union shall define and pursue common policies and actions, and shall work for a high degree of cooperation in all fields of international relations, in order to [among other things] safeguard its values, fundamental interests, security, independence and integrity.

Values as foreign policy

The notion of the assertion of the values of the European was already declared as the aim of EU foreign policy, for example in the Treaty of the European Union, Article 22:

The Union shall define and implement a common foreign and security policy covering all areas of foreign and security policy, the objectives of which shall be [among other things] to safeguard the common values, fundamental interests, independence and integrity of the Union in conformity with the principles of the United Nations Charter (1992).

Values in the European Security Strategy

Similar value formulations are expressed again in the 2003 European Security Strategy, 'A More Secure Europe in a Better World', which describes the strategic objectives necessary to 'defend its security and to promote its values' (2003). The strategy opens by framing the new 'global challenge' facing Europe as one where there are 'increasingly open borders in which the internal and external aspects of security are indissolubly linked'. The 'key threats' to Europe mapped out in the document are terrorism, the proliferation of weapons of mass destruction, regional conflicts, state failure and organized crime. The strategy underscores the fact the none of the new threats to Europe is entirely military, nor can be addressed by entirely military means. It asserts that a number of non-military instruments (political and economic pressures, humanitarian efforts) must be taken into use in order to address them. These will, the document affirms, rely on a mixture of 'intelligence, police, judicial, military, and other means' (Biscop, 2005; Council of the European Union, 2003).

Values in the Internal Security Strategy

Against the background of a more or less realized Schengen *acquis*, the EU faces the considerable challenge of establishing and organizing the institutions, agencies and, not least, the principles that will organize the internal security after the suppression of the internal borders. The market security provided by a liberalization of international trade within the EU produces, simultaneously, the horizon of more wealth and a multiplication and diversification of security needs. Traditional external concerns, it is true, are displaced toward the external borders and, to some degree, the variety of external affairs issues channel through a increasingly porous internal structure to take a place in sub-European, national, regional or local bureaucracies. This migration in tasks and competencies, far from aligning itself along simple internal–external vectors, opens a vacuum, and with it a kind of Aristotelian *horror vacui*, an anxiety for the very emptiness that enables its structurally necessary liberties. A new concept and new strategy is the response: *The Internal Security Strategy*.

For the authors of the Internal Security Strategy, the provision of security has two aspects, structural and substantive:

> For citizens of the European Union, security is one of the main priorities. The EU multi-annual work programmes have already provided a good pragmatic basis for strengthening operational cooperation, but now a larger consensus on the vision, values and objectives which underpin EU internal security is required.
>
> (Council of the European Union, 2010)

The pragmatics being in place, the principals values that will 'underpin' internal security need to be clarified. It is in part the purpose of the ISS document to do just that. The documents both articulates and claims the presence of a consensus of security values. The 'values' of European construction ('human rights, democracy and the rule of law') are here most often evoked as the basics of a European culture of value. These values, undifferentiated and unqualified, play two different roles in this document. In their first role, values are linked with security itself such that security is understood as conceptually co-determined by values. In essence, security is not thinkable without values.

> Europe must consolidate a security model, based on the principles and values of the Union: respect for human rights and fundamental freedoms, the rule of law, democracy, dialogue, tolerance, transparency and solidarity.

The kinds of security foreseen through the ISS is in some sense, through the suppression of such values (i.e. military power, technologies of violence, autocracy, etc.), colluding with an 'other' security, different, more refined, presumably more secure, more 'value'-able, more noble, etc.

The second role or position of values in the ISS document has been directly and intentionally threatened by the composite threats that make up the new landscape of threat in Europe:

> The main crime-related risks and threats facing Europe today, such as terrorism, serious and organized crime, drug trafficking, cyber-crime, trafficking in human beings, sexual exploitation of minors and child pornography, economic crime and corruption, trafficking in arms and cross-border crime, adapt extremely quickly to changes in science and technology, in their attempt to exploit illegally and undermine the values and prosperity of our open societies.

From the hydraulic discourse of security versus values often heard in public debates, whereby the one is increased while the other is proportionality decreased, the ISS document moves to a logic whereby the provision and assurance of security does imply a trade-off of values. Here, even the non-terrorist authors of security threats – criminals, traffickers, pornographers – adapt with the very aim of attacking values.

Shared values form the basis for a certain community, a community of values from which meaning, legitimacy, initiative and aspiration flow unequally, and with them the constitutive insecurity that structures the horizon of their future loss.

Community of values

The understanding of community presented in Chapter 5 presupposes a discourse, be it academic or popular, and a political position relative to that discourse. What is the discourse of community? The division of labour of academic fields, particularly in modernity, has given rise to a number of different, sometimes overlapping, discourses of community. We might name *social, cultural, political, technological,* and *economic,* in addition to our primary object, community of *values.* The differences between discourses of community rests upon their differing systems of reference and valorization, and their differing logics of inclusion and exclusion. Variations in discourse thus give way to a politics of community. Academic debates within these fields turn not only around the content of supposed communities, but also around the borders that articulate them, and the logics and forces of inclusion and exclusion that structure them.

From a phenomenological point of view, the rise in the concept of community responds to a generalized sense of crisis in the social sphere, in other words to a sense of loss of community. As Hobsbawm put it in *The Age of Extremes,* 'Never was the word "community" used more indiscriminately and emptily than in the decades when communities in the sociological sense became hard to find in "real life"' (Hobsbawm, 1994: 428). The modernity of the concept of community is related to its crisis, to its insecurity. Communities multiply and overlap, producing criss-crossing identities and loyalties. Neither the predicates that determine communities are stable nor the body-political that represents them to both community members and non-members. As we have suggested earlier, this sense of insecurity is associated with the rise of a certain 'multiculturalism' and the notion of multi-layered awareness known as *glokalisation.* Because of migration and refugee movements, cultural identity becomes more intermingled, making community boundaries more porous. Global awareness has given force to local legitimacy and cultural sovereignty. The local is legitimated against a wider supra-local horizon. In terms of the semantic or symbolic structure, a community is not only a social praxis, it is also a system of meaning (Anderson, 1991; Cohen, 1985). Both access to community and access to understanding a community are determined by codes of conduct and semantics of the community's actions.

A community of values, then, is a community whose belonging is determined by a shared set of values. This shared-ness plays out differently relative to the two axes of community mentioned earlier: community as a set of predicates and community as a body. If a community is a set of predicates, then the predicates of a community of values are values. The catalogue of shared values becomes distinct in relation to other communities that do not possess the same values, or which possess a different composition of values. Thus values are relative to the other, to the non-community member, to the immigrant, to the other religion, the other culture, etc. No community of values is based on one value alone. Predicates are always multiple. The interplay of values forms the unique character of the community as a body: the composition of the community has a value in itself on par with the constitutive values.

A community of values is also a thing in itself, actively implicated and involved in the formation and mutation of values. The community itself has a certain value, both to members and non-members of the community. The community is inherently conservative, regardless of the actual values involved in its constitution. Any community, including a community of values, thus tends toward its own self-preservation.

By *value* we understand an abstract notion whose concrete realization is estimated, by common consensus, relative difference, or absolute authority, as being of significant worth. Without endorsing a *politically* relative view of value, it must be admitted that no value has absolute value. Something is *a* value from the moment it has more worth than something else. Whether the source of this worth is implicit or not does not change the relative nature of its value-ness. The *source* of values of communities is inevitably occult. This fact contributes to preserving its relativity, by assuring that any absolute reference, historical or otherwise, is implicit, not explicit.

These basic ideas and definitions open on to the first paradox of the community of values: values are both universal from the point of view of the community, and particular and situational from the point of view of moral communities. As abstract concepts, values are only meaningful to the degree that they are considered universally valid. If a value is not everywhere and always a value for the members of the community, then it is not a value at all.

The community as a whole is defined by its values as against other entities, other groups, individuals and communities, which do not possess its values. In this sense the universal nature of the given values depends upon there particularity, on the opposition to the situations where they are not valid. Supposed universality makes visible *internal* divergence or particularity. The value principles upon whose consensus the community is formed does not guarantee their concrete universality, their universality in effect. Indeed the very presence of the universal principle is a reminder that the reality to which it refers is not yet universal.

The community of values is always disjointed with respect to its own boundaries. Moreover, it is both lesser than and greater than its boundaries. Any community of values is characterized by internal heterogeneity, strife, disagreement, political friction, etc. On the other hand, a community of values always exceeds the political boundaries of which it is constitutive. Any community of values constitutes itself by relating to others. It thereby lies partially beyond its own conceived borders. In other words, the existence of the community of values depends upon a kind of negative relation to its other.

Based on its supposed universality, the community of values aims at the other as an object of its action. It must relate to the other individual, the other community, the other moral ideal, even though it is foreign to him/her. In other words, it is the essence of a community of values to fail to be a successful community of values. A community of values is the movement of a necessarily paradoxical non-correspondence between the conceptual and the empirical. A community of values is therefore one that is constantly self-interrogating, constantly forming a new idea of itself based on the ever-changing empirical landscape of that which it seeks to encompass. The movement is dialectical, swinging from the articulation of moral assertions or norms to the identification of the empirical reality of existing and already valid values.

Insecurity of a community of values

Security is the condition of being secure, of being protected from or not exposed to danger, 'freedom from doubt [...] from care, anxiety or apprehension; a feeling of safety or freedom from or absence of danger' (OED, 1971). Security is thus a negative category, a state of *absence* on two different levels. It is both the objective *absence* of (or freedom from) threat and the absence of *anxiety* or *apprehension* of threat. As we pointed out above, security, in contrast to safety, refers to a sphere of potentials. It relates to a field of presumed, though actually unspecified, danger. This virtual association of security links it with its second quality. The relationship to an unspecified field of dangers is inseparable from the *experience* of this danger. Thus a kind of phenomenology of security comes into play. Security is a lived phenomenon, an experiential concept.

To what extent does the classical model of *security community* relate to the concept of *community of values* developed above (Adler and Barnett, 1998; Deutsch, 1957b; Kitchen, 2009; Rieker, 2006)? On one level, a security community and a community of values are essentially different; on another they are similar. Their difference relates to the threat to which they are opposed. A *security community*, according to the classical definition, is one whose common basis is the threat from which it offers freedom. The threat is generalized according to any number of categories, provided that the threat is an existential one, that is, that it its achievement potentially leads to the dissolution of the community. A *community of values* is of a different order, though its *security* is based on a structure analogous to that of the security community in general. It is related to the existential threat of dissolution. The common basis of a community of values is a set of values. The perception of threat to moral values is the basis for the creation and evolution of institutions that secure such values. These institutions are the prime force for changing the self-understanding of threat to the values of the community.

The common basis of the community of values is a set of values. What would the realization of an existential threat to that community, namely its destruction, actually mean? If security is to be understood as the presence of unspecified threat and the experience of that threat, what would the result of the collapse of the security of the security community mean? What does the threat to which security refers actually threaten? What would the execution of such a threat imply? Two strange and disconcerting answers impose themselves.

First, the logic of security does not contain a logic of destruction, only a disposition for the unspecified *potential* for destruction. It is the *threat* of danger and not danger itself that constitutes the essence of security. Threat in the security community has no real referent, only a virtual or potential one. Or, to put it another way, the threat at the basis of a security community is self-referential. Threat refers only to threat. There is no external or transcendental danger, at least not relative to the security community, which would be the outcome of the collapse of the security community (Agamben, 1993; Badiou, 1995).

Second, what would the collapse of a community of values actually mean? The key to understanding the life of moral values in time is the insight that values *cannot be pulverized*. No objective violence, no degree of absence of concrete incorporation of values, can serve to annihilate them. If we understand moral values to be purely principled, timeless, placeless concepts, then it goes without saying that no empirical change, creation or destruction can threaten them. One might imagine that those individuals who share the moral values that constitute the common basis for the community of values are dispersed, killed or otherwise eradicated, but the values themselves are never exposed to threat.

Thus the reactionary battle cry of popular politics: 'We must militarize in order to protect our values' rings empty. Values themselves are never under threat, can never be eradicated. If the community of values is threatened, this threat surrounds only the cohesion of those who share the moral values in question. Neither the subsistence of the shared values nor their sharing is empirically in doubt, only the *cohesion* of those who hold them. That cohesion is extra-moral. It does not belong to the community as such, but precedes it and remains external to it. Consequentially, the only community that can actually be utterly and outrightly dispersed is one in which the there is no common basis, in which there are no common predicates or properties.

What then is the security of the community of values? Against what must the community of values be secured? To make a community of values secure would not imply eliminating the *objective* threat to the moral values. The insecurity of a community of values would correspond to the menace of disruption of the self-constituting dialect between value and reality. The only menace to the community is values, the loss of the process of its self-constitution, the play of community: idea-reality, value-institution. To eliminate insecurity would be to eliminate the possibility of freezing the internal dynamic of community.

The menace to the community of values is thus not the destruction of its moral values. It is, rather, the interruption of the link between the abstract values and the institutions, large and small, that first concretize them, then contribute to the dynamic of their evolution. The threat is logically double: either calcification of the relation between ideal and concretization at the heart of the community, or its uncoupling. The ability to act as a community of values, and the ability for the members of a community of values to act individually, depends on their ability to take cognizance of the values they are enacting. The community of values is a community that knows itself as such, reacts to the scope and limits of its own application. The community of values is thus not the static existence of the set of values that makes up its foundation. It is, rather, the process of questioning of the application of its own principles.

The community of values is thus, *by necessity*, insecure. If it were not insecure, it would cease to be 'moral'. The threat to the community concerns the openness to moral questioning, to moral ambiguity. The community of values is not a collective attachment to a normative checklist. It is a formation confronting the ethos of threat implicit in any question of values.

What is the relationship between a community of values and its security? What does it mean to say that a community is insecure? The consequence of these reflections is that a community of values is *necessarily* insecure. The 'value' of the community of values lies precisely in its insecurity. If it were not insecure it would cease to be of 'value'. The value of the community of values lies in its very insecurity.

11 The modernity of a cosmopolitan Europe

Nothing is more modern than modernity, yet nothing is so old. This is because a tension lies at the very heart of the notion of modernity. 'Do we live in an enlightened age?' asked Kant in his 1783 *An Answer to the Question: What is Enlightenment?* 'No,' he answers himself, 'but rather in an age of Enlightenment' (Kant, 1983a: 45). In his stunning *We Have Never Been Modern*, Bruno Latour makes the troubling claim that the repertoire of modern critical analysis has always been internally inconsistent if not outright contradictory, and, more importantly, that we have always been at home in the non-modern world, living comfortably with hybrid combinations of natural and social objects-subjects (Latour, 1993). For Kant, as for Latour, modernity is a certain way of thinking, a perspective on the world that is also a perspective toward one's self. Modernity, according to Latour, is an aspiration toward a concept, which, paradoxically, excludes itself from realization. It is the insight into a homogeneous set of principles that exclude realization.

Common for all great diagnosticians of modernity is the insight that modernity is not simply a turning point along one great linear path of self-unfolding historical facts. It is a way of thinking, of conceptualizing. To the degree that it is the quest for a kind of unity – of religion, culture and state – it is a methodology, a philosophical anthropology of human life, in which the human subject is autonomous and the world fragmentary (Delanty, 2000: 11).

Modernity is, on the one hand, a temporal notion, a dimension of historical or temporal present-ness, or past-ness of differentiation from the past, of change and transformation, of newness, of a relation to present events, living people, recent memories, actions over which we have control, events that effect directly our lives (OED, 1971). Modernity thus refers to a process of transformation of change, a spaceless notion of transformation. What is modern is new. In this mode, modernity also contains a subtle normative dimension, a temporal hubris, a set of implicit value claims about the past versus the present, the civilizational position of society in a long-term sliding mode.

On the other hand, modernity is a historicized category referring to a broad constellation of social, cultural, religious and political formations. Modernity in this sense is a certain form of social life, marking the *end* of a certain historical evolution, growing out of particular concrete historical changes: the secular state and polity, capitalist economy, social formations of the division of labour and relations to secular culture (Hall et al., 1992). Among other things, historical modernity refers to the emergence of a certain kind of *institutionalization* of the nation-state from a historical situation in which traditional institutions and structures dominated. In traditional societies, the structure of family, village and church determined the shape and self-understanding of the individual subject, providing role, a meaning and a set of collective references – what we commonly call *political identity*.

This notion of *self-understanding* is central to the notion of modernity, both in terms of its historical emergence and its continued evolution. Modernity refers to a kind of relationship to one's self, an understanding of one's present. It is a self-understanding, an understanding of the world projected through an understanding of one's self in the world and in time. In the following we will re-cast political modernity as a world order in which the structures and constellations of *power* undergo an important transformation, one that will have long-ranging consequences for the singular form of European construction known as the European Union.

Political culture is a constellation of meanings, values, symbols, ideas, knowledge, language and ideology that constitute political activity recognized as such. Political culture is the available set of concepts and ideas, categories of understanding and means of expression that render political reality understandable, and which ascribe to it the moral, economic and social values it might seem to have. Thus where the conventional measures of modernity – processes of economic, social and political development – possess clear, even material, measures, these measures are determined by the political culture of a society.

In other words, political culture does not precisely reflect modernity. It is, rather, constitutive of it. In some sense the very notion of political culture is at odds with the movement of political modernity. It is thus incorrect to simply state that modernity has had an impact on political culture, as our session title suggests. Political culture produces modernity in the sense that it produces concept, meanings and values that are then co-opted by the social sciences and deployed in order to legitimate political activity, for the modernization of politics corresponds more or less to a double evolution of (1) narrowing the reach of the concept to techniques of political action and control, and thereby (2) to an instrumentalization of politics.

The modernity of European corresponds with the modernity of a certain idea of the 'social'. Traditionally, modern societies are identified with the changes brought about by the emergence of industrialization in the 19th century. Moreover, the very notion of modernity is inseparable from certain transformations in the nature and methods of scientific investigation. Social science, in particular, and modernity are reciprocally determinate.

Firstly, the fundamental *intellectual* impetus of modernity is arguably the Enlightenment, both the European (as expressed in authors like Kant, Voltaire, Montesquieu, Diderot and Rousseau) and the so-called 'Scottish' Enlightenment (exemplified by Hume, Smith, Fergusson and others). Enlightenment is first and foremost a *critical movement*, a critique of traditional political authority and the central ideas that support it, ideas such as *progress, science, reason* and *nature*. The *social sciences* are canonized, as we know, around the turn of the 20th century, by the founders of modern sociology: Durkheim, Weber, Simmel and Tönnies. Their impulse continues the critique of traditional conception inaugurated by Enlightenment *philosophes*.

Secondly, modernity is substantively, as well as temporally and spatially, heterogeneous. It can be related to a composite set of movements and developments operating in different domains, at different velocities and in different places. According to this analysis, there is no single, causal view of modernization. *Economic modernity* is understood as a certain phase in the development of economic relations, characterized by the spread of commerce and trade, markets, a new division of labour, new forms of consumption. The evolution of *social modernity* involves the shift from agrarian to industrial forms of production. These are accompanied by shifting conceptions of the private and public spheres, the family, gender and class differentiation. The characterization of *political modernity* arises from the study of the emergence of the modern state. The present is hereby conceived as the outcome of a movement of the classical European empires, the feudal states, the estate system and absolutism, to the form of the modern nation-state: encompassing conceptions of political authority, secular power, legitimacy and sovereignty. Lastly, *cultural modernity* is associated with awareness of the importance of moral, social and political values, meaning and symbolic structures in the modern self-understanding. Thus studies like Weber's protestant ethic, Freud's civilizational critique, or Lévi-Strauss' structural analysis of social life all testify to a need for differentiation of the cultural dimensions involved with internal integration and differentiation of societies and their relation to other societies.

Social science methodology and social identity

The methodological problem that attaches itself to social scientific research on identity is straightforward. If one attempts to collect *objective* knowledge on a social scientific object, then all objects offer problems, for the social scientist is always necessarily implicated in the object of research by the very act of carrying out the research. This is a fundamental insight of social science methodology today. To work in a scientific way implies making choices, applying rules and criteria, making use of models that are subjectively determined, models that do not belong to the object, but which are formulated or construed prior to the object. The historian must always choose archive material based on incomplete background knowledge, that is knowledge that is only possible or conceivable after the research is complete. Sociologists take their material from human subjects, which can never avoid investing such objects with their own subjective points of view. Political scientists study political action, which is based on subjective attitudes about power, meaning and politics. The list goes on. Scientific objectivity reveals itself everywhere as problematic in terms of its own lack of scientific foundation.

Unfortunately, the problem becomes even more complex when one considers the theoretical consequences of studying social constructions and social identities in the social sciences. What is the *objective* expression of identity? What or who speaks for what we are? Or to express the problem in still another way, who speaks when 'the European' speaks? Who speaks when the Italian, the Norwegian or the Maldivian speaks? Who speaks when 'I' speak? Who is objectively in a position to give an adequately objective expression for who or what I am?

Already in the 18th century, well before the formulation of what we today call the social sciences, Kant gave a convincing answer to these ensemble questions. He does so by introducing a fundamental differentiation between facts – let us define them as 'naturally occurring phenomena – and our rationality – or conscious understanding of such facts. His differentiation builds upon the distinction between two concepts: *phenomena* and *noumena*. Kant defines *phenomena* as objects that we perceive as objects. In other words, he articulates the distinction between things as they actually are (*von ihrer Beschaffenheit an sich selbst*) and the way in which we understand them (Kant, 2007: 142–3). There is a kind of double-ness in these phenomena: we have the *object* in our view, but it is inseparable from knowledge of the fact that we have the object in view. *Noumena*, on the other hand, are objects that are merely thought, but which do not have their origin in an empirical reality. A *noumena* is not an object of our sense but a thing-in-itself (*Ding an sich*). A thing-in-itself is the object prior to perception, prior to understanding, conceptualization or rationalization. It is an object before it becomes an object for our consciousness,. The thing, such as it truly is, in and for itself, not merely inaccessible for human consciousness, is non-understandable, non-conceptualizable, it doesn't even belong to the category 'object'. The object is not itself without the subject, which makes it understandable or 'objectifiable'.

The other side of Kant's reasoning is that all objects of thinking are objects of thinking by virtue of being organized and structured by the categories of understanding given beforehand in the human intellect, or intuition, as Kant would say. Understanding is necessarily a process of de-limitation, a process of differentiation, which creates the object in conformity with the categories that make the world what we would call 'understandable'.

The interest of Kant's theoretical results for the social sciences is that we now understand that empirical research does not simply deliver things (facts) such as they *are* – as facts – but such as they appear to us and become understandable. Facts that have become objects for understanding are already no longer facts but rather a mirroring of how understanding is structured. We can only understand facts after they have been filtered through understanding. Moreover, the *difference* between an object of understanding and the object as such *can itself not be the object of understanding.* The difference between them is neither fact nor understanding. It exists in a kind of no-man's land between and beyond the two. Knowledge of the world that is gathered from empirical perception is not pure knowledge. It is knowledge based on a certain kind of perception. Knowledge of the world that is gathered from empirical perception is not 'pure' knowledge. It is knowledge based on a certain kind of perception. (ibid.: 143–4).

The central question that we ask in what follows is: Where should *European construction* and the European Union be situated in the complex world of political institutions that have marked the history of European modernity? In order to answer this question, we take up the basic principles of one theory of modernity that has had particular influence and longevity in the last decade, namely that of the sociologist Ulrich Beck. This theory is, in particular, characterized by its concept of a 'second modernity'.

Beck's theory of risk society

According to Ulrich Beck, modernity has not always been a self-reflexive disposition. His view of modernity grows out of an analysis of the nature of change, not only from traditional to industrial societies but also from industrial societies to post-industrial societies. His theory is empirically based on concrete changes in the organization of social life. Just as the modernization processes of the 19th century displaced that class-based agrarian society of the previous period, modernization today displaces the 'traditional!' industrial society. However, in opposition to the replacement of one social structure by another, the modernization process we experience today has no 'other' to which to relate. The new ('second') modernization process is the development of a relation with modernity itself. This is what Beck describes as the difference between 'simple' and 'reflexive' modernization, modernization of tradition and modernization of industrial society (Beck, 1992: 21). European societies have suffered from the 'myth' that the industrial society, with its categories of self-understanding through work and life, production and consumption, economic growth and technical and scientific rationality, was the last phase of modernity and could not be surpassed.

This is what Beck calls the 'legend of the industrial society'. This legend, invented in the 19th century and dominant in all forms of social life structures, social classes and casts, and nuclear families, is the normalization and linearization of careers. For Beck, these are the basic principles of individuality in the modern social setting. And it is these principles that are called into question by the advance of a new kind of modernity, the second modernity. Their traditional anchoring is disturbed, uprooted and demystified.

The reflexive modernization of the industrial society has two primary dimensions in Beck's theory, in terms of a process of risk production and in terms of a process of individualization.

The first primary characteristic of this new social disposition is the institutionalization of risk. By this Beck does not mean simply the appearance or presence of risk in everyday life, but rather the *production* of risk as an unpredictable by-product of industrial production. Whereas in simple (first) modernity such risks were calculated into the logic of production and work, in the second modernity, such risks are unpredictable by-products, incalculable risks. The other side of advanced modernity in Beck's account is more common. It involves a variety of processes that lead to individualization, the breakdown of traditional collective structures and the rise of individual rights, obligations and privileges. This process takes place within three sectors in European society: the bourgeois public sphere, the family, and employment and education.

Yet in contrast to what Beck identifies as the postmodern vision of modernity, which postulates the failure, the exhaustion or even the impossibility of the modern project, Beck interprets modernity as a success story, as a social evolution that, based on its implicit criteria and ideology, more than met its ideals:

> Reflexive modernity opens the possibility of a creative (self)-destruction for an entire epoch, the industrial epoch. The 'subject' of this creative destruction is not crisis, but rather the *victory* of western modernisation.
>
> (ibid.: 64–5)

It is, in effect, the *success* of modernity, not its failure, that causes the conundrum of our time. The theory of modernity is an attempt to seize both the movement of emancipation and rationalization and the side-effects it implies. As industrial modern becomes obsolete, its belief in rationality, its technical magic, becomes demystified and secularized, and a *second* modernity emerges, its contours still un-sharp because of the dilemmas and ambivalences it contains and even advances.

The European *cul-de-sac*

The theory of reflexive modernization is a critique of the relationship between a certain self-understanding in time and the institutions that pretend to concretize it. In this sense, modernity is a process of historical realization of a kind of social and cultural identity. At the same time, and inversely, the nation-state institutions that carry out the functions of modernization seek their legitimacy in these social and cultural identities. It is, therefore, not by chance that the public institutions of the nation-state are founded and developed in relation to society's sense of self. It is the idea of a collective entity that gives force to the concrete construction of it. In other words, one notion or other of social, cultural, even historical fabric is fundamental for legitimating the public works carried out in their name. Ideas ultimately give rise to actions.

The relation between *ideas* and *actions* is the domain of politics. It is here that political systems unfold and the symbolic and real play of power takes place. It is also the domain of *science*, most importantly human and social science. As we noted above, the rise of the human and social sciences is inseparable from the rise of the modern nation-state. By this we mean that science provided the tools, the methodologies and, from a certain point of view, the content of the nation-state. Yet the relation between the nation-state and the social and human sciences that support it cuts both ways. The nation-state, with institutional set-up, its political powers and ideologies, also contributes decisively to forming the premises for the very social sciences that support it. The human and social sciences are determined by the nation-state, not only in their function but also in their *method*. This determinate nature of social scientific methodology is what Beck calls 'methodological nationalism'.

The term 'methodological nationalism' is derived from Anthony Smith's usage in the theory of nationalism and refers to the analytical assumption that the society and territorial state are reciprocally adequate, and indeed exhaustive (Smith, 1971). The concept of methodological nationalism implies that the essential methodological categories necessary for the analysis of society are already determined by the categories, concepts and assumptions and presuppositions implicit in the social understanding of the nation-state. In other words, the nation-state is not only a political form; it is, *firstly*, an *epistemology*. It is not only a certain set of principles about political organization, about the relation between political organizations, the structuring of authority, power and legitimacy within a state. It is a structuring agency for knowledge about society, culture, politics, etc. in the nation-state. It provides the means to understanding political forms, the means to organizing knowledge, in general, and knowledge about the political, about the nation-state, in particular. It structures and organizes categories and concepts that determine our understanding of society: cultural identity, religion, class relations, labour, ethnic belonging, demographic de-limitations, economic categories, value determinations, etc. It is, indeed, most commonly the nation-state and its agencies that concretely organize and finance social-scientific research through nationally co-ordinated and systematized institutions, funds, research councils, etc. These institutions not only organize the distribution of financing but also the structuring of research categories and projects of 'national interest', knowledge distribution and valuation, research teams and institutes, as well as networks of research and higher education.

Secondly, methodological nationalism contains a *normative* dimension. The link between the nation-state and the institutions of research and development that it supports and promotes are determined in part by relations of power, of value, of national or other political priorities. The ideas of interest to the social and human sciences, to the organization, a financing and manning of research, is riddled with political, ethical, deontological and other value-based choices and prioritizations. In this sense, the methodological nationalism that first establishes the nation-state institutions of research simultaneously systemizes and aligns them in terms of values that are external to them. Science is laden with issues of value; yet these values are not 'originally' or 'naturally' a part of science. They are ascribed to science by the political systems that surround it, provided through institutional mechanisms that make scientific research possible in the first place.

Moreover, claims of state power and control not only provide the institutional value-framework for research; they also justify and provide the legitimacy to establish and maintain the very object that the sciences are mandated to research: 'society'. In essence, the instruments and concepts directly involved in maintaining a researchable notion of 'society' are explicitly and implicitly provided by the state. The state orients and legitimates fundamental rights, education systems, social policy, party politics, official language, literature, police forces, etc. (Beck, 2000: 64–5). All of these contribute to determining, *avant la lettre*, the objects of social science research.

Thirdly, methodological nationalism implies a set of *ontological* claims, a set of assumptions about the being in the world of the social, of the particular kind of existence society has, its necessity and its contingence. In the optic of the nation-state, society is presented in a particular form, a form that is taken as 'natural', as 'given' (ibid.: 64). The relationship between society and nation-state, between the particularities of the social and the historical and geopolitical particularities of the nation-state are difficult, if not impossible, to put into question within the paradigms provided by the nation-state.

Taken together, these dimensions of methodological nationalism make up what Beck calls an 'architecture of thought, action and living', which structures the way 'national' social sciences are capable of researching and understanding nation-state society. This is the 'container' theory of society, in which the territorial state, its normative, epistemological and ontological foundations, are also the basis of society, such as it is understood by social scientists and, through them, provided to politicians and bureaucrats as the basis for political decision-making and action (Beck, 1999b: 115; 2000).

Globalization

Beck's most recent work is based on a critique of methodological nationalism and a critique of the blindspots inherent in methodological nationalism and an attempt to explore alternative platforms on which to base social-scientific research. Beck begins his critique through a reinterpretation of the concept of *globalization*. The working theory of the critique is that, since it is the nation-state-based limitations of the social sciences that are the implicit presuppositions of society's understanding of itself, these presuppositions need to be unpacked and deconstructed. The most direct and important critique of the nation-state is *globalization*.

Globalization is, according to Beck's definition, 'the processes through which national states and their sovereignty are criss-crossed and undermined by transnational actors with varying prospects of power, orientations, identities and networks' (Beck, 2000: 11). It is perhaps uncontroversial to note that globalization does not supplant the nation-state. Globalization takes the nation-state as its starting point and prerequisite. In this sense, the trace of the nation-state is necessarily present in any post-national constellation. Globalization does not, however, leave the nation-state untouched. Rather, it brings about a fundamental mutation in the nation-state through processes of geographical expansion, international trade, global networking of finance markets, the growing power of transnational corporations, the evolution of information and communications technology, the universal demands for human rights, global culture industries, the emergence of a post-national, polycentric world politics, in which transnational actors grow in power and number alongside governments, the emergence of the question of world poverty, the issue of global environmental destruction and transcultural conflicts in one and the same place (ibid.).

Methodologically, this observation boils down to what Beck calls the 'container-theory of society' which builds upon three fundamental assumptions: (1) sovereignty and security, (2) cultural homogeneity, and (3) the priority of the state with respect to society, in short, the unity of territory, sovereignty and state (ibid.: 23–4).

The essential consequence of this understanding of the relationship between state and society is methodological. It is only natural that social sciences, which emerged at the end of the 19th century should be structured by this fundamental relationship. Or, as Beck puts it, the social sciences *interiorized* the territorial organizational framework of the nation-state. The social sciences develop quite naturally in correspondence with primarily state-based institutional mechanisms (Beck, 2000: 25).

Not only the field of sociology, as Beck suggests, but arguably the human sciences as well, are born in the latter third of the 19th century parallel to the bureaucratic, legal, institutional scientific refinements of the modern state. The social and human sciences are founded upon institutional arrangements, university structures and financial provisions bound to the rationalization of the modern nation-state. In short, the rise of the social sciences in general is co-terminous with the rise of the modern bureaucratic nation-state. Indeed, classical social science (Weber, Simmel, Tönnies) is in many regards closely intertwined with the analysis of and legitimization of the nation-state and its institutional arrangements (Lepenies, 1981). Thus not only is the nation-state the primary referent of the original social sciences, the social sciences constitute a significant means of legitimizing the state.

It will come as no surprise to many that the sensible way out of the *cul-de-sac* of methodological nationalism will lie on the European plan. The answer to the blindspots and dead-ends of the nation-state-based social and human scientific research must be research based on a European paradigm, a European optic. The way out of the *cul-de-sac* of the national perspective is a shift to the European level, and to a perspective that embraces Europe's process of reflexive modernization.

The cosmopolitan perspective

Beck's earlier account of risk society was, as we have seen, based on the postulate of a two-phase modernity. Simple or first modernity, by virtue of its own success, its own over-production of rationality and 'calculability', is overridden by a second, complex modernity. The second modernity, in contrast to the first, is unable to rationalize its successes, unable to calculate the quality and quantity of its by-products. The 'logic of singularity' of the first modern is surpassed by a logic of plurality, or, to use Beck's metaphor, the 'Newtonian theory of society and politics of the first modernity' is surpassed by a 'Heisenbergian logic' (Beck and Grande, 2007: 29). The common conception (and self-conception) of the first modernity was as an eternally self-present process producing what, predictably and rationally, it could be expected to produce. The notion that it could do otherwise, that it might be cracked or fissured, is unthinkable within the concept of (first) modernity. The thought that it might produce its own excess, its own risk, was excluded. Or, as Beck puts it, 'the idea that the foundation of modern society, in the same way as its victor, was porous, dissolved or its meaning transformed, is totally foreign to the classical thought of the social sciences' (ibid.: 29).

The social-scientific assumption upon which the study of Europe and European construction is based, observes Beck, is dualistic. It is fundamentally a logic of us and them, national and international, domestic and foreign. It is, in other words, a logic of 'either or'. This is the logic of singularity proper to the first modern. This logic is being replaced by the logic of plurality. The logic of 'either or' is replaced by that of 'both and' (ibid.: 29).

The methodological alternative to the blinding limitations of methodological nationalism is thus to open a new methodology with a European lens.

Yet the consequence is not merely a methodology appropriate for observing issues that arise in Europe, for confronting the *factual* challenges of observing more objects with a wider scope. Rather, it is to Europeanize the national perspective, to Europeanize the way in which we conceptualize and analyze any social-scientific object, not just those that fall under the rubric 'European'.

This *cosmopolitan vision* thus calls into question the fundamental principle of the national perspective, namely the conviction that 'modern society' and 'modern politics' are organized exclusively according to the logic of the nation-state. The cosmopolitan perspective problematizes the fundamental presumptions and assumptions of the conventional social sciences. In *The Cosmopolitan Vision*, Beck outlines six 'principles and errors' of methodological nationalism. He corrects the categorical conception that society is subordinated to the state. In classical political thought, this is the case (Beck, 2006: 27; 2004: 44). This is not because of some tradition of conceptualization of society and state, but rather as a necessity of the acceleration of the first modernity. The state creates institutions of containment and security that on the one hand permit the national society to live and flourish in peace and prosperity of the kind set out in the promise of modernity. On the other hand, it *hinders* the emergence of alternative or non-national forms of society or social order. Potential alternative social forms face an environment without institutional support and security, centres of knowledge, finance, etc. In Beck's terms, this is the epitome of the 'container model' of social science self-understanding. Only a territorially based system of categories, politics and social categories is viable. A territorially based notion of the social is thus the only possible alternative.

The cosmopolitan perspective proposed by Beck opposes the notion that the world-view of the social sciences is determined through the opposition between the national and the international. The notion of one singular national society whose frontier is somehow identical with the nation-state borders makes little sense. The cosmopolitan view sees society as plural – as societies – overlapping, intertwined and in 'marble cake' formation. It is both multicultural, multi-ethnic, multilingual, etc. It is European, sub-European, trans-European, sub-national, regional, local, etc. The notion of national society, from this point of view, is thus more or less senseless. It corresponds with little other than itself (Beck, 2006: 28).

Any social science methodology equipped to capture 'national society' would only be self-referential. And, in fact, this is essentially the trap that the national social sciences fall prey to. Their methodology is dominated by the universal false deduction from particular national society to universal society, according to which one's own society is unavoidably construed as society itself. This is the error of much of classical sociology (Marx, Weber, Durkheim) and is to some extent corrected by techniques of comparison, both national and international. But these correctives do little to correct or adjust the methodological (i.e. conceptual) problems inherent in the concept of national society (ibid.: 28–9).

This socially based false deduction has a cultural counterpart. Method-ological nationalism, in its tendency to identify society with nation-state, produces certain presumptions about the nature of culture and cultural plurality within the nation-state. Two alternative errors are common. Either one tends toward universal equalization of cultures ('McDonaldization') or one tends toward a position of incommensurability, of universal non-comparability of cultures. The first alternative corresponds to what is often criticized as a certain 'postmodernism', 'anything goes', or, in Beck's words, as 'flat cultural cosmopolitanism'. This version of cultural plurality is conceived as a montage without criteria, as a universal compatibility of all cultural artefacts proper to nation-state territory. All objects can be associated with each other *without* producing meaning, *without* intelligibility arising from the connection itself. This conception does not stand up to a dialectical understanding of the relationship between concept and object. Such a perspective would claim that if two or more objects can be associated, then they can, and are, in fact, conceptualizable together, and thus produce coherent meaning as an ensemble. The second alternative supposes the *incompatibility* of transnational cultural objects. It promotes the primacy or necessity of the national as the nexus of culture, history, memory and language. National cultural objects belong together with other national cultural objects and cannot be abstracted. This point of view disregards *otherness* in a way analogous to how the first model disregards *sameness*. The radical otherness with which one would be required to dismiss all other cultural objects than one's own would call into question the very substance of one's own culture. The degree of isolation required in order to defend the conviction that culture is strictly autonomous would eliminate one's own sense of self as an alternative to other selves.

These conundrums lead to the conclusion that the perspective of methodological nationalism is, by and large, essentialist. It can only separate or distinguish what is culturally and politically woven together. The historical sub-text of any nation-state reveals its origins in an other – be it historical, cultural, social, constructed through war, migration, globalisation, etc. Something non-nation-state-orientated is inevitably at the origin (or at the very least related to the origin) of the nation-state (ibid.: 32–3).

In summary, the relation between the two methodological perspectives is essentially asymmetrical. The national perspective excludes the cosmopolitan perspective, while the cosmopolitan includes the national. These structural errors of methodological nationalism are all associated with a failure to draw the consequences of what Beck calls a shift from a logic of 'either or' to a logic 'both and'. The exclusionary logic of 'either or' inhabits and organizes methodological nationalism, while the inclusive differentiation of 'both and' organizes the grammar of methodological cosmopolitanism (Beck and Grande, 2007: 29).

Europe as a research object

Research on Europe in the social sciences has remained imprisoned between two alternatives: the federalist approach that negates or disregards national politics and international political identities, and intergovernmental approaches that essentially reduce European questions to matters of inter-state politics. Methodological nationalism thus leads political theory to a *negative definition* of Europe. It is based on a national-institutional understanding of a national sphere of action, a kind of zero-sum game: what strengthens Europe weakens the nation-state.

Methodological cosmopolitanism evokes a *positive definition* of Europe. The zero-sum game logic of 'either or' is replaced by a positive-sum game of 'both and', in which benefits of power, influence and development on the European level do not correspond with diminished power on the national level (ibid.: 5–6).

A fundamental insight, and warning, of Beck's theory of modernization on the European level is that the methodological cosmopolitanism of the 'both and' does indeed *supplant* the 'either or' of methodological nationalism. It is not a question of 'either or' between the 'either or' and the 'both and'. They are compatible with each other and, indeed, must exist alongside each other. But just how? The logic of 'both and' does not adequately describe, from a certain point of view, the dynamic relationship between the different levels of identity and institutionalization in the European reality. Consequently, it cannot be the basis of a coherent and comprehensive methodology. The nature of self-understanding, the kind of self-understanding that is presupposed by Beck's theory of European social fabric as a relationship to itself, is necessarily more complex. The *phenomenology* of the cosmopolitan perspective requires a far more dialectical theory of the self and other, of methodological subject and methodological object.

When we put into use the logic of 'both and', then any given subject can possess multiple positions on the subjective landscape, can hold multiple identities, which are both meaningfully related to each other and at the same time not entirely reducible to each other. One can indeed be Norwegian and Scandinavian, both European and non-EU member, both immigrant and citizen, etc. Here we are not just speaking of empirical facts that we now understand to be compatible with each other, even though we once thought they were incompatible with each other. We are speaking of a system of adjacent realities and identities, a way of being many things *and* not threatening one's own identity.

Or, to put the phenomenon in even more philosophical terms, following Kant's epistemology, we might say that such facts about ourselves are already no longer facts, but rather a mirroring of how our understanding of the world is structured in our own rationality. They are a mirroring of a kind of human methodology at a deeper level. The *subject* of sociology is not simply a broad-minded collector of facts, a bucket of knowledge that is merely filled up, transported and emptied. Rather, it is a container that is transformed by each and every fact. For this reason the very *experience* of the apparent incompatibility of identities must also be an object of our questioning. How does the European *subject* change, dialectically, as a relation between subject and object. The cosmopolitan gaze is not only the 'both and' collection of incompatible facts, but one of a *particular experience* of incompatibility that is projected on all facts as universal.

Conclusion

The concept of Europe first arises with the question of the institutionalization of European identity. In other words, the concept corresponds to the *need* for a concept, and to the need to *concretize* the concept and confirm it by institutionalizing it. The concept of Europe functions like a collective attempt to convince ourselves that such a thing actually exists. It is a structural concept, a structural logic, which repeats itself again and again through European history. The great 'Europe builders', from Alexander to Genghis Kahn, to Charlemagne, to Caesar, to Hitler, fight for an expanding geopolitical Europe and contentious *concept* of Europe. If one is to focus upon the modern narratives of Europe, one sees clearly that it is the feelings of crisis that connects them all together with a sober institutional architecture.

During the interwar period there emerged no less than three important attempts at institutionalizing a certain understanding of Europe: the 'pan-European' project created by Coudenhove-Kalergi in 1923, the project for the 'United States of Europe' in 1929, and Aristide Briand's 'Society of Nations' in 1929. After World War II, the project was again taken up, this time by Jean Monnet, Robert Schuman and a group of European technocrats, who saw in the project of European construction an answer to the darker moments of modern European history. Their work led to the signing of the Treaty of the European Coal and Steel Community in 1951.

These are the *institutional* measures that mark our time. What is the conceptual logic on which they repose? Just like any nation-state, Europe as a concept has its own set of borders which form the framework for the content of European institutions. Europe, which perhaps constitutes the broadest category of any of the individual nation-states that constitute it, is itself structured by other forces, as something external to itself. Europe is always European *conceptual* and *social scientific* politics precisely because it is not created through real-political forces alone. The European is created in the crossfire between the European *self* – which, in principle, does not yet exist – and the European other, which it does not yet know.

12 The new *nomos* of Europe

Only a few months after the Schuman Declaration in May 1950, the basis of the Treaty of Paris one year later, and thus the forerunner of today's European Union, another engaged European, the controversial Weimar jurist Carl Schmitt, published his paradigm-rattling *The* Nomos *of the Earth in the International Law of the Jus Publicum Europaeum.* For many years leading up to the publication of *Nomos*, Schmitt had argued that European jurisprudence was all but obsolete, cut off from its sources and under the negative influences of an increasingly technological culture (Balakrishnan, 2000: 5; Dyzenhaus, 1998). This way of thematizing European intellectual evolution converges with the array of political positions that mark Schmitt's intellectual career. He is, by and large, indifferent to traditional left–right oppositions of traditional politics, seeing them as secondary to his project of re-founding contemporary jurisprudence. Through his career, he adamantly argued for the autonomy of the sovereign state, seeing in its decline the loss of legitimacy, the weakening of economic integrity and the detachment of law from its historical roots. In the *Nomos* book, he focuses on the relation between European and international jurisprudence, and what he calls the 'spatial order' that has always supported it. In his analysis, Schmitt describes the end of a global era and the rise of a new era, starting in the mid-1940s, that is approximately simultaneous with the origins of the European Coal and Steel Community.

This chapter investigates the degree to which the historical confluence of European construction and the Schmittian European *nomos* bears any deeper, more substantive, links. It will advance the hypothesis that Schmitt's critique of what he called *European International Law* reflects to a compelling degree the complex geometry of the emerging European legal system. By examining the architecture of European law in the light of Schmitt's concept of *nomos*, it attempts to contribute to clarifying the unique logic of legitimacy and authorization that make up the European juridical space.

Schmitt the European

Schmitt's own philosophical relation to the idea of Europe varies vastly in the course of his career. From a certain point of view, one might say that his career consisted of nothing less than an ongoing critique of the premises and consequences of the 'European project'. Schmitt bursts what he sees as the conceptual and political limitations of the nation-state in an original way that has consequences both for our understanding of the national and the European.[1] John P. McCormick has charted the conceptual contours of four distinct relations to Europe through the course of Schmitt's career (McCormick, 1997: 133–41). According to McCormick these phases are: (1) Europe as a form of neo-Christendom, a position set out in *Roman Catholicism and Political Form* (1925), (2) Europe as Central European political-cultural anchorage, primarily in the essay 'The Age of Neutralizations and Depoliticization' (1929), (3) Europe as interwoven with a German dominant *Grossraum*, and (4) Europe situated in the evolution of law, space and sovereignty in *The* Nomos *of the Earth* (1950).

Schmitt's earliest consideration of the notion of Europe and its contribution to contemporary European ideas is a critique of the political function of Catholicism. This function is expressed both as the political form of the catholic tradition and as its substantive values. In terms of the formal characteristics, which give the book its title, Schmitt advances a critique of modernity as the rise of instrumental rationality.

> In almost every discussion one can observe the extent to which the methodology of the natural-technical sciences dominates contemporary thinking. For example, the god of traditional theological evidence – the god who governs the worlds as the king governs a state – subconsciously is made the motor impelling the cosmic machine. The chimera of modern big-city dwellers is filled to the last atom with technological and industrial conceptions, which are projected into cosmological or metaphysical realms. In this naïve mechanistic and mathematical mythology, the world becomes a gigantic dynamo wherein there is even no distinction of classes.
>
> (Schmitt, 1996: 12)

The instrumental rational course taken by the European cultural evolution consequently threatens the transmission of the substantive values of European religious culture, including the central tenets of authority, collectivity and individuality. Yet for Schmitt, what is in the end more decisive for the cultural trajectory of Europe is not the *theological* content of Roman Catholicism, but rather the shifting nature of *the political*. Catholicism is 'eminently political' in contrast to the superficiality of political rationality of our time (ibid.: 16). To the newly evolved 'political mechanics' of economic and military means of power in Europe, Schmitt opposes the

Catholic Church as the 'the consummate agency of the juridical spirit and the true heir of Roman jurisprudence' (ibid.: 18).

In Schmitt's second phase of European orientation, the 'Age of Neutralization' essay positions Germany and central Europe relative to Russia under the sign of the technology (Schmitt, 1993). Schmitt sees European culture in general as structured and marked by a 'neutralization process', whereby the centre of European spiritual heritage transitions from a more theological to metaphysical and moral, and finally to an economical, rationality. In this phase of Schmitt's understanding of Europe, the axis of analysis shifts to the German–Russian dimension, the role of France in European intellectual affairs is toned down and the spectre of unbridled technological development is put in the foreground. Schmitt's earlier emphasis on the need for a historical awareness of the intellectual *status quo* of Europe takes, in the 'Neutralization' essay, the form of a renewed emphasis on the present and coming mutations in the nature and understanding of technology and the unique form of rationality it embodies: 'technicity (*Technizität*)'.

> The process of continuous neutralization of various spheres of cultural life has reached its end because technology is at hand. Technology is no longer neutral ground in the sense of the process of neutralization; every strong politics will make use of it.
>
> (ibid.: 141)

Schmitt's analysis of European intellectual history focuses here on the notion of neutralization brought about by the influx of technology in European life.

The central European emphasis of the 'Neutralizations' essay is continued in the following phase of Schmitt's European trajectory, covering his association with National Socialism and represented by the lectures and writings on *Grossraum*. The *Grossraum* concept points toward Schmitt's later analysis of the European *nomos Grossraum* to the degree that it builds upon the need for a general reevaluation of the notion of international legal order in terms of its concrete spatial determinations. In this sense the concept represents the basis for the spatially oriented legal analysis of the *nomos* book. 'International law (*Völkerrecht*) as *jus gentium* is, as a law of peoples, first and foremost a *personal* order, that is, it is a concrete order determined by the one's belonging to a people or a state. [It is, however] not only personally determined, but it is also simultaneously a concrete *spatial order*' (Schmitt, 1991: 270). *Grossraum*, in Schmitt's European vision, is thus not only a geopolitical concept, so often the object of reproach, but also a *metaphysical* one, linking the spatiality of geopolitics and international law to the Earth. International and European law are, without doubt, *about* space, they *refer* primarily to space. According to Schmitt, they must also be conceptualized as being spatially determined themselves.

The *nomos* book represents the fourth and final phase of the evolution of

Schmitt's thinking on Europe (Schmitt, 2003). It widens the scope of Schmitt's juridical pessimism from the main themes of his career – sovereignty and legitimacy on the German national level – to questions surrounding the status of international law. Whereas in the 1963 foreword to *The Concept of the Political* (1932) Schmitt sums up the constellation of the writings that aimed to fully analyze this new situation: the Hugo Preuss book (1930), *The Protector of the Constitution* (1931) and *Legality and Legitimacy* (1932) concern the new challenges surrounding domestic politics. *The Concept of the Political* deals with the evolution in inter-state relations, and *The Nomos of the Earth* deals with the same set of mutations as they play out on the macro-historical world level (Schmitt, 2004; 1930b; 2007). In kind with his claims about the withdrawal of jurisprudence in the national framework, Schmitt develops an extended historical analysis of the decline of the Eurocentric order of international law, beginning with Hellenism and reaching its nadir in the post-war institutions of international law. Its focus is, first and foremost, but not exclusively, the universe of international jurisprudence surrounding the League of Nations, though its roots extend all the way back to the post-Napoleonic Monroe Doctrine (1823).

What is innovative about Schmitt's historical demonstration of the decline of the European jurisprudence is its correlation with the decline of a certain European *spatial* order. According to Schmitt, the long evolution in the relation between humans and the Earth has been decisive for the nature of traditional legal order. The historical links to European international jurisprudence (*ius publicum Europaeum*) have decayed with the old world order that supported them. The modern conception of territoriality is a Cartesian one, it maps according to a linear logic, a fixed set of principles or concepts (sovereignty, deed, ownership, belonging, rights, etc., on to a fixed spatial template). Space is, in effect, a given, universal and ubiquitous. This conception accompanies the evolution of the concept of nation and the nation-state paradigm of sovereignty, the very fabric of international law. Schmitt's insight, as we will see, evolves from a critique of the fixed-ness of the spatial linking of international law (Varga, 2007).

If Schmitt is correct in his prognoses about the end of a global era and the rise of a new yet uncharted world order in the mid 1940s, then the architects of the nascent European Coal and Steel Community face the same conditions, and must carry out their work with the same cultural, social and juridical raw materials, against the backdrop of the same concrete historical experience. The fundamental insight of the era, for observers as different as Schmitt and Schuman, was that the essential values of our time are transnational and extra-territorial, and that they defy, for structural reasons (Schmitt) or by historical contingency (Schuman), the political and legal institutions of our time.

This chapter will attempt to continue the trajectory of Schmitt's historical analysis of the *ius publicum Europeaum*, suggesting how its central concepts and theses map on to the grand geopolitical and civilizational project of

European construction from 1950 to 2004. It will explore the applicability of the concept of *nomos* for the nature of EU evolution, and interpret general elements of the European legal system in terms of the concept of *nomos*.

The *nomos* of the Earth

The *nomos* book thus lies at the intersection of a number of concerns that preoccupy Schmitt throughout his career. Schmitt looks to gather the threads of a certain interpretation of world history, both in a unitary and unifying Hegelian sense, but also in a specific sense. Europe's history, from Schmitt's perspective, is inseparable from a certain experience of *space* and *place*. History, and its correlates, politics and law, is spatially determined. For this reason, *The* Nomos *of the Earth*, is as much a theory of historiography as it is political or legal theory. If the work is to be understood in its empirical dimensions, it is by identifying the concrete specificity of international law and to map these specific determinations on to the large movement of world history. The *nomos* book in this sense is an attempt to historically link fundamental changes in the nature of international jurisprudence with changes in the cultural, social, political and *spatial* order of the world.

Conceptually, Schmitt hooks his analysis on the multivalency of the historical concept of *nomos*. In ancient Greek, *nomos* is defined as 'that which is in habitual practice, use or possession'. From this basis it is thus variously translated as 'law' in general, as 'ordinance', 'custom', derived from customary behaviour, from the law of God, from the authority of established deities, or simple public ordinance. *Nomos* also means 'law' understood in the sense of rationality, the 'reigning' order of things, or what we would today call 'discourse'. *Nomos* is also linked to the word *neimô*, meaning 'to deal out', 'distribute' or 'dispense'. The concept is thus also associated with being a hub or distributor of meaning or rationality, both in the physical and metaphysical sense of the word, the logical organization of things in space and time. This component of its meaning is what links it to the notion of *extension*, the spatialization of rationality. (In modern Greek, a *nomos* is a prefecture or county in the sense of a distribution of legitimate authority in a given place. *Nomos* thus implicitly links to the deployment or application of power across a given territory (Liddel and Schott, 1940).

Nomos thus refers to both spatial territory and the political or legal rationality that is valid for that space. It points to the *order* established through an appropriation of de-limited territory. To Schmitt's reading, a land seizure (*landnahme*) is a seizure of land, which not only constitutes a shift of property but which also simultaneously orders the Earth rationally and thus posits a distinct and ordered relationship between the political subject of power, ownership and political action. It also designates the act of establishing order, of logic or rational discourse through the original partitioning of land (Schmitt, 2003: 341).

The most significant aspect of *nomos* for our purposes is, however, the way in which it gives a certain kind of reality and meaning to pure emptiness of what is sometimes called 'Cartesian space'; that is purely formal, empty or meaningless spaces. When territory is partitioned or divided through acts of war or politics its rational organization is not simply changed along spatial lines, its administration crystallized in terms of formal laws or rules. Rather, the land seizure productively shapes the dynamics in, above and all around it. Like the shift from Cartesian space in the field of political geography, Schmitt intends the concept of *nomos* as a polemical alternative to the positivistic understanding of legal order that he sees as bureaucratically encroaching on European jurisprudence in his own time, the '*situation établie* of those constituted dominates all customs, as well as all thought and speech', reiterates Schmitt in the *nomos* book. 'Normativism and positivism then become the most plausible and self-evident matters in the world, especially where there is no longer any horizon other than the *status quo*' (ibid.: 341).

Nomos is thus to be understood as a kind of antidote to the instrumental prescription of law, which somehow preexists it or which somehow preexists the territory over which it has jurisdiction. On the contrary, the meaning of territory, of inhabited or uninhabited space, of the *territoriality* of the territory arises with its *nomos*. This is what Schmitt understands when he calls *nomos* 'constitutive'. *Nomos* makes out the very territoriality of territory by organizing the meaning of its space, by organizing its spatiality. It is indeed an ordering of reality, but one which orders reality by constituting it. As we will see, this constitution of the territoriality of territory simultaneously institutes a relation to international law, its meaning in space and the meaning of space for it.

Schmitt draws his understanding of the term *nomos* from a distinct period in history: corresponding to the transition from wanderer society to the society of fixed and land-based households, from the *nomad* existence to the *oiko-nomein*, the land-based order of the household. In these terms, Schmitt marks off three distinctive historical-spatial *nomoi*, or 'orders' of the Earth. The first is the mythological stage, from prehistory to the 15th century age of discovery. The second is the period from the 15th century to the early years of the 20th century. The last, still unconceptualized, according to Schmitt, extends from the Treaty of Versailles. In the era before the planet was conceptualized as a finite totality, space was ultimately free. The question of organizing it in terms of international law never occurred since it was never conceptualized as a thing in itself. It *was* reality itself, the ultimate and transcendental backdrop to all things. According to Schmitt, this situation began to evolve in the 15th century. The 'Age of Discovery' opened the face of the Earth to apparently infinite land appropriation, thus transforming the essence of space itself. Instead of the geopolitics of discrete and finite territory, a geopolitics of open territory began. Land appropriation throughout the 15th to 17th centuries went effectively unopposed.

This change in spatial and thus geopolitical consciousness was, in Schmitt's view, decisive. Even the pre-Renaissance spatial consciousness that saw Rome or Jerusalem as its centre knew that such a religious or political geography related to an enemy other, be it invading Germanic tribes or Islam. The Renaissance period, on the other hand, was characterized by a lack of opposition to spatial appropriation (Schmitt, 2003: 87).

During the Middle Ages, Europe was, of course, not divided into states in the modern sense. For this reason and others, international law in the modern sense was not possible. Today we think of states as having undisputed political control over their own territory, independent of external political control. Indeed, it is the foundational notion of international law. By contrast, medieval kings shared power across a number of axes: internally, with their barons, each of whom had a private army; externally, they were obligated to show some sort of allegiance to the Pope and to Rome. The discovery of sea routes to the Far East and the (re)discovery of America, the European sea powers transcended the medieval political limits on their power, disrupting the political order and leading to the emergence of the concept of the sovereign state in the modern sense, first in theory, in the 16th century, by Bodin, then in effect in Spain, then France. The Treaty of Westphalia inaugurated *ius foederationis*, giving approximately 300 political entities, essentially made up of the remains of the Roman Empire, the right to enter into alliances with other political entities under certain conditions (Cassese, 2001: 20–1; Malanczuk, 1997). Although a number of European states emerged as dominate (France, Sweden, The Netherlands), in terms of the right to form alliances and engage in state-to-state diplomacy, they were approximately equivalent in juridical terms. A legal order emerged based on the diplomatic and political structure of these equivalencies: the *ius publicum Europaeum* (Koskenniemi, 2002: 418–25).

The fundamental consequence of this evolution was the recasting of war as secular. The complex mix of religious, sectarian, inner-political power struggle was replaced by a system in which territory became the primary demarcation of political power and where the logic of inside/outside took hold (cf. Teschke, 2003; Walker, 1993). The 'humanization of war' was the direct consequence of the redrawing of political lines in terms of nation-state territory. Modern international law was founded upon the codification of the new norms of war as inter-state instead of religious (Schmitt, 2003: 141).

The new international law, *ius publicum Europaeum*, was in essence a formalization of the rules of war that made sovereign states its distinct and territorially anchored moral subjects. Wars were henceforth fought between *justi hostes*, just or correct enemies, specified as legal personalities in terms of a common European code of conduct, based on the partition of lands and the identity of moral personality, justice and territory. In moral terms, wars were henceforth only waged between equals. The European continent, controlled by the *ius publicum Europeaum*, became a homogeneous moral space in which the rules of war, the forms of opposition, were specified in advance by the codes of inter-state activities. *Ius gentium* (law of nations) and *ius inter gentes* (law among nations, inter-national law) mapped directly on to each other. Indeed, they were indistinguishable.[2]

In Schmitt's view the reality of the world order has left this legal order far behind. In *The Concept of the Political*, for example, he describes the end-point of this long process of decline in which:

> the entire structure of state-based concepts that the Eurocentric political and legal sciences had built up through 400 years of intellectual labors. The state as model of political unity, the state as bearer of the most astonishing of all monopolies, namely that of the monopoly of political decision, that glimmering work of European form and occidental rationality, has been dethroned.
>
> (Schmitt, 2004)

By all evidence, the era of the grand European legal order is behind us, and yet the quandary that characterizes our time, according to Schmitt, is that we seem unable to dispense with the 'classical' political and legal concepts forged in the 16th and 17th centuries and developed without imagination since then. According to the classical model, he argues, one differentiates clearly between the interior relations of the state and external relations, domestic affairs and international affairs. Once upon a time, the state was the privileged arena for exercising the political. It was the site where 'the political' was understood as determining inter-state relations. According to the classical model, the state was an integral political actor, turned toward the outside, toward relations with other states. Domestic order and security were the responsibility of state-controlled police. The 'criminal' was understood as a domestic, civil, legal category, while the 'enemy' was understood as a category of international relations, and peace was understood as absence of war. In Schmitt's radical reconceptualization of 'the political', particularly in his 1929 essay 'The Concept of the Political', he refers to a primordial entity of human existence, based on the relation of self to other. In Schmitt's terms, this appears as 'friend' and 'enemy', though this must be understood as preceding individuality, personality and any political institutions of the state.[3]

In *The Concept of the Political*, Schmitt underscores that the concept of the political presupposes a *plurality* of political units. There can be no political unity without the opposition of that unity to another (Schmitt, 2004: 54). This essentially Hegelian insight is the basis for Schmitt's understanding of the situation of the international system. The political world is a 'pluriverse', not a 'universe': no state represents humanity. Indeed, in Schmitt's notorious formulation, 'whoever says "humanity" is deceiving' (ibid.: 55). Does the European Union, with its institutional make-up and transnational *acquis communautaire*, simply extent the trend of *ius gentium* as distinct from *ius inter gentes*, which Schmitt decries in the two 20th-century attempts to establish a new global *nomos*? Does the system of European Union law offer something new?

The European Union and the *ius publicum Europeaum*

Before turning to our analysis of the EU legal system, we linger at another late text in which Schmitt considers the notion of a European legal order after the League of Nations: 'The Plight of the European Legal Sciences', from 1943 (Schmitt, 1957). In this essay, written at approximately the same time as *The* Nomos *of the Earth*, Schmitt evaluates what he sees as the state of the art of the European jurisprudence and, in doing so, comments on the nature of European community in terms of actual and possible legal framework. The article is both an evaluation of the relationship between the centuries-old European jurisprudence and the European scholarly traditions into which it is situated, and a diatribe, typical for this period in Schmitt's life, against legal positivism (Carrino, 1999).

For Schmitt it is, again, burgeoning legal positivism, which has shaped and determined the evolution of the informal European legal community. According to this model, which Schmitt sees spreading and developing throughout Europe, the formal validity of laws lies exclusively in its propositions, combined with a state that is willing to enforce them. According to the positivist position, laws are by and large instrumental: their validity is identical to the force of their implementation. For Europe, politically torn and tattered after two world wars, no substantive foundation for law seems available. Here Schmitt is referring to individual European nation-states and the aspects of a shared legal order they manifest. The prospect of a common European legal system in the sense we see it today in the institutionalization of EU law is distant since, as he explains, there is precisely no common political will to enforce a European law if there were to be one. This is, of course, true for the state of European solidarity in 1943.

Schmitt then unites his critique of the state of jurisprudence in Europe with a parallel attack (in the *nomos* book and elsewhere) on the destitute tradition of *ius publicum Europeaum*, European law of nations (Schmitt, 1957: 386). From the perspective of legal positivism, state law and international law have fallen completely from one another. They have, according to Schmitt, two distinct sources of law and procedural principles. The internal and the external are thus alienated from each other and a kind of political realism has become the abiding theory of politics (de la Grange, 2002: 141, Koskenniemi, 2002). The domestic and international belong to two utterly different spheres, and have no conceptual or even practical communication with each other. Contracts and agreements made between European states have, for the positivist, formally speaking, nothing at all distinct in comparison with contracts and agreements made with non-European states.

The fact that two European states might enjoy an international agreement, as opposed to having one with a non-European state, is strictly a matter of coincidence (Schmitt, 1957; Slaughter, 1997, 1995).

Here the assumption upon which Schmitt bases his lament over the absence of a coherent (non-positivist) legal order is precisely the same assumption he criticizes elsewhere in his assessment of the international legal order (League of Nations and UN), namely that it is an amalgam instead of an interconnected, organic legal system. The strange reality, however, as Schmitt underscores, is that the European states share similar or identical legal systems to form the basis of a legal community. The more or less absolute juridical equivalence of the individual states' international legal systems and the identical ethical, political and cultural status of their legal personalities renders *ius publicum Europaeum* obsolete and also uninteresting for the present.

The new European *nomos* will not be a legal order in which all European nation-states adopt one and the same parallel legal system, thus sharing a single tradition that is unaffected by national particularity, not like a re-transmission of Roman law as a 'spiritual and intellectual Common Law of Europe' (Schmitt, 1957: 392–3). This would be the opposite of the 'atomi-zation' of the nation-states which Schmitt so vehemently attacks in his evaluation of the League of Nations and the UN. Yet a true *ius publicum Europaeum* will need to be both more and less than a shared tradition, passively adopted. It will need to repose upon *both* shared traditions *and* national, individual and case-based particularity. As it happens, something like a trans-sectorial legal order has indeed begun to emerge in Europe and continues to develop.

With the adoption of the Lisbon Treaty, the process of European integration has advanced further than any of the historical European utopians had dreamed. Yet what does it mean for a given institutional set-up to be European? Just how European is the European Union legal system? (Niess, 2001; Burgess, 2002). The question of the fundamental sense of Europe and what kind of institutional set-up it calls for is far from resolved (Pageden, 2002: 33–4; Passerini, 2002a). European unity remains something other than the unity of Europeans. Nor is it constituted by the unity of its political institutions, government, legislatures or courts. It is something more, though clearly something less as well.

Schmitt's stand-or-fall criterion for the validity of an international organization is precisely that it should *not* be *international*, rather *inter-national*. From a juridical perspective it must reattach the wayward fellows *ius inter gentes* and *ius gentium*, while at the same time recognizing the pragmatic, post-Hegelian impossibility of cultural, political and legal universality in any institution, be it local, national, or supra-national. The defunct League of Nations was doomed to failure since it permitted the international law to crumble into a formalistic consolidation of national actors in an era when both politics and jurisprudence played the strings in a different register of meaning and power; a simple, particularistic link between a finite number of nation-state entities, whose political substance remained to be unpacked in order for it to participate in the cultural organization of the continent.

As we will see, however, European Union law occupies a strange and complex position between an international law model and a federal model. European construction has developed a kind of jurisprudence that communicates with national legal traditions in the tradition of common law, based in culturally determined norms and customs. It thereby appeals to universal principles and the formalism of an international civil code. Where international law has four interrelated types, (a) treaties and conventions, (b) customary law, (c) general principles, (d) standing court decisions (Cairns, 1997: 71), European jurisprudence, as we shall see, has an even more complex set of sources. The recurring challenge for the European Court of Justice (EJC) has been to navigate the terrain between the general scope of international law, law established between member states, law established between member states and non-member states and the growing corpus of law established *sui generis* between the EU and member states.

This is not the place to rehearse the many utopian histories of European construction, some more viable than others. A unique chronology can be charted according to whether one is concerned with the geographical conceptualization of the European continent, the ebb and flow of something called the European spirit, the seemingly unavoidable economic nature of its institutions or the contours of its legal institutions. Each is constructed upon a myth of origin and shared destiny, of *alpha* and *omega*. Each is teleological in design, aiming, with varying degrees of pragmatic fulfilment, at an integral 'Europeanization' (Burgess, 2003).

European history has never been a chronicle of facts and events that unfolded in a place called Europe. The history of Europe is a cosmology, a myth of foundation that unites heaven and Earth, the geographical continent and the people who have inhabited it (Passerini, 2002b). It is narrative bound together as a system of ideas, constituted through traditional, physical, moral and encyclopaedic history. It has never simply been the story of politics played out on a continent already constituted, already shaped. The history of Europe is the history of the interpretations of the myth of Europe, including the geographical one. Though no less indeterminate than other narratives, the geographical narrative of Europe is primeval among narratives. The 'great events' of European history, that is, those deemed worthy of inclusion into the canon of histories, official or unofficial, of Europe are both transnational and transterritorial (Delouche, 1992; Duroselle, 1990: 11–14).

The European *nomos* as a topology of values

The new geopolitical configuration that emerged from the Treaty of Westphalia was based on the concern for security. Even though the political landscape was considered a thing apart, European culture has been at pains to see itself in terms of particularity. Indeed, the European cultural self-understanding is anything but particular, it is the very invention of universal pretension. Shadowing the intricate transterritorial character of European jurisprudential thought, the newly forged Treaty of Lisbon sets out a conceptualization of the European, which, like the logic of value itself, defies the territorial confines of the European continent.

As the Preambule of the Treaty states:

> Drawing inspiration from the cultural, religious and humanist inheritance of Europe, from which have developed the universal values of the inviolable and inalienable rights of the human person, freedom, democracy, equality and the rule of law; Recalling the historic importance of the ending of the division of the European continent and the need to create firm bases for the construction of the future Europe; Confirming their attachment to the principles of liberty, democracy and respect for human rights and fundamental freedoms and of the rule of law [...] [the plenipotentiaries] have decided to establish a European Union (2008).

Europe's past is conceived of as the foundation for the values of its present and its future. There is, according to the Preamble, inspiration to be found in the past, inspiration that also contributed to developing the inviolable and inalienable 'universal values' of our present. As discussed in Chapter 10, those values, though universal, must be posited again as the basis of the Europe of today, in order to both overcome the divisions of the past and forge together the common 'destiny', which, even though it is the destiny of Europe, appears to be sufficiently threatened to require inspiration from the past in order to safeguard it. An insistent though fundamentally unstable notion of universality inhabits these opening aspirations. On the one hand, the cultural inheritance of Europe's past is the origin of the universal values of the present, the basic political principles that guide the European construction of our time. On the other hand, however, that past is one of division and clashes, division that must be overcome in order to deploy the values, which, nonetheless, were valued before, toward the uniting of our present, which finds itself under the inspiration of the past. Thus the strange logic of universal value: universalism of the past is fissured and must be transcended in order to achieve universalism.

This is the tension between a transcendental notion of universality, a notion whose origin and destiny are doomed to remain invisible like Schmitt's mystical origin of international law, and a kind of normative universalism, a universalism-to-be, a universalism understood as in some sense already here, but nonetheless necessary to effectuate and operationalize in and through European construction. Despite its 'bitter experience', and with no implicit knowledge of the future, Europe will continue along its path, choosing its unavoidable destiny.

The universalism of European cultural history thus obeys a conceptual topography that we are at pains to map onto its physical geography. This is so for two reasons: first, because geography is never purely physical geography; it is always made conceivable, understandable, communicable by a network of ideas about place, space, emptiness, etc., which do not collapse onto it. Second, conceptual topography of any kind contains an implicit reference to the materiality of things in space and in time. One does not precede the other; both render transcendence *strictu senso* meaningless. In the eyes of the Treaty, Europe is both a place and a transcendental, extra-spatial entity, a set of ideas and values, which by their very nature are transnational and international.

Thus the themes of 'territoriality' and 'territorial cohesion' recur again and again in the Treaty's provisions. Despite the fact that the European Union remains a geopolitical entity whose physical boundaries are beyond dispute, the cohesion of its territory is explicitly posited as codified and institutionalized, something *to be reinforced*. Among the EU's objectives formulated in Article 1 is the promotion of 'economic, social and territorial cohesion' (Treaty of the European Union, 2008). At the same time the Union will seek to maintain and respect the 'territorial integrity' of the member states, 'maintaining law and order and safeguarding national security (ibid.). EU citizenship includes the right to work and reside freely within the territory of member states (ibid.), to enjoy rights of EU citizens in the 'territory' of third states. It becomes evident that, on the one hand, the classical notions of nation-state self-constitution and relation to others is clearly valid and in vigour; on the other hand, the repeated reaffirmation of the notion of territoriality nearly reads like a throwback to a time when the notion had far less anchorage in time and tradition. The notion of territoriality is reiterated precisely because the Lisbon Treaty comes to the fore in a moment when territoriality has never been so precarious, never so distant from its own self-evidence.

In this sense it is also remarkable that a new figure of spatiality emerges from the draft constitution, equally marking the *nomos* of the EU. The value abstractions announced and confirmed in the draft constitution are repeatedly associated with an *area* or *zone* with 'soft' or variable borders. Thus, 'the Union shall offer its citizens an area of freedom, security and justice without internal frontiers' (Treaty of the European Union, 2008).

In terms of its neighbouring states, the European Union shall 'also promote an amorphous space of influence, 'an area of prosperity and good neighbourliness, found on the values of the Union and characterized by close and peaceful relations based on cooperation' (ibid.). It shall also 'constitute an area of freedom, security and justice with respect for funda-mental rights and the different legal systems and traditions of the Member States' (ibid.). The values of the European Union are not positively and indistinguishably attached to singular individuals or institutions, not even to particular determinations of space such as borders and walls. The

European values to be institutionalized in the Lisbon Treaty correspond to semi-amorphous areas, to a zone of value, non-linear and non-discrete.

The Charter of Fundamental Rights contained within the Treaty lays out an unsurprising set of traditional European values, based on the UDHR tradition of humanist principles, supplemented by global capitalist notions of free movement of goods and market liberalism. *Values*, moreover, are a central theme through the text. Most significant for our purposes is that despite the distinct European tradition, geographically discrete and territorially sovereign, Europe nonetheless constitutes an amorphous 'zone' of values and rights (ibid.). This '*area* of freedom, security and justice, without internal frontiers, and an internal market where competition is free and undistorted' does not map onto the political geography of Europe; rather it draws its own value-topology in a Heideggerian fashion. Simultaneously, the Treaty insists on one of the primary international values, namely the maintenance of 'territorial cohesion and solidarity' amongst Member States.

This is only one form of the great paradox of our time, cooked down to the term 'glocalization': globalization opens the horizon for ubiquitous experience of ideas, which by the reverse-awareness of the particularity of the local are overturned in their universality. This is the truly Hegelian moment of global society: the universality of universal precepts is overturned by the universally valid experience of their specific application and applicability in particular settings. Market liberalism, to take the most prominent example, and a central tenet in European construction, is only universal to the extent that it can be applied in the individual global settings that were completely unforeseen by those who first formulated the principle. In terms of the Preamble, the European values will be spread to all Europeans, all who fall under the same umbrella of Europeanness will be respected for their difference, precisely because they are different, weak, deprived.

By the same token, national individuality is not opposed to European identity. The national schisms that brought the European wars of the past are not in some sense exceptions of history, a temporary derailment of the true European history. Nor are they are inferior moments in the construction of a higher order of civilization. The dialectical experience of conflict-in-unity is the very essence of European thought, both on the political level and in the domain of jurisprudence. Without the geographically based cultural heterogeneity on this otherwise homogeneous peninsula, the notion of a European unity would be unthinkable.

This set of ideas stands in contrast to what Schmitt rejects in the League of Nations model of international organization, namely that it homogenizes the member states, reducing their political subjectivity and legal personality to mere straw men. They become mere political and juridical atoms with no internal politics or interpretive jurisprudence. The far more dialectical self-understanding of the draft EU Constitution conceives of the political subject and legal personality of Member States and the EU as *permeable*.

The European legal order

A similar evolution can be observed in the European legal order. International law in Europe (distinguished for the moment from the European legal order) is spatially determined and this determination in space has varied widely since the rise of the notion of international law at the beginning of the 20th century. Just as Europe has been continuously politically reordered and restructured in the course of the last century, so has this spatialization reproduced itself in the conceptualization of Europe in international law. Schmitt sees the most prominent illustration of this phenomenon in the lateral incision across the geographical East–West line. This bifurcation of the geographical, political cultural, and even spiritual Europe, is only the most visible of the spatial reordering that marks Europe's historical transitions. These changes have significant consequences for the spatial character of international law. This is particularly the case during the Cold War, when a variety of different planes, zones and spheres of political and legal influence were simultaneously operative. International law was at once universal and bipolar, homogeneous and heterogeneous.

Europe is also divided along a North–South axis, separating Greece, Portugal, Spain, southern Italy and Ireland from the 'rest' of Europe, both in terms of economic welfare and in terms of cultural, social and spiritual values. The European system of norms is also torn in two across the trans-Atlantic axis. After 1990, the abiding bifurcation dissolves, the fall of the Berlin wall brings with it the end of communism, the unification of Germany, the collapse of East–West European multilateralism, and fresh eastern European aspirations to join the economic development of the rest of Europe (Gautron, 1999: 6–7).

The *Wende* of 1989 brought about a new shift in this spatio-cultural constellation. Among many other macro- and micro-political changes, the role played by inter- and non-governmental organizations exert influence in Europe and elsewhere, take on greater geopolitical and geocultural importance. The dismemberment of the former Soviet Union into a number of states, restructuring the former Yugoslavia and Czechoslovakia, created new states and new constellations of norms, laws, rights and values, and made more or less unequal transitions to both market rules and legal norms at differing speeds. Juridical questions related to borders, monetary zones, trade and taxes, armaments, security and rights of individuals and citizens become suddenly more complex.

By the same token, a new kind of juridical cosmos has evolved linked to the institutional evolution of the European Union. On the most general level, the multiple enlargements of the Union (or earlier, Communities) itself has widened and transformed the juridical horizon of national law, including not only European member states, but also non-European states and the framework and parameters that determine their relationship to the

EU at large and the EU member states in particular. To this can be added the expanding spheres of influence of the Council of Europe, the OSCE and OECD. Each of these institutional matrices carries its own political and legal sub-structures, which interact with and influence the political and legal structures of the states they concern. The synthesis of these new legal and political frameworks makes up what we call the new *nomos* of European jurisprudence.

Though debate among political scientists surrounding the question of what kind of political entity the European Union actually is has not abated, there is consensus among legal experts that it constitutes a *sui generis* phenomenon of jurisprudence. EU jurisprudence distinguishes itself from both classical international law and all types of federal jurisprudence. As the Court of Justice of the European Communities stated in the oft-cited 1963 judgements by ECJ Van Gend and Loos.

> The Community constitutes a new legal order of international law for the benefit of which the states have limited their sovereign rights, albeit with limited fields, and the subjects of which comprise not only member states but also their nationals. Independently of the legislation of member states, community law therefore not only imposes obligations in individuals but is also intended to confer upon them rights which become part of their legal heritage. These rights arise not only where they are expressly granted by the treaty, but also by reason of obligations which the treaty imposes in a clearly defined way upon individuals as well as upon the member states and upon the institutions of the community.
>
> (ECJ, 1962b)

Even before the advent of the Treaty of European Union in 1997, in which the notion of Europe as a community of shared values first arises, the Court of Justice was struggling to draw the consequences of a system of legal ties without precedent. Also in the well-travelled Costa vs. ENEL case, the judgement makes visible the way in which social and political systems of legitimacy struggle to find their anchoring point legal system:

> By contrast with ordinary international treaties, the EEC Treaty has created its own legal system which, on the entry into force of the treaty, became an integral part of the legal systems of the member states and which their courts are bound to apply.
>
> (ECJ, 1962a)

Yet instead of one axis of comparison in the political sphere – an assembly of nation-state-like structures – the question of the status of the EU system is inevitably one that moves between the norms of national law and the categories of international law.

One way of studying the nature of changes in European law is to begin by plotting its 'origins'. When legal scholars speak of European law, however, they do not presume that law is a purely theoretical construction or that it has a distinct beginning and end. Rather, it is understood as emerging out of a concrete political, cultural and social setting. Moreover, they presume that legal systems build from a heterogeneous field of sources, ranging from customs to both formal and informal rules and regulations (Evans, 1998; Cairns, 1997; Chalmers and Szyszczak, 1998; Hunnings, 1996; Winter, 1996).

In formal terms, European law is conventionally divided into three layers: primary sources, secondary sources, or legislation and tertiary sources. The *primary* sources are derived from two basic sources. First, there is law stemming from formal treaties signed in the name of Europe and which designate the conditions of the adherence to the treaties. Second, there are the treaties entered into by the European Union (or Community) with third parties, whereby the EU (or EC) is presumed to be a sovereign unit. The formal framework of European law itself makes up the *secondary* source. It is commonly distinguished by three levels of legislation: (1) regulations, (2) directives, and (3) decisions. Finally, the *tertiary* sources of European law link to the basic practices of jurisprudence such as they emerge from the work of the European Court of Justice. These include the actual case law of the European Court of Justice, the basic legal principles that are adopted in the ECJ, the general principles of public international law, in addition to the acts of law adopted by representatives of member state governments (MacLean, 2000).

These three layers are structured in order of descending level of abstraction. The primary sources articulate the most general level of abstraction, linking to the most general principles of rights and philosophical traditions. They express the historical identity and design of the European project. This is the level of international politics in its meeting with European law. The secondary level is more concrete and context-specific, incorporating the more technical elements of regulation and governance. The tertiary level is the sphere of legal communication between member state institutions and between legal and regulatory institutions across nation-states. To these can be added the national law and international public law.

The new *nomos* of Europe and the topography of European legal *cosmos*

The interaction between these different layers and sub-layers, with their varying degrees of legitimacy, politicization and anchoring in customary law, is complex. The scientific response to this complex cosmos of legal substances is the theory of competences. The theory of competence has emerged and developed as a kind of legal regulation of the hierarchies and sub-hierarchies of power and legitimacy. The concept of 'competence' replaces in some sense the notion of authority in the unique sphere of European law. Competence is the fundamental attribution of law. It designates the foundation or source of jurisdiction and the basis of legitimacy for any given field of legal issues. Competence only emerges as the result of an attribution of competence by a competent authority. Competence gives rise to competence. In this way a kind of meta-competence is the precondition for competence, commonly called the 'Kompetenz-Kompetenz' question.[4] However, though the competence–competence feedback displaces by one level the question of the origin of legitimacy (Schmitt would say, and Derrida after him, the 'mystical origin of competence'), it simply displaces it by one level, replacing the original competence by an original attribution of competence (also known as the 'transfer of sovereign rights') (Schmitt, 1996; Derrida, 1992a).

The European legal system thus has a kind of porosity. It is, not by chance but necessity, contaminated by what is outside it. The sovereign border of EU law, the distinguishing line between what belongs and what does not, is traversed by flows of cultural meaning, of legitimacy and competence, both nourishing the system and taking nourishment from it. Thus, in contrast to a federal law model, according to which competence springs from a substantive foundation, the European system seeks a kind of organic organization along lines of varying intensity, unstable geometries and sources of varying depths. In certain situations, the EU even possesses competencies drawn from substantive, unquestioned member state sources, which leave it susceptible to the degrees of co-ordination of authorities (competences) that are outside itself (Gautron, 1999).

The European legal order bends and stretches the traditional concept of legal personality and does not a little mischief to the notion of the political subject. At the moment of Schmitt's *caesura* at the end of World War II, the sanctity and autonomy of the individual is set for epiphany in the Universal Declaration of Human Rights (UDHR). In other words, the *individual* is constituted on the international scene in terms of his/her rights. The document is also the inaugural use of the term 'human rights' in an international setting, adopted by the General Assembly of the United Nations. The individual and the human rights attributed to it thus acquire the legal force of international law. Although international law does not come close to exercising universal jurisdiction, there hardly exists a more encompassing expression of universality in the sense Schmitt wishes to construe it in the new *nomos* of the Earth than the notion of human rights. Few dispute its validity, though interpretations of its precepts are *legio*. The Declaration refers both to rights of nations and individuals. Nations are guaranteed the right to self-determination and to property; individuals are guaranteed the rights to life, liberty, freedom, freedom of thought, expression and assembly, in addition to a wide set of rights involving access to legal process.[5]

The self-evidence of the formal validity of a fixed set of principles of human rights has been tested with increasing frequency. End-of-millennium multiculturalism has put into question the special version of universalism embodied by the UDHR (Beck, 1999a; Grimm, 2000). Political disdain for the UN and the impracticality of human rights have grown in kind with the US global hegemony (Guantanamo, Abu Ghraib).

In Schmitt's eyes, the United Nations suffers from the same untimeliness as the defunct League of Nations. It is essentially the institutionalization of a covenant regulating the relationships between sovereign states, one which remains incapable of conceptualizing their porosity. Though it is clear that the UDHR concerns most directly individuals, its mode of application has typically been through the authority of the nation-state.

In terms of European Union politics, the UDHR provided the inspiration for the drafting of the European Convention on Human Rights, which was adopted in 1950, less than two years later (Alston and Weiler, 1999; Cohen-Johanthan, 1989). It plays a central role in the Treaty of Rome (establishing the European Community) (1957). Article 13 specifies the European Community and European Council will seek to 'combat discrimination based on sex, racial or ethnic origin, religion or belief, disability, age or sexual orientation'. Article 177 mentions 'human rights' explicitly, admonishing that 'Community policy in this area shall contribute to the general objective of developing and consolidating democracy and the rule of law, and to that of respecting human rights and fundamental freedoms' (1992: Articles 13, 17). The Treaty of Amsterdam (1997) reaffirms these general notions of human rights in the foundation of the European Union, stipulating it as 'founded on the principles of liberty, democracy, respect for human rights and fundamental freedoms, and the rule of law, principles which are common to the Member States' (1992: Article 11). The notion of human rights is also the object of a wide array of legislation in force and in preparation.

The Treaty of European Union also plays the role of bringing the Common Foreign and Security Policy (CFSP) into formal existence. Remarkable in this context is that the object of securitization is not only to ensure the security of Europe in a conventional sense, but also 'to safeguard the common values, fundamental interests, independence and integrity of the Union in conformity with the principles of the United Nations Charter'. Lastly, the TEU sets out the conditions of membership of the Union, which include an acceptance of the principles of human rights as set out by the UN Charter (1992: Article 49).

The extra-territoriality of EU human rights politics is co-ordinated by an essential *ius gentium* in the sense that it comprises both a politics of *internal* and *external* human rights. The explosion of migration across and on the periphery of European space reopens issues of racial, religious and cultural discrimination in the European Union. Global migration patterns have transformed cultural unities into patterns of flow, mingling and imbricating traditions of ethnic and cultural identity within and outside the EU.

Three other recurring principles have marked the singularity of the European legal order: direct effect, supremacy and subsidiarity. *Direct effect* can be defined in broad terms as the mechanism whereby a European citizen can rely upon a provision of EU law before his or her national courts. The national courts are required to acknowledge, protect and enforce the rights conferred by the provision (Cairns, 1997: 84). The notion of direct effect thus sets EU law aside from other international institutions in the sense that it relates directly to the individual. Whereas international law and international organizations confer rights and obligations on nation-states, EU law has the ability to exercise jurisprudence in an individual capacity. Individuals have a set of transnational European rights, which at the same time are protected by the jurisdiction of the national courts. *Supremacy* assures the precedence of EU law in cases where it comes into conflict with national law.

These structural principles are not formally assured in EU treaties. On the contrary, they have grown informally through the corpus of case material that has developed throughout the construction of the European system. The principles of supremacy and direct effect have a clear impetus: they move the centre of gravity of European jurisprudence away from the nation-state level and toward the EU level. This shift was perceptible throughout the 1980s and woke the concerns of the European public sphere, yet most were convinced that its national institutions would not be threatened by EU construction (ibid.: 96–7). In this atmosphere, the concept of *subsidiarity* was developed, both in legal cases and in the political discourse surrounding the Delors presidency of the European Commission. It was codified in EU law through the Single European Act (1986). The Act stipulates that the European Community should act only to realize the objectives of its environ-mental policy where these objectives could not be attained better on the level of the national authorities. The principle was later codified in the TEU in terms of *competence*, specifying that 'in areas which do not fall within its exclusive competence, the Community shall take action, in accordance with the principle of subsidiarity, only if and insofar as the objectives of the proposed action cannot be sufficiently achieved by the Member States and can therefore, by reason of the scale or effects of the proposed action, be better achieved by the Community'.

The triple mechanisms of direct effect, supremacy and subsidiarity thus put into place a regulation of the porosity of nation-state sovereignty. They organized an international legal order in which the currents of universality are supplemented and supplanted by those of particular rights and obligations. It thus transcends the classical 'monist–dualist' dilemma, which Schmitt bemoans in the 'Plight' essay of 1943. That controversy pits those who, like Kelsen, see national legal orders as 'creatures' of international law (monists) against those who, like Triepel and Anzilotti, argue that national legal orders were separate legal orders that resisted the penetration of international norms (Witte, 1999: 178). The European legal system, if only by default, resists both poles of the debate.

Conclusion

To the extent that the evolving European legal system is not, at present, nor aspires to be, a global legal system, a new global *nomos* (in the sense of a world order based on the appropriation, disappropriation and distribution of the Earth), it cannot fill the void left by the collapse of the *ius publicum Europeaum* bemoaned by Schmitt. This impossibility lies in the far more modest aspirations of European construction, in the nature of the concept of *nomos*, in the finitude of the history of global expansion and in our experience of the finitude of our planet. The decline of the universal legal order, including international law is not the fault of the UN and other global organizations. This decline and uncertainty of conventional legal categories produces a certain insecurity all on its own: while it is difficult to present decisive evidence, it might be suggested that a component of the scepticism to the project of European construction shown by the French and Dutch in the 2005 referendum on the European constitution, and the Irish in 2008, can be attributed to a missing certainty as to the structure of sovereignty within the porous architecture of the EU institutions.

Four correlations can be made with Schmitt's theoretical perspective relevant to the recently frustrated but ongoing process of European construction. First, the blurring processes that Schmitt observed early in the 20th century have continued. The basic oppositions that Schmitt diagnoses in a number of his writings (inside/outside, war/peace, combatant/criminal) hold true, more so in our day than ever before. Second, there will never again be a global legal order. This is the consequence of the concept of universality itself. Both experience and the logic of universality teach us that a universal system is only universal in opposition to another. As Schmitt admonishes in *The* Nomos *of the Earth*, until outer space becomes a true space for conquest and appropriation on a grand scale, the global state will remain a fiction. Third, on formal legal grounds, the European legal system, with its dialectical mix of 'limited' universality and local particularity, the variety of its sources on different levels of European life, is in some sense one answer to the problem posed by Schmitt. The European legal sciences have already survived their own fissuring into legitimacy and legality. Moreover, the breakdown of international law into international politics is not a menace to European civilization, as Schmitt might see it, but rather inherent in the system of European law. Fourth, the extension of Schmitt's analysis beyond the 1950s into the era of European construction confirms Schmitt's diagnosis, while at the same time suggesting that he was too pessimistic in his characterization of the European legal order. A kind of new *nomos* is emerging to respond to the challenges he perceived. It is characterized by a multicultural flux of values, which have a systematically blurry connection to territory, function in a global economy, and are protected by a security agenda that reaches beyond the 'traditional' international space of Europe.

This is the new European *nomos*: a new spatial order, based not on space-ordaining law, but building upon on a new ordering of peoples, culture and value in space.

Notes

1 Useful analysis of the background of Schmitt's European perspective can be found in the *Telos* group's analysis of Schmitt. A selection includes (de Benoist, 1999, 2003, 2004; de la Grange, 2004, 2002; Marder, 2008; Arditi, 2008; Gottfried, 2008, 1998; Gare, 2002).
2 The link between Schmitt's European vision and the question of a European identity (cf. de Benoist, 2004).
3 In the earlier essay, 'The Problem of the Domestic Neutrality of the State', Schmitt explains how the already dominant practices of economic *laissez-faire* liberalism were not adequate to ensure the non-politicization of domestic life. The state today – meaning, above all, but not exclusively, Germany – is an 'economy state', but it is not equipped with an 'economic constitution' (Schmitt, 1930a: 41–59). The way out of this predicament is, in true Schmitt form, to strengthen the state sovereign, and dampen the party-political pressures.
4 'Competence', in the language of the European legal system, denotes the authority of a person or institution to make certain kinds of decision.
5 General Assembly of the United Nations (1948). Universal Declaration of Human Rights; http://www.hrweb.org/legal/udhr.html. Verified 6 July 2005.

13 A federalist Europe between economic and cultural value

In December 1945, Denis de Rougemont stood before a meeting of the fledgling Movement of European Federalists and delivered his now renowned 'Message to Europeans'. Lying in ruins after yet another unthinkably destructive European war, Europe, to de Rougemont, was in a situation of grave danger. The deep wounds dividing Europe he saw as not only material but also spiritual. 'Europe is threatened,' he proclaimed,

> Europe is divided, and the greatest threat comes from its divisions. Impoverished, burdened by the barriers that hinder the circulation of her goods, but which are incapable of protecting her, our disunited Europe is marching toward its end. No one of our countries can alone aspire seriously to defend her independence. No one of our countries can alone resolve the problems with which the modern economy confronts her. In the absence of a freely consented union, our present anarchy will expose us tomorrow to a forced unification, either by the intervention of an empire from without, or by the usurpation of a party from within.
>
> (cited in Deering, 1991: 425)

Later the same year, de Rougemont set out the two fundamental consequences for the mission of Europe:

1. The political union of our peoples is henceforth the condition not only of their survival but also of the just exercise of their world function.
2. This union must take a form dictated by structures, both historical and living, of the complex organism of our culture: that is, a federal form.

> (de Rougement, 1966: 420)

In this chapter we explore the relationship between European cultural identity and the institutional structure built in its name by focusing primarily on the federalist vision of Europe and the politics of economic unification

that have led Europe to the remarkable step, on January 1, 1999, of renouncing all national currencies in favour of a European one. The chapter will proceed in three steps. Firstly, we will argue that the federalist movement contains a normative core based on a notion of collective cultural value in the work of Spinelli, Monnet and Schuman. Secondly, we will present the philosophy of money as an attempt to link value in general to the phenomenon of money in particular. Lastly, we will update Simmel's vision by presenting some of the general critiques of the new liberal economics in Europe.

Federalism in the prehistory of the European Union

The concept of federalism has followed a long and illustrious path in European history. The origins of the word 'federal' can be traced to derivations of *foedus* (treaty) and *fidere* (trust). A *foederatus* is a *confederation,* a union or association bound by a contract, a contract not only anchored in a notion of legality, but also whose authority is bound by confidence, trust, affinity, empathy and conviction. The first English language use of the term 'federal' is ascribed to the 17th century puritan colonists of north America who spoke of a 'federal theology', a covenant between God and the settlers of the New World, later expanded to comprise the 'federation' among the new states. By the same token, though the term 'federal' has had a considerable career in the evolution of the European political landscape, its widespread modern meaning comes from the federal constitution of the United States in 1789 and, in particular, the political principles developed by writers such as Alexander Hamilton, James Madison and John Jay. Philosophers and writers as diverse as Kant, in *On Perpetual Peace* (1795), Madame de Stael, Constant, Mazzini, Hugo, Proudhon, Mill, Freeman and many others kept the notion vividly alive throughout the 19th century, increasingly associated with the question of war and peace.

   The birth of modern European federalism is often attributed to Altiero Spinelli, ex-communist and anti-fascist militant, who, together with Emesto Rossi, composed what has come to be known as the *Ventotene Manifesto.* The text, written in 1940 and smuggled from exile into occupied Europe, gave an impetus to the nascent federalist movements carried forth through wartime illicitness by members of the Italian and French resistance movements. It became the central statement for the early European federalist movement. The political impetus for that movement's public legitimacy has, arguably, to thank Winston Churchill. Churchill, who long supported some sort of notion of a European Union and had spoken repeatedly of the formation of a Council of Europe, made a watershed speech in Zurich in September 1946. In his speech Churchill decried the 'Babel of jarring voices' among the victors of the war, and the 'sullen silence of despair' among the vanquished. The remedy, he proclaimed, was to recreate what he called the 'European family', by providing it with a structure 'under which it can dwell in peace, safety and freedom'. This structure was a United States of Europe. 'If Europe is to be saved from infinite misery, and indeed from final doom, there must be an act of faith in the European family and an act of oblivion against all crimes and follies of the past' (Churchill, 1994: 6–7). The speech reinvigorated the movement for European unity and led to the creation of the European Union of Federalists in 1947 and to the formation of the Council of Europe.

In the eyes of the European federalists, the Council of Europe was a failure. It did not possess, so they claimed, the institutional powers necessary to impose the supranational resolutions it made. Jean Monnet, who had political experience from the League of Nations, the National Liberation Committee and the London resistance, and had been appointed Planning Commissioner for the French government after the liberation, saw the Franco-German tensions as the primary threat to European peace and stability, and turned to the principles of federalism in his famous memo to the Minister of Foreign Affairs Robert Schuman. In consultation with Chancellor Adenauer, Schuman released the memo that was to be known as the Schuman Plan, in May (Schuman, 1950).

The Schuman Plan was the first concrete federalist project on the European scale. The plan argues that solidarity is threefold, a dialectical relation between the civilization's ethical and cultural community, the wisdom of ages and the concrete institutional matrix that will bear forth that cultural heritage. As Jean Monnet noted in 1952, 'The life of institutions is longer than that of men, and institutions can thus, if they are properly constructed, accumulate and transmit the wisdom of successive generations' (Monnet, 1952).

According to Schuman, Europe's battles are classically familial. In his memoirs, *Pour l'Europe,* he describes the construction of Europe as the reunification of a community already bound by common interests. For Schuman, the first step in the re-engagement of the European clan is the creation of a system of economic co-ordination and regulation based on the principles of market liberalism and the free flow of capital, which have become the European *mantra* of today (Schuman, 1964; Burgess, 2001b: 315f).

The great challenge of European construction in the eyes of Schuman was to give political-institutional flesh and bone to the deep ideals and interests in the hearts of Europeans. 'The true European spirit is the recognition of the realities, the possibilities and the obligations in the presence of which each of us places himself beyond frontiers, beyond our antagonisms and our resentments' (Schuman, 1964: 26). In other words, the unity that we are to seek is not *external,* not derived from the contingent, circumstantial or occasional characteristics that make individual groups what they are. These are mutable, variegated and unstable. The unity that must be sought is *internal,* based on the 'organic structure' of Europe.

> The unity of Europe will be accomplished neither uniquely nor
> principally by European institutions; their creation will follow the
> progression of spirits – whence the importance of a free circulation of
> ideas and individuals between the European countries. Those countries
> that refuse this notion exclude themselves in principle from Europe.
>
> (ibid.: 30, 48)

The European Union is, in this vision, an immense transcription machine,
a conduit between the material values of the national political economy and
the spiritual, cultural and moral values of the European cultural heritage.
The question for the future architects of Europe is just how this transformation is to take place: According to which rules of transcription can the
values that unite the European family be embodied in the political and
economic institutions of the European Union?

Value after modernity in economic theory

Three essential paradigm shifts mark the end of the modern and the passage
to the postmodern understanding of political economy: (1) from *classicism*
to neoclassicism, (2) from neoclassicism to Keynesianism, and (3) from
Keynesianism to monetarism.

Where classical theory represents the value of an object as *stable*, derived
directly from the labour costs necessary to produce it, neo-classical theory
sees value as momentary, variable, provisionally attributable to the
desirability of the object. Value is dependent upon unpredictable fluctu-
ations, passing fashions and subjective representations of desire. According
to neoclassical theory there is no objective universal measurement of value,
no regulation of exchange in a position of absolute mediation.

Henceforth, value does not pass from the object to the moral constitution
of the subject; rather, it is produced by the subject. The discourse of demand
and desire, consumption and satisfaction enters explicitly into economic
theory simultaneously with the rise of the international stock markets. The
question of value is placed on the order of the consumer. This re-tooling of
the notion of value takes place against a clear ethical backdrop. Not only is
the struggle to acquire and preserve what is valuable continued within a
different paradigm, but also the struggle for what constitutes value becomes
more explicit. Instead of basing itself on a world of indigence, poverty and
disuse, neoclassical theory is based on a world of abundance and satiation
(Goux, 2000).

According to neoclassical theory, the economy achieves equilibrium when
the supply of and demand for money are equal. This equilibrium
presupposes a dichotomy between the 'economic or monetary sphere' and
the 'real sphere'. The economic or monetary sphere consists of the mass of
money, theoretically defined by monetary authorities, which influences
nominal prices. The 'real sphere' consists of a certain number of material

givens: material resources, technologies, inclinations of real individuals, etc. Keynes vigorously denies the theory of a dichotomy consisting of two differing 'spheres' with two independent orders of economic variables (Burgess and Stråth, 1999). For Keynesianism, money is completely integrated in the function of the real economy.

According to Keynes, money cannot be abstracted from its psychological, social and cultural function. Thus Keynes breaks with neoclassicism, and his view of employment as a function of monetary policy sees price as a function of monetary policy. According to Keynes, money plays a certain psychological role in a world dominated by incertitude. Political economy on the individual level is a question of confronting the uncertainty of an unknown future. The political conclusion drawn by Keynesianism is that there is a certain economic efficacy in social protection.

The latter half of the 1970s sees the renaissance of a neoclassical current, which in general explains the crisis of the early 70s by reproaching European governments for too much state intervention under the influence of Keynesianism. In 1978, the Chicago School economist Milton Friedman was awarded the Nobel Prize in economics. His theory of monetarism based on a theory of 'rational anticipation' completed the removal of the last traces of Keynesianism and the re-establishment of neoliberalism as the *status quo* of American–European economic thought. Friedman's neo-quantitative theory returns the discourse of flexibility to the economic dimensions that Keynes had placed at the centre of policy-making. Equilibrium is a function of flexibility, that is to say, a function of uncoupling prices and salaries, as much as possible, from economic manipulation. The individual is seen as a rational actor capable of anticipating work well beyond the present.

Thus, while Keynesianism sees money as a deeply interpenetrating element of the sociocultural fabric of society, Friedman and neo-quantitative or monetarist theory see money as being socioculturally neutral. Money is understood as passive, foreseeable and independent of the sphere of the 'real', The rise of quantitative analysis ('econometrics') and computer-generated economic modeling only serves to strengthen the perspective that political economy is an object for mathematical science, that the unifying dimension of money is an instrumental matter, that cultural self-understanding on any level is basically exhaustible through technologies of identity.

Georg Simmel's *Philosophy of Money* focuses not on the economic science of money but on the structural relation between value and money. It presents, in Simmel's words, 'the pre-conditions that – situated in mental states, in social relations and in the logical structure of reality and values – give money its meaning and its practical position'. It relates money to 'the conditions that determine its essence and the meaning of its existence' (Simmel, 1978: 10). In this sense, it is not 'economic facts' that are the object of the *Philosophy of Money*. The purpose of the analysis is, rather, 'to derive from the surface level of economic affairs a guideline that leads to the ultimate values and things of importance in all that is human' (ibid.: 12).

In this sense, value has a metaphysical status. It is not simply one property among others. Rather, in neo-Kantian style, it is a comprehensive form or category relating to the being of a given object in relation to a given subject (ibid.: 26). Objective perception is not given. It arises as a process of valuation. 'We live in a world of values which arranges the contents of reality in an autonomous order' (ibid.: 25). Like immediate being itself, value cannot be logically demonstrated. Rather it is an original form of our imagination, of what we perceive, experience or believe. Like being, the foundation of value seems to point elsewhere, to a non-present, unspecified foundation. But if we are to follow the trail back to the foundation, we find that it is only a conviction, an affirmation or a recognition. We can only assert the value of a given object by its relation to other objects. All demonstrations of value are an invocation of the need to recognize that there is an object of the same value that has also been recognized (ibid.: 27). Value is not a quality but a structure, indeed constituent of the very structure of reality. Value inferences, says Simmel, are simply the disclosure and clarification of the conditions under which values are realized, without at the same *time* being produced by these conditions.

Thus value is a kind of no man's land of the social matrix. Value is not objective, not a fact. And yet, the subject is indifferent to the value of the object, in the sense, the essence or existence of the subject is not dependent upon some factual value. The subjectivity of the subject is never called into question or brought into play (ibid.: 29). Moreover, like subjectivity in general, valuation is dependent upon a certain historical development. The distinction between subject and object, and the place of valuation in the field of tension between them, is subject to evolution. A reconstruction of Simmel's understanding of this evolution reveals much about Simmel's theory of modernity and the place of value in modern reality.

In a work reminiscent of Weber's historical analysis of ideal types, Simmel plots the evolution of the subject–object constellation from its origin in *Indifferenz*. Consciousness begins as a kind of original unity in an undifferentiated state 'in which the ego and its objects are not yet distinguished' (ibid.: 29–30). Value emerges when humans depart from the original condition of *Indifferenz*, when we become conscious that all needs cannot be immediately satisfied. An object is desired and a means must be used to acquire it (ibid.: 31). *Value* corresponds to the perceived distance and desire created by the distance between subject and object. This perception creates the experience of value.

The development of the distance between objects and subjects is the historical process of cultural evolution and growth. Culture produces an ever-widening 'circle of interests'. The terminus of the historical development of culture is the quite gloomy vision of the technical form of transactions that we see in modern society. Here the domain of value is detached from the domain of the personal and the interpersonal (ibid.: 78).

The end-point of Simmel's reconstruction of the evolution of money in its social context is the transition to the functional character of money and the subsequent decline of the substance of money (Poggi, 1993: 158–63). In the early modern period (Renaissance), money was not yet completely abstracted from the substantial value to which it referred (Simmel, 1978: 84). Money becomes increasingly institutionalized, increasingly involved in a developing public sphere, increasingly a public commodity. Money becomes de-personalized and related to a central institutional organization. The value of money is more commonly associated with the *guarantee* of an agency or institution, namely more or less detached or independent from the act of exchange.

Money can be used in an ever-increasing number of ways, corresponding to an ever-increasing number of value types. Relativism establishes 'the (mutual) condition of things' as 'their sense' (Poggi, 1993: 172; Simmel, 1978: 118). Social reality is thus 'de-substanialized'. Modernity creates multiple societies.

Money makes visible the relativity of social reality, disclosing the 'formula of being'. At the same time the function of money becomes more and more associated with the concentration of values. Not only does the quantity of money increase, but also, in time, the extension of money increases as well. More and more objects are touched by and associated with money. In this way money tends toward its 'pure concept' and away from its attachment to particular or individual substances. Thus, money is involved in the general development, which in every domain of life and in every sense strives to dissolve substance into free-floating processes (Simmel, 1978: 170).

In this way, and despite Simmel's emphasis on the growing functional quality of money, his reconstruction is not a modern story of simple alienation, the detachment of symbol and thing, or signifier and signified. The growing functional side of money carries with it a conceptual or spiritual element. The relations between the contracting parties who use money guarantees its continued function.

Monetary Europe and the federal subject

The blueprints for the European house have undergone immense changes since the proto-federalist vision of Jean Monnet in the early postwar years. According to both Simmel and his successors, the value that forms the culture - the spiritual and ethical basis of the European community - is *praxis*, a process of production.

The question posed by a number of sociologists of money such as Bourdieu, Le Barron, Aglietta, Marechal, Goux, Henaff and others is meant to re-insert value into the philosophy of social relations (Goux, 2000; Bourdieu, 2000; Le Barron, 2000; Aglietta and Gerschlager, 2000; Maréchal, 2001). Whereas the Walrusian neoclassical model focuses on formulating the conditions of general equilibrium in which an autonomous sphere of exchange is modelled according to more or less abstract principles of satisfaction, Aglietta develops a reformulation of equilibrium as a problem based on social parameters (Aglietta and Gerschlager, 2000: 104).

Money thus makes a new entry, not as a frictionless conduit of value, timeless and placeless, but as a mode of regulation. It re-acquires the kind of thickness it possessed once upon a time, in Keynesian theory. It is no longer conceived as transparent but, rather, as both socially connected and capable of exerting political pressure in a way that had long been considered obsolete.

For neoclassical econometrically based theories, the economy is not 'real'. It is a virtual system, an abstract linking of values in flux. In terms of moral or aesthetic value, money is utterly neutral. For the theory of regulation proposed by Aglietta, money is a tool for effecting social and value-based changes. For classical (and neoclassical) theory, money does not do anything, has no concrete grasp on reality, is never a determinate of the social, the cultural or the ethical.

Such a theory of regulation boils down to a theory of the economic subject. If we presume that the economic subject is predefined - that it exists before economic transactions take place – then economic relations are secondary to the subject. The economic subject is thus completely auto-nomous and thereby unaffected by the consequences of the general economy. Economics thus becomes a system of general equilibrium. This system presumes not only the autonomy of the economic subject but also its anonymity. None of the economic subjects invokes the personal identity of itself or any other. Moreover, the equilibrium in question is utterly detached from the economic subject. It is an equilibrium of prices from which the satisfaction of individual subjects is derived.

According to this classical conception, money is purely instrumental. It has no personal or social dimension. Money is one object among others. The alternative proposed by Polanyi, Aglietta and others turns this model on its head (Aglietta and Gerschlager, 2000: 113–14; Polanyi, 2001). It follows that *confidence*, the basis of monetary value, is produced within economic rationality. Confidence is stabilized by elements within the system. A theory of money, which conceives of the economic subject as a product of exchange, will also see confidence as a product of the hierarchy of values. 'What is hierarchical is the common representation - a common good. In order to found confidence, something other than repetition and incorpo-ration is necessity. One requires an opening toward the other' (Aglietta and Gerschlager, 2000: 115).

In modern, market-based democratic societies, this notion of socially produced confidence is extremely problematic. It will not take place within the strict boundaries of political economy, but rather through the formation of a public sphere, and a general public sphere of legitimacy: the European Parliament.

14 War in the name of Europe and the legitimacy of collective violence

European construction, as we know it in the early 21st century, is arguably a late phase of a long utopian project of unification and rationalization dating back to the Roman Empire, perhaps even to Alexander and the Hellenistic period. The particularly *modern* segment of that enterprise, however, begins with the innovations in the international state system brought about by the Treaty at Westphalia in 1648. At Westphalia, war in Europe was transformed into European war.

The notion of 'war in Europe' builds upon a geographical de-limitation. The conflicts of the Thirty Years' War were atomized conflicts played out side-by-side on one great battlefield of Europe. But they were fought in the name of local, even feudal, interests. The new world order at Westphalia gave content to a universal concept of sovereignty. It thereby also gave content to a universal concept of war, a concept based on new notions of sovereignty, collectivity, recognition and political rights. War was no longer war in Europe, but rather European war. The modern European versions of the questions of just war and peace, from Hobbes to Michael Walzer, build upon the conceptual tools and political materials provided in this new international system. The purpose of this chapter is to formulate a special case of the question 'What is Europe?' by asking 'In the name of what Europe may just war be waged?'

The very old question 'What is Europe?' can be reformulated in a number of ways and answered from a number of angles. One may, for example, answer the question of what Europe is by seeking out its origin, by trying to find out what it *originally* was and by identifying with that origin, its eternal essence. Or one may adopt a psychological approach to the question by surveying and cataloguing what Europeans feel when they feel European, or a more social-behaviourist approach by studying the 'impact' or change in behaviour as a function of changes in the European political or social reality. Or one may adopt a more simple, geopolitical approach to the question by asking what *territory* corresponds to the term Europe.

This chapter will take a *pragmatic* approach (in the sense of Pierce or Dewey) to the question of what Europe is. In other words, it will reformulate the question based on the presumption that Europe is what Europe does.

More concretely, it will ask what acts may be carried out *in the name* of Europe? What institutions can be built and what concrete policies can be embarked upon in the name of Europe? Or to be brutally direct: what violence can be undertaken in the name of Europe?

Not incidentally, the Treaty of the European Union takes explicit steps toward the development of a European military, by articulating the founding terms of a Common Foreign and Defence Policy for the European Union. Just how 'European' is the European Union's military policy? What is the European substrate in the notion of a European defence and security identity. Finally, and more concretely, what did the role of the European Union in the Kosovo crisis of 1989–99 have to do with European values, culture and destiny? In many ways, this question simply boils down to a question of sovereignty in a classical sense. In other ways, however, the Kosovo crisis demands a new analysis, a new model of understanding of international relations, with new consequences for an equally new and unheard-of political entity: the European Union.

What is war waged in the name of Europe? The following attempts to develop this question and provide some contours of a response through a simple and relatively conservative reasoning. I will begin by returning to the classical principles of the Augustinian just war tradition, and extracting one of its central principles, that of *right authority*. This principle will then be put into relation with the classical principles of war and sovereignty of Grotius and Hobbes. These notions will then be confronted with the 20th century challenge of globalization and the so-called post-national constellation. Finally, I will ask under what conditions the European Union's ambition toward a unified European concept of security can fulfil the conditions of a European war. I will conclude with several comments on the European security and defence identity in the context of the Kosovo crisis.

The Just War tradition

There seems to be no avoiding the notion that war is *always principled*. The theoretical problem arises with the notion of giving *order* to the principles. Even before Augustine's well-known formulations of the principle of just war, Roman law created the categories designed to associate the notion of an ethnic or cultural collectivity and the rights provided by that collectivity. The *jus ad bellum* tradition articulates a number of themes concerning the ways in which one may rightly or justly resort to war. In the Thomasian rendering, these criteria are: just cause, right authority, right intention, proportionality of ends, last resort, reasonable hope of success, and aim of peace. I will focus on only one of the classical means to justify the use of violence for the attainment of political ends: *right authority*.

'Right authority' is often used synonymously with 'sovereign authority' or 'competent authority' – quite simply, limits the right to authorize force to sovereign political entities. This core concept of right authority has the *prima facie* effect of favouring certain interventionary uses of force in the interests of internationally recognized standards of justice. From this principle, one might argue for the right to use force if necessary for such purposes as combating international terrorism, responding to other forms of international lawlessness such as the traffic in illicit drugs, or systematic and sustained violations of universally recognized human rights (Johnson, 1999: 31–2).

The principle of *proper authority* also raises questions about intervention under international auspices. Clearly, international organizations up to and including the United Nations, lack sovereignty in the traditional sense. Thus the question immediately becomes: Without sovereignty, is there any right to authorize force? Classic just-war doctrine would say no, reserving that right to sovereign states. Still, in contemporary debate, international authorization for interventionary use of military force is often claimed, though on the basis of *consensus* (as in the Security Council resolutions relating to the Gulf War and to the United Nations protective force in Somalia) rather than sovereignty.

The question for us remains: Assuming that *right authority* is a legitimate source of moral justification for military intervention, to what extent can the European Union be said to possess right authority in some radically new sense? In order to develop our reasoning in the direction of an answer to this question, we must first turn to the conception of *sovereignty* in the classical tradition, and ask in what way the globalization of the late 20th century has brought changes to that conception.

The classical model of sovereignty

Grotius

In the history of political and legal theory, the thinking of Hugo Grotius has endured by virtue of the fact that it formulated a new system of ideas at a conjuncture in the history of European geopolitics, namely the decline of the international order of the Middle Ages. The concept of sovereignty in the Middle Ages was based on two pillars: the ecclesiastical authority of the Church of Rome and the political order of the emperors. But by the time Grotius wrote his principal work, *De jure bellie ac pacis* (1620–25), the economic, social and spiritual orders that had dominated were disintegrating and the Thirty Years' War was raging across Europe.

By the conclusion of the Thirty Years' War, there was clearly no chance of recovering either of the two pillars of the Middle Age order. Thus Grotius set out to formulate the principles of a new, humanized order based on law. The new international order built upon the presumption that juridical thinking was the new science of that age, and that such thinking would be capable of founding *universal* principles, principles applicable across the European geopolitical spectrum.

The foundation of that universal anchoring was double: on the one hand, the notion of *natural law,* on the other the notion of *contract.* Like the Stoics, Grotius derived the principles of natural law from reason and the rationality of humans. And in the shadow of his master, Erasmus, Grotius developed a humanized notion of the *contract (pacta sunt servanda)* as the highest authority within and between states.

Hobbes

The sovereign remained the anchoring point of the political and legal system. Hobbes formulates the logic of the sovereign in its most forceful form in his writings from the 1640s and 50s. Hobbes shares the two foundational principles of Grotius: the rationality of human enterprise based on the law of nature and the force of the social contract. Yet, as is known, Hobbes refused the notion that humans were *naturally* social or political. The state of nature is pre-political and pre-social.

The social contract in the schema of Hobbes is thus a counter-natural moment, a rational gesture with the aim of self-preservation. The social contract is the agreement between individuals founding civil society not to resist the commands of the sovereign. The contract is rational only to the extent that the egotism out of which it springs, is inherently rational. The notion of justice is entirely related to the contract. It is completely humanized, independent of any transcendental authority. To be just is to heed the contract; to be unjust is to deny it. Injury is the non-performance of covenants.

This notion of justice implies a fundamental broadening of the notion of just war. Objective justification for war is no longer necessary since it is fear of one's enemy that is the source of civil society, and thus the source of the notion of justice contained in the civil contract. In this sense, Hobbes introduces an essential distinction between *justice* and *legality.* For Hobbes, it is possible to speak of the legality of war without making reference to a transcendental notion of justice. The political union, just like justice and injustice are defined in terms of legality, that is, in terms of correspondence or non-correspondence with the contract on which the union is based.

This brings us finally to another essential innovation on the part of Hobbes: the legal fiction of the sovereign as a person. Based on his notion of the civil contract, Hobbes reasons that duty is only duty to one's self. There is no duty to any other individual. The fiction of the sovereign as a person creates a political subject with a will that can represent the will of all others. The legislation of the sovereign is the self-legislation of all political subjects. All political subjects can and should regard the actions of the sovereign as their own actions. The sovereign *is* the political union. How does the process of globalization, which has so marked the last two decades, effect the notion of the sovereign as a unified, singular political subject of sovereignty formulated by Hobbes?

Globalization and post-national sovereignty

The European postwar period is marked by a transformation in the notion of sovereignty as a political function to sovereignty as a function of economic variables. In the immediate postwar years, the Bretton Woods system, together with the IMF and the World Bank, assured a regime based on a balance between nationally determined economic interests and the ideals of international market liberalism. When this system collapsed in the early 1970s, a new constellation of transnational liberalism emerged in which the international mobility of capital and labour, and the post-Fordist ideology of 'flexibility', were central. In this regard, multinational interests and organizations became the most well-defined competitors of the European nation-state (Habermas, 1998a: 119).

A new sociology of globalization has gone to great lengths to map out the changes in social structures and forms of society in the moment *national* society becomes *transnational* society, moving beyond the territorial boundaries and institutions of the traditional European nation-state. Ulrich Beck, for example, formulates the question of globalization as the question of what he calls 'second modernity', in which the notion of global society displaces that of the national society (Beck, 1999). A broad definition of globalization would include a consideration of worldwide expansion of telecommunication, mass tourism or mass culture, mass technology, arms trade and ecological overload. A more narrow definition involves the exploding of national borders and the obsolescence of national categories, values, controls and rights.

Globalization goes beyond the displacement of sovereignty and power from one political subject to another. It involves a change in the very concept of sovereignty, that is, in the concentration of power and the legitimacy of that concentration. The ebb and flow of money, the velocity of exchange, the resistance and pressure of convertibility, replace the subject–object relation of traditional understanding of power.

Among the more radical political questions that are formulated in the wake of these changes is the following: Is democracy still the most relevant source of legitimization in an era of declining democratic participation, progressive detachment of dynamics of power from democratic control mechanisms, failing correspondence between national democratic political organs and transnational political issues and restructuring of the European polity?

First, we must underscore that the post-Westphalian era of the nation-state marks not only the emergence and development of modern juridical principles of rights and national sovereignty, but also inaugurates the development of the principles of international law, which expand and modernize the principles of the just-war tradition. The obsolescence of the nation-state opens a complex set of questions about the sovereignty of territorial states, about the protection of rights and laws based on cultural collectivity, and about democratic legitimacy in general. In *The Post-National Constellation*, Habermas plots out four immediate consequences of such decay: (1) the effectiveness of state functions, (2) the sovereignty of the territorial state, (3) collective identity, and (4) the democratic legitimacy of the nation-state (Habermas, 1998a: 105–22).

In the era of globalization, the nation-state is increasingly powerless with regard to control and administrative functions traditionally based on the state. As a consequence, one can observe a general decline in the coherence of traditional systems of international collaboration such as the UN, the OECD, NATO, etc. In their place, international 'regimes' emerge – informal international arrangements and accommodations steered by 'soft power' become more dominant.

The question of the decline of democratic legitimacy of the nation-state clearly concerns the question of national legitimacy. The classical idea of the right to national self-determination is no longer supported by a collective national polity, but rather by sub-national units – that is, by a complex and composite cultural substrate – or by supra-national interests. In what way does the European Union enter the fray of globalization?

The European Union is neither an intergovernmental agency nor a complex set of transnational interests. It is, however, an aspirant for displacing, to one extent or another, the European nation-states. The degree to which such a displacement is desirable or even possible is, of course, a matter of considerable debate. Euro-sceptics, market-Europeans, Euro-federalists and partisans of 'global governance' compete for legitimacy in this political, social and juridical debate.

What does it mean to Europeanize war? This question boils down to asking whether or not the European Union can, in any sense, displace, reverse or replace the ailing nation-state as a sovereign basis for just war. Or, the more primal version of this question: In what sense can the EU constitute a sovereign body in a post-national reality?

Attempts at the reconstruction of an internally based polity as a basis for post-national sovereignty have been variable. The 'return of the social' in European politics can very well prove to be the beginning of a new kind of sovereignty built upon an internal coherence of European peoples (Hoffmann, 2000: 193–5).

In post-Enlightenment political theory, the notion of national sovereignty is complemented by that of universal rights. Kant's *Metaphysics of Morals* (1797) introduces a radical concept of freedom and a new concept of legality. *Legality*, for Kant, implies that all laws shall be simultaneously coercive (*Zwangsgesetze*) and norms based on duty (*Pflichtgesetz*). In other words, a law is duty-based coercion. It is coercion, which I in my freedom choose for myself. Sovereignty, for Kant, combines the force of law (*Zwangsgesetz*) and moral obligation based on universal rights (*Pflichtgesetz*). It seems to me that this Kantian formula remains viable on the European level. The universal rights proper to the European cultural tradition (*Pflichtgesetz*) fit the bill, while the question of a monopoly on power (*Zwangsgesetz*) seems to be the final element necessary in the construction of a European cosmopolitan sovereignty (Kant, 1996). What effect can this juridical pair have on the aspiration for a European military force based on European sovereignty?

Evolution of the notion of European security

The Treaty of Lisbon opens a new chapter in the story of European construction. Like the tradition of just war, this innovation can be traced back to the international political order established at Westphalia in 1648. Its more immediate prehistory, however, begins in the post-WW II era of European construction (Stråth and Magnusson, 2001).

The Schuman Plan of 1950, in its principles as well as in its intentions, is the direct predecessor of the TEU. Its aim was related to the security threat posed by the lingering tension between France and Germany, and to a desire to address the possibility for repeated conflict through political union of one kind or another. The Schuman Plan was a relatively moderate approach to the problem, based on the unification of the coal and steel industries of the two countries. Security was immediately associated with economic interests.

This association became the bulwark of European construction in the Treaty of Rome and all of its revisions up until the Maastricht Treaty, when the notion of security at last saw the light of day as a matter of geopolitics, rather than as a subdivision of national and international economics.

Interestingly enough, this division in thought about Europeanization comes at a conjuncture in the *conceptual* history of geopolitics. At the very moment when European geopolitics and international economics are distinct in the Treaty, the very *concept* of geopolitics is completely saturated with the economic underside of globalization.

For a complex set of reasons, which we have only begun to document, the European Community from the 1950s to the 1980s evolved in the direction of an economic community. This 'economization' of the early European construction, begun by the Treaty of Rome in 1957, had an important side-effect in the area of security: it cultivated an entrenched dependence on the United States. The attempt by France to create a European Defence Community, and, later, the Fouchet Plan, were both too little and too late.

The Delors era of the 1980s relaunches a reinvigorated European Community with the Single European Act and its famous '4 liberties' based on a principled set of economic necessities for the establishment of a European common market. Riding upon the impetus of the European economic construction, the Maastricht Treaty was signed in 1991, establishing the European Union and announcing its five primary objectives: the standardized *aquis communautaire*, a common currency, the enhancement of a system of interior co-operation, European citizenship, and the 'affirmation on the international scene of the European identity through the development of a common foreign and security policy'.

I would like to develop the meaning of this identity and its place in the logic of sovereign war and peace, on the one hand, and just war on the other. My argument has three moments. First: security presupposes identity. Second: political economy is a viable identity formation. And third, security, political economy, and identity converge in the concept of *security identity*.

First, and as we have seen, the Hobbesian model of sovereignty is based on the formation of a political identity and of the collapsing of the national interests on the *persona* of the sovereign. The Westphalian model of national sovereignty is impossible without this notion of the concentration of the essence of the nation onto one unified, coherent and homogeneous identity. In the post-national constellation associated with the development of the European Union, this identity remains indispensable.

Second, European identity has settled into a privileged form of collective expression in the discourse of political economy. Common values and interests, shared heritage and ambition find their most pronounced articulation in the economic version of these notions: monetary value, shared monetary interest, harmonization, common culturally determined economic policy such as the CAP, etc.

Third, these strands of security and identity, connected and simultaneously held distinct by their mutual consolidation through the discourse of economics, have at last converged in the TEU as *security identity* (Hoffmann, 2000: 190).

The evolution of the notion of security has been further shaped by changes in the *nature* of Europe's geopolitical 'others'. As Pierre Hassner and Jacques Rupnik have recently pointed out, the discourse of cultural collectivity and democratic values, in relation to which the notion of European security has evolved, takes another aspect from the point of view of eastern and central Europe. From the western European point of view, the EU is understood as an embodiment of European democratic values. On the other hand, from the eastern point of view, it is NATO that is the primary purveyor of democratic values, and the EU is primarily perceived as a bureaucratic-economic organism (Hassner and Rupnik, 1999).

The apparent irreducible kernel of the European *troika*: European identity–economy–security plays the paradoxical role of both motor behind a common foreign and security policy and its impediment.

As I suggested above, national identity in the form of a national polity, is the traditional basis for the legitimacy of military action in relation to other sovereign nation-states. Transferring that kind of legitimacy to a European level implies reformulating the concept of polity in European terms. A clear strategy for such a reformulation was clearly by way of the notion of a European identity. Indeed the theme of collective interest and shared values recurs again and again in the official documents related to the construction of a European common foreign and defence policy.

To be sure, the concept of European identity has had an intriguing career in the post-WWII process of European construction. It is first launched in the Commission's 1972 Declaration on European Identity, which defines European identity based on three pillars: (1) common heritage, interests and special obligations within the community, (2) the 'dynamic nature' of European unification, and (3) the extent to which the Nine were 'already acting together in relation to the rest of the world' as it is formulated in the 1972 Declaration on European Identity (European Commission, 1973: 492). All three are based on internal unity, heritage and internal coherence with regard to the rest of the world. That 1972 Declaration was part of a tactical effort to relaunch the process of European construction, which was, however, floundering in the economic crisis of the early and mid-1970s.

In the subsequent lull in political activity, from the 1970s to the late 1980s, the concept of identity went under cover only to re-emerge later as the anchoring point for the notion of a European *defence*, in Article J (Title V) of the Maastricht Treaty, and simultaneously in the negotiations between the Western European Union and NATO, in conjunction with the ratification of the Amsterdam Treaty in 1997.

In the Maastricht Treaty, the notion of European identity was inscribed in the discourse of the 'third pillar', the Common Foreign and Security Policy, attached to the logic of international strategic otherness of Article J. The Common Foreign and Security Policy includes 'the eventual framing of a common defence policy, which might in time lead to a common defence' (Article J.4). This implementation should serve, according to the Preamble, to reinforce European identity and its independence in order to promote peace, security and progress in Europe and in the world.

Up until Maastricht, 'European identity' was used to denote the cultural unity-in-diversity of Europe, thus informing in widely divergent ways the legitimizing way in which the Europe Union was to be constructed. Maastricht reduced the concept of identity in the best case to a basis for international diplomacy or, in the worst case, to a quasi-militarized kernel, a celestial fix from which to navigate a defence policy in an increasingly complex global battlefield.

Parallel to the launching of the Maastricht Treaty, the western European Union – the conglomerate of EU nations that belong to NATO – made its own declaration of new principles, coining the expression 'European Security and Defence Identity', which it declares as its responsibility to develop. ESDI is conceived as a sort of conduit with the North Atlantic Alliance, and at the same time an assertion of difference, of unique interests, aspirations and capabilities, also on the military level.

The final brick in the evolution of the concept of European identity is the development of the European Security and Defence Identity. The

European Council, in its meeting in Cologne in June 1999, made bold use of the post of High Representative to appoint Javier Solana, former Spanish Foreign Minister, Secretary General of NATO during the Kosovo crisis, and later Secretary General of the Western European Union (Hannay, 2000). The Kosovo crisis brings the European Union face-to-face with the realities of its role of its new 'security identity'. A new Europe meets a new concept of security.

The Kosovo test

In the best dialectical fashion, the Kosovo crisis was both the test of the new European security policy and the reality that created the policy. The short version of the story is that the European Foreign and Security Policy was extremely weak when put to the test. The crisis underscored, among other things, the disunity among the European nations, the discontinuity between the EU and NATO, and, not least, the continued dependence on the Americans, both militarily and diplomatically.

The principle facts of the crisis are well known. In 1989, Kosovo is, for all practical purposes, erased from the Serbian political map. With it, disappear the political rights of Kosovars. In the period 1989–98, Belgrade refuses any form of dialogue with the moderate Kosovar Albanians, provoking the formation of the UCK. By 1998, Belgrade is thus furnished with a justification for the repression of the UCK, making no distinction between partisans, non-partisans and civilians. This leads to the UN Resolution 1203, in October 1998, demanding a ceasing of hostilities. The hostilities nonetheless continued through the negotiations at Rambouillet, which ended in February 1999. After the Raçak massacre on January 15, and repeated threats of bombing, NATO forces began bombing on 24 March 1999.

The run-up to the bombing in April 1999 was framed by a complex network of competing institutional and state competencies. This included a strange interplay of diplomacy, humanitarian reasoning and more or less impotent military posturing between Richard Holbrooke, mandated by the UN Security Council, the OSCE mandated by the EU, and NATO, which boldly forged the new concept of 'humanitarian air strikes' in order to grant legitimacy for its own military action.

All the major international bodies swiftly condemned the action by the FRY/Serbs, but no coherent action was taken to back up that condemnation. No action was found to be adequate to the *principled* charges of injustice. The question thus stands as to whether such 'coherent action' to 'back up' moral condemnation is at all possible. Is there a concept of *security* that adequately embraces a set of moral principles and at the same time the set of military tools capable of enacting them?

The Kosovo crisis is, for all intents and purposes, the child of the Westphalian international system. Yet we can stretch the point further by saying that the Kosovo crisis was an *unavoidable* consequence of the Westphalian international system. For the irreducible paradox at the heart of the crisis is that both the *principles* put into practice by the Kosovar Albanians in forming the UCK and the *principles* deployed by the Serbian leadership were derived from that system. Both were 'legal' in terms of international law. Both were based on rights and rule of law. According to the tenets of international law, Belgrade's intervention in Kosovo was legal in the sense that it fell within the bounds of national sovereignty and of the right to exercise a monopoly of state violence within that framework. The UCK's assertion of Kosovar Albanian rights was also legal, based on the tenet of 'national' self-determination of peoples. It must be added, however, that the original intention of the latter principle is to protect the rights of peoples under colonization.

The NATO bombings – the 'humanitarian bombings' – were considered illegal by most because they were not sanctioned by the Security Council, the only organ considered capable of providing legitimacy to such international action. Those who ordered the bombings argued simply that they responded to the *spirit* of previous resolutions, if not to the *letter*. From another point of view, the western allies argued that the strikes were legitimate because they were carried out in the name of preventing humanitarian catastrophe. From the point of view of international law, this argument is simply invalid.

It is not at all clear that the Common Foreign and Security Policy, which was finally formulated in the Maastricht Treaty will become a 'defence ministry' – the legitimate military wing of a sovereign state in the classic modern manner. Indeed, the more likely evolution of the post-national constellation in Europe is the further transformation of the discourse of economics as the discourse of security. Despite the fact that the European arm of NATO, the Western European Union, announces its future European military entity as an *identity*, the economic power of the European Union seems to be the weapon of global politics.

Long before it gave itself an official Foreign and Security Policy, the EU was involved in foreign and security policy. The tool of that policy, aside from traditional diplomacy, was economic encouragement and sanctions, humanitarian aid, promotion of dialogue and encouragement of the respect of human rights. Yet, without doubt, the EU inhabits a middle ground between civic power and military power. Foreign policy identity has always been articulated as economic identity (Adam *et al.*, 1999; Hoffmann, 2000).

This is part and parcel of the structural logic of the European public sphere. Those with legitimacy in a certain area of policy cannot act; those without it do act. At the very moment when the European Union is eager to posit its security identity, that identity seems to belong to another plane. The interpretation of the Kosovo situation by the international community was schizophrenic in just this way. All considered Kosovo the 'powder keg' of the Balkans. Yet precisely this realization led to hesitancy (Weller, 1999: 33). The emerging international constitutional system has a negative feedback loop: the need for action leads to the impossibility of action.

The classical explanation of the failures of Europe in this dark hour of its 20th century history would argue that there is only a shaky coherence in international politics because of a complex network of crossing interests. An alternative explanation would be that these inconsistencies are imminent in the very *concept* of security. The post-Westphalian concept of security, in order to be security, must harbour and even nurture the tension between the unity of interests and the disunity of the sovereign self.

Utopia is just not what it used to be. Primarily because war and peace are not what they used to be, and thereby security is not what it used to be. The EU failed in Kosovo, not merely because it had a bad policy, or lacked political will or military muscle to back it up – NATO had all these and failed as well – but also because the post-national constellation is still forging a new understanding of what peace and security actually mean.

Conclusion

The many faces of European security

The value-laden nature of security and insecurity has contributed to a fragmentation of both perceived European security threats and European approaches to these perceived challenges. The adaptation of European institutions to this new reality has been difficult, thwarted by the wide variations in cultures of law enforcement, border control, intelligence and diplomacy, and, not least, new cultures of fear and prudence. In our time it is clear that there is not one European security, only European securities.

This shift to a new security environment has at the same time brought a shift in the areas of focus of security thinking in Europe and, accordingly, a re-tooling of the roles of security institutions, the scope of their responsibilities, the European partners they work with, the international rights regimes they answer to and the source and nature of the threats they are confronting (den Boer and Monar, 2002; Bigo, 2000; Grabbe, 2000; Haack, 2006). This new security continuum of internal and external security has created a novel situation whereby concepts and institutional arrangements traditionally aimed at internal security challenges (police, national and local information, administrative authorities, social agencies, etc.) become increasingly challenged to address matters traditionally reserved for the external security professionals (military and international police forces, foreign affairs officials, international legal agencies, diplomatic corps, etc.), while the latter are increasingly required to deal with matters reserved for the former.

European construction and the globalization of security

In general terms, Europeanization has taken the form of a certain kind of globalization. From its very first manifestations in the Coal and Steel Community (1951) to its pillarization in the Maastricht Treaty (1993) to its economization in the European Monetary Union (1999) and, finally, to its re-tooling as a fully-fledged global actor in the Lisbon Treaty, the European project has evolved as an attempt to provide institutional responses to global processes. The general characteristics of the globalization process are well known. They centre in one way or another on the weakening of the sovereignty of the modern nation-state, on the development of transnational networks and institutions, and on the global flow of information, capital and human beings (Burgess, 2000; Burgess and Stråth, 2001; Delanty and Rumford, 2005; Bigo, 2002; Risse, 2005; Tonra, 2003). Thus, in a general way, one can observe, in a time-frame that reaches not only to the postwar European construction, but also centuries back, a growing porosity or even blurring of nation-state borders. This large-grain definition of globalization can be plotted far into the past, with origins and forms that precede by far the modern, technology-driven, flow-based conceptions. And yet if we are attentive to the distinct metaphysics of globalization, then its core experience can be related to a general experience of interconnectedness with the foreign and experience of the 'world' as otherness, and of this experience-of-the-world as threat and insecurity (Appadurai, 2001; Bamyeh, 2000; Bauman, 1998; Featherstone, 1990).

In the hectic months and years between the Yalta summit of February 1945 and the Schuman Declaration in May 1950, the globalized security challenges of World War I were addressed by the architectures of the European project as a need to deploy a certain set of unifying principles of market liberalism to the divergent economic interests of a Europe torn by war. Globalization was seen as a set of economic interdependencies on a global scale. The rest of this story is well known. The early form of Europeanization that responded to it was a market liberal perspective designed to enhance the free movement of goods, services and workers (Burgess and Stråth, 2001). Through setting up the European Coal and Steel Community in 1951, postwar Europeanization came to mean an enforced dismantling of national borders in terms of trade and commerce: the harmonization and externalization of border controls and the free flow of goods, services and capital. This globalizing political transformation was primarily a legal and institutional process. It consisted in part in dismantling of institutional inconsistencies between the original member states and, in part, of strengthening common institutional logics and procedures (Cowles et al., 2001; Risse, 2005). This gradual institutional-ization of the ideology of free movement of goods, services and capital, together with the evolution of transnational economies, naturally led to a gradual dismantling of the EU's internal borders. It also led to the emergence and generalization of a kind of European political sovereignty. This consolidation, *sui generis* in nature, is still evolving today, and is the object of ongoing scholarly and political debate (Balibar, 2004; Bellamy and Castiglione, 1997; Carlsnaes et al., 2004).

With the gradual – though still relatively marginal – harmonization and co-ordination of institutions of governance at its internal borders, a growing porosity of national borders developed and began to be felt in terms of an interlinking of national economic and political institutions in Europe. In this way, at least at first glance, Europeanization has taken the form of a globalization project in tune with its time. At the same time, however, the implementation of this version of Europeanization has, in more recent times, revealed the institutional difficulty of harmonizing and standardizing widely differing institutional cultures with their distinct cultural and social value premises. The shared economic interests of the Member States of the European Union did not – and still does not – constitute an adequately common ground for institutionalizing the universal core of Europe. The relation between Member States among themselves, relative to the EU, and as a component of the EU's relations to the geopolitical reality outside of the EU, continues to evolve.

Globalization has also brought significant changes to the present threats landscape. There is thus a consensus today, both among scholars and practitioners, that a wide range of security threats, both new and traditional, confront both states, individuals and societies. New forms of nationalism, ethnic conflict and civil war, information technology, biological and chemical warfare, resource conflicts, pandemics, mass migrations, transnational terrorism, and environmental dangers challenge the conventional means of understanding threats and of assuring the security of all regions of the world. The growing awareness of these new threats is challenging the way in which the principles and tasks of security scholarship are presently understood. No one state can manage the array of threats to its own security, nor can any one state manage the threats to the security of its neighbours both inside and outside Europe. In the globalized setting, the challenge of maintaining security is no longer limited to the traditional foreign policy and military tools of the European Member States.

Migration and the shift of internal/external borders

Starting from the immediate post-Cold War environment, but then intensifying after 11 September 2001, the phenomenon that has had the most significant consequences for the course of European security thinking is the problem of migration. Not only have patterns of migration flows changed significantly in the last decades, but also an increasingly globalized awareness of the migration of both European citizens and foreigners, both within and toward Europe, has had growing political consequences. Perhaps even more important is the impact it has on the European sense of self, of cultural values, social conventions, human rights and citizenship. Thus in cultural terms, the challenge of migration reaches deep within social and cultural boundaries and – problematizing their self-understandings their rules of inclusion and exclusion and the ways of circulating with each other.

In a parallel way, the management of security in Europe has faced considerable challenges in the new era of globalized threats. The threats facing Europe, no longer exclusively 'hard', but rather often 'soft', no longer respect the geopolitical borders of the nation-state and the European Union. More importantly still, they traverse and resist the institutional 'borders' and arrangements traditionally designed to manage them (social agencies, informational authorities, police, etc.). The most significant effect of this shift is that the lives of citizens are no longer regulated at the physical borders. The border operations traditionally provided for by the nation-state (border controls and security guards, passport authorities, etc.) have, in this way, been shifted outward. At the same time, a growing number of European and international organizations took on increasingly dominant roles entirely detached from nation-state sovereignty, further contributing to the interrelatedness of non-national institutions and regions, and further weakening both the role and capacity of traditional sovereignty arrangements.

On the theoretical plane, this shifting of the border between the internal and the external can be traced to changes in the notion of sovereignty and the role of the state in the protection of its citizens. Yet while the newly institutionalized blurring of internal borders is a direct consequence of political interventions in inter-state sovereignty arrangements, with the aim of increasing efficiency and efficacy of operations at the inter-state level, a number of important changes can be observed along the external borders of the EU. These changes, while more and more commonly observed, remain, in general, inadequately theorized (Walker, 2007; c.a.s.e. Collective, 2007; Salmon, 2006; Rieker, 2006; Ekengren et al., 2006; c.a.s.e. Collective, 2006; Wivel, 2005), in particular, the question of changes in the security architecture of Europe. Since the end of the Cold War another intensification has taken a clear form: the security threat to Europe increasingly identified as 'transversal', that is, anchored in immigrant or minority milieus. The sphere of internal crime-fighting and external war-making were henceforth blurred (Bigo, 2000).

The management of insecurities through technology and the development of new technologies of security are increasingly becoming a policy priority for the European Union and its member states. This new emphasis on technological responses to insecurity is justified in governmental arenas through the argument that this drive is rendered necessary by the environment of new global threats of the post-bipolar era. The novelty of this environment, it is claimed, lies in the transnational and asymmetric dimension of danger, and thus in its unpredictability, as compared to the previous period. Threatening developments, in this perspective, range from transnational organized crime to illegal migrations, and include various forms of political violence, including new forms of warfare. New technologies of control and surveillance, which rely in particular on evolutions in technologies of information and communication (TICs), are, in this perspective, deemed crucial, because they supposedly permit to move beyond reactive measures, developing the capacities of security agencies to anticipate threats and act proactively.

The logic of value in the internal/external security continuum

The challenge of managing migration has led the evolution of security thinking in Europe headlong into its own value-based foundations. Europe is often construed (in particular by Europeans) as a project based on a set of shared values. It is these values that permit the EU to constitute itself as a quasi-sovereign political body, endowed with the legitimacy necessary to execute monetary policy, enact law and deploy a foreign and security policy (Burgess, 2008). Such values are thus the alpha and omega of the security in the broad sense of the project. Security is a state in which the wellbeing of individuals, groups or society is in terms of what it values, be that a certain form of life, language, religion, wealth or power. If the European Union faces new security challenges, these are deeply related to the political, social, cultural and ethical values with which it identifies and with which it differentiates itself from what is outside it. The internal/external security continuum corresponds to an encroaching ambiguity of the 'inside-ness' and 'outside-ness' of security practices.

The conceptual logic of the border always implies a set of values distinguishing the codes of behaviour of the in-group from the codes of the out-group. From the point of view of individuals, the border separates those who belong from those who do not belong, it protects and shelters, ascribes privileges and obligations. From the point of view of society, the border takes the individual into a system that controls and monitors him or her. Borders in this sense protect from the threatening others who are outside of the collective while simultaneously protecting society from the others that are within.

In a traditional sense, Europe's security has historically revolved around the presumption of a distinct set of European values. These values, which are embedded in a wide range of treaties and legal and policy documents, are presumed to be shared by all Europeans, thus forming the foundation of European identity (Burgess, 2002, 2008). Thus European security identity stems from the political notion that such distinct European values are to be defended, indeed defending Europe is identical to defending these values. However, like values in general, the European values, be they political, legal, social or cultural, are by no means restricted to the political borders of Europe. The prevalence of values, their validity and significance, varies as a function of political, social and cultural change. Thus to the security challenges that traverse the internal/external security must added another challenge, that of the continuity and coherence of the value-based premises that both support Europe as a distinct identity and exceed its political borders.

In this sense, Europe's external borders are not, and never were, simply physical barriers. They are also demarcations between 'value zones' where certain regimes of social, political, legal and moral rights are distinctly valid and where others are not. Yet from a pragmatic point of view, Europe's borders also represent the limit that differentiates what security practices may be implemented – tools and means of policing and criminology, diplomatic protocol, and military modes of operation, etc. The borders differentiate institutional interests and aims, and the complex interplay of European and international political norms and codes. These ethical borders of Europe are clearly not identical to the physical borders of Europe. Rather, they form a system of value-based principles and practices that both circumscribe the physical borders of Europe, and also give them political, social and cultural legitimacy. Why then do European security practices struggle at present to adapt the institutionalized logic of physical borders to the evasive and complex ethical borders that reflect the threats of the present time?

This evolution in the complex set of ideas surrounding internal and external security takes place parallel to a consolidation of a European internal and external security identity. In other words, at the moment where the complexity of threat to Europe reaches a high point, the political principles of inclusion and exclusion, defence against foreign and domestic threats, protection against crime and refuge and shelter put into question the meaningfulness of differentiating between internal and external security. As European law- and policy-making becomes more distinct in its broad expression of the political principles of internal and external security in Europe, the practices of security in Europe are being put to the test by transnational security threats.

What are the *practices* that make up the internal/external security continuum? How do they support and legitimate the implicit logic of ethical values that, in turn, structure the continuum of security practices In Europe? We can distinguish four main dimensions or sub-themes of internal/external security practice, each with its own approach to the value dimensions of securing Europe: (1) the proliferation and intensification of security technologies for surveillance and border control, (2) hybrid legal solutions to the new trans-border legal dilemmas, (3) challenges to traditional nation-based criminology and policing practices, and (4) challenges to the value orientations of CFSP/EDSP implementation. All four grow out of conceptual and political traditions based on a relatively clear distinction between the internal and the external.

Proliferation and intensification of security technologies

Through the last decades – but in particular since the attacks of Madrid – technological approaches to security have become widely prioritized. This resort to a technological management of insecurities is, however, not just a natural and functional outcome of the existence of new threats and the availability of technologies. Two dynamics can be underscored. On the one hand, we can observe a certain evolution in security technology. It is dependent upon material feasibility, but it is also informed by developments among the professionals of the security industry, as well as by their relations with policy-makers and analysts. On the other hand, we are also witnesses to the emergence of ever-new applications of technologies of security. Technology is not an autonomous phenomenon (Väyrynen, 1998). It develops within an environment where threat is perceived, a social and cultural setting where its need is conceptualized, and a place and space where it is deployed.

While some security development initiatives still focus on traditional, reactive/defensive technologies (e.g. the Galileo system and its application for border control), the main focus of security technology programmes in Europe today is on the intersection between biometrics and databases (O'Neil, 2005; Ross and Jain, 2007; Lyon, 2008). The development of such technologies converges with the rise in prominence of discourses and practices of anticipation and pro-activity in the management of insecurities. The connections between these processes and, in particular, the role played by the professionals of the security industry in the promotion, funding and adoption of new technological instruments, remains understudied. It is clear that the blurring of the traditional distinction between the practices of internal and external security is further accelerated by this technological innovation in the management of insecurities, which allows for activities of control and surveillance to expand beyond borders and into the future. Practices such as the use of biometrics and databases or the provision of risk analyses based on profiling, are increasingly becoming components of the activities of security agencies (Liberatore, 2007).

Such practices have significant ethical implications closely linked to new technologies of control and surveillance, and bolster the capacity of security agencies to intrude into the private lives of EU-citizens and non-citizens alike. They create major potentialities of encroachment upon fundamental rights and freedoms. They have, in other words, important ethical implications, the most consequential amongst which is the risk of discriminating, through information processing, against whole categories of population.

Legal practices of the internal/external security continuum

Whereas external security is understood as external security in relation to something other, something beyond the state's borders, something different, *internal* security, by contrast, refers to insecurity of individual citizens and society relative to themselves, relative to other people living within a state's borders. This distinction, however, itself entrenched in international politics, becomes increasingly more difficult to uphold. It has been progressively weakened together with the dichotomy of law (binding judgements and principles of legality) and politics (from diplomacy to war). In this sense, the growing acceptance of security as an individual right in European case law seems to be a factor that influences the relationship between internal and external security. For example, the expanding recognition in the European Court of human rights duties to be respected abroad by the European Member States challenges traditional understanding of the states' duties in and outside the territory (Amoore, 2006; Germain and Kenny, 2005; Olsen, 2004).

In the same vein, the theory of the state of exception and the legal/political questions connected to it impinge on the core of the EU and member state security policies. These questions concern the tension between governance through law and governance through management, and bring to the fore concrete questions related to judicial protection, such as the role of national courts and of the European Court of Justice, and to accountability (de Hert, 2005a, 2005b; de Hert and Gutwirth, 2003). Data protection has become equally unstable in recent years. The relation between First Pillar and Third Pillar data protection provisions remain unresolved in the new ambient insecurity. The relation between the SIS II regulation and the Visa Information System is illustrative of this gradual change, as is the link between EU security networks EUROPOL, EUROJUST, EURODAC and FRONTEXT, and the exchange of information between them. The blurring of the distinction between internal and external security parallels that between the concepts of war and crime and the evolving discourse concerning collaboration between security agencies and institutions at the national and western level (police, intelligence services, military professionals, private security institutions) (Anderson and Apap, 2002; Apap and Carrera, 2003).

As a consequence, a new set of legal safeguards will need to be developed based upon new methods of collaboration and data sharing relative to migration. In addition, there are new legal challenges to be faced in the fields of domestic legislation and anti-terrorist legislation. It will survey the state-of-the-art of domestic anti-terrorist legislation in EU countries, evaluating them in terms of standards of protection (checks and balances) for individual liberties provided in the European Convention on Human Rights and clarifying the conditions for the application of Article 15 of the Convention, which allows contracting states to derogate from the rights guaranteed by the Convention in time of 'war or other public emergency threatening the life of the nation'. Given its intrusive effects on individual liberties, there is a need to consider a review of the procedure for the adoption of anti-terrorist measures and laws (Guild, 2004, 2007; Kuijper, 2004). Internal/external security parallels the transformation of violence and conceptions of criminality, and determines juridical means for hindering intelligence services from contributing to a merging of internal and external security rights. In this sense, the shift of the logic and rules *inside* the state, and the rule of law, will have consequences for the notion of international human rights.

The shifting role of security professionals

Illegal activities across national and European borders have expanded steadily in the last decades. A wide range of contraband, human trafficking, narcotics and weapons is not only a threat to society itself, but also linked to global networks involved in financing terrorism or other illegal activities. The international character of such criminality puts it in proximity to forms of political violence, or ethnic or sectarian conflicts. Thus in the sphere of criminal violence, the local, national and international levels are become easily overlapping or mixed. These significant changes in the landscape of crime, all of them, to a greater or lesser degree, caused by changes in the European security landscape, have distinct consequences for law enforcement on the nation-state level. National law enforcement agencies are forced to make a transition from policing on a national level to policing in an entirely different European theatre of not only norms and laws, but also of cultures of criminality. The means and legitimacy of police activities have been dispersed internally and externally (Walker, 2000), and have become the subject of 'multilateralization' or 'pluralization' (Crawford *et al.*, 2005) and of privatization and 'nodal' security orientations (Johnston and Shearing, 2005). The forms of authority and democratic control have thus been put under pressure by a new era of policing tasks as well as by encroaching mutation in the nature of police work. The tasks and responsibility of maintaining civil law and order can no longer be successfully carried out based on, or by reference to, a local level. In the last decades, Europe has undergone a number of significant transformations in the use of technology with the aim of managing insecurity. These transformations are to be understood in the context of the growing de-differentiation between previously distinct activities: fighting wars abroad, controlling populations at home and managing the border between these two spheres. The European Union stands as a clear illustration of these evolutions. The military is involved in activities within the territory of the Member States, but also abroad in missions of international police. Police agencies have invested in the European arenas, and policemen are sent abroad to conduct crimefighting and liaison activities. Border-guard services no longer operate at the borders between the Member States of the EU, but in other spaces inside the national territory (e.g. airports or train stations) at the borders with non-EU members and beyond.

Particularly noteworthy are the ethical consequences of three kinds of challenges to policing security in Europe: ongoing and emerging informal networks of police professionals, new modes of inter-governmental co-operation and emergent supranational institutions. All three types of development in policy involve co-operative arrangements and exchanges of both information and service traditionally anchored in locally based institutions organized and supported by value systems proper to one environment. The norms and codes of transformation of information and services also traverse value-borders, characterized codes, norms and practices that map poorly or not at all unto corresponding categories in other national environments or on different levels in the global policy systems (Sheptycki, 2004, 1998). Facilitating this transition has been a primary task of the Justice and Home Affairs Unit of the European Council (Council of the European Union, 2002, 2005b).

Cross-border value issues in CFSP/ESDP implementation

Among the most unambiguous transfers of political concepts from the nation-state level to the level of the EU in the process of Europeanization is that which concerns CFSP/ESDP. Though there is considerable disagreement about the appropriate scope and degree of that transfer, it is, by and large, considered to be, formally or technically, the least problematic process (Howorth, 2001; Wessel, 2003; Winn, 2003). Traditionally, foreign policy and defence and security strategy have projected the face of the EU to the external world, while the threat of terrorism, even in its earlier 20th century European forms, was a matter of home affairs. This changed considerably after the attacks of 11 September 2001. The threats to the one began to flow into and enhance the threats to the other. The European response to the attacks was to revise the understanding of security and its protection by taking into account the increasing porosity of the security borders.

The Madrid bombings on 11 March 2004 led to an intensified reflection on the nature of threat to Europe, and set in motion a number of important political activities with the aim of securing the EU against terrorism. Here, though the terrorist threat to Europe concerns primarily the lives of Europeans on EU territory, the link to external threats becomes immediately evident. As Commission President Barroso declared following the Madrid bombings, 'Terrorism is a global phenomenon, and the struggle against it must therefore be carried to the world stage' (Barroso, 2005). The Commission's 2004 communication *A Strategy on the External Dimension of the Area of Freedom, Security and Justice*, declared that:

> menaces such as terrorism, organised crime and drug trafficking also originate outside the EU. It is thus crucial that the EU develop a strategy to engage with third countries worldwide.
>
> (European Commission, 2005)

And on 17 December 2004 the Council adopted its *Conceptual Framework on the European Security and Defence Policy (EDSP) Dimension of the Fight against Terrorism*, including measures for support to third countries, rapid response protection, intelligence and crisis management, all based in mechanisms and tools stemming from external defence and security mechanisms (Council of the European Union, 2004). 'No purpose is served,' summed up

Commissioner for Justice, Freedom and Security Frattini, 'in distinguishing between the security of citizens inside the European Union and those outside'. Nonetheless, he concluded, the key to succeeding in the struggle against terrorist threat is that the EU must 'project its values' (Frattini, 2005).

It is thus clear that hybrid approaches are necessary for complex challenges. Cross-pillar approaches are emphasized repeatedly in strategic thinking about terrorism, most prominently in the four pillars ('Prevent, Protect, Pursue, Respond') of the *Counter-terrorism Strategy* (CEU, 2005a). Yet this hybridization of the security practice redoubles the complexity of analysis and policy-making in at least three important ways. Firstly, it opens the question of translating the political, social and cultural values of Europe into foreign policy principles applicable to the rest of the world and, in particular, to those who would do harm to Europeans. The challenge of the 'projection of values' is one that recurs constantly in the plans of attack of the European Neighbourhood Policy. Secondly, the multiplication of institutional actors and agencies responsible for security, thus combining institutional loyalties through complex, overlapping systems of accountability, and in which flexibility and suppleness are necessary virtues, leaves them less accessible to democratic oversight and control (Guittet, 2006: 138). Thirdly, In the Council's four-pillared approach to terrorism set out in the *EU Action Plan for Combating Terrorism,* powers of action, access to information, border system monitoring and police co-operation are opened and redistributed to actors who previously had little to with them (CEU, 2006). Each of the four measures requires a re-tooling, relating to individual citizens in ways that have not been their usual purview.

Throughout its brief and rich history the European concept has undergone striking changes. From the free flow of goods in the Treaty of Paris, to the monetary principles of the EMU, to the pillarized architecture of the Maastricht Treaty and finally to the integrated institutional design of the Lisbon Treaty, the European self-understanding has, in part, clung to an original globalized vision, in part adapted to a changing world. Security has always played a part in this story, but never with the same intensity as it has in the post-Cold War and, in particular post-9/11 and post-3/11 world.

The most recent and most significant evolution in the European security reality is the gradual detachment and shifting of the internal and external security borders from the national and European physical borders. As we have seen, this shift has had two main effects. First, it has continued in the fulfilment of a central ambition of the European project, shifting the legitimacy and functionality of security services to the European level. This has enhanced and rationalized in a number of ways the assurance of security in the European Union. Secondly, it has created synergies, collaborations and constellations in the European security architecture that were not foreseen by even the most recent visionaries of the European project. We have argued that a key to linking and understanding the common ground for these two movements is the notion of value. By unpacking the conceptual relation between security and value, then reviewing four institutional arrangements in view of the security-value concept, we have suggested that both the long-term continuity and more recent ruptures and discontinuities in European security thinking can be plotted and understood as negotiations of value. The technological impulse so prominently guiding European security thinking today will not realize its potential without the insight that the threat to Europe is a threat to its values, and that values, fluid and amorphous as they are, are not objects like any others.

Bibliography

Adam, B., David, D., Dumoulin, A., George, B. and Remacle, E. (1999) *La nouvelle architecture de sécurité en Europe*. Brussels: GRIP.

Adler, E. (2008) The Spread of Security Communities: Communities of Practice, Self-Restraint, and NATO's Post-Cold War Transformation. *European Journal of International Relations*, 14, 195–230.

Adler, E. and Barnett, M. N. (1998) *Security Communities*. Cambridge, MA: Cambridge University Press.

Agamben, G. (1993) *The Coming Community*. Minneapolis, MN: University of Minnesota Press.

Aglietta, M. and Gerschlager, C. (2000) L'euro, avec ou sans confiance? Comment créer une nouvelle valeur. Preface et entretien avec Michel Aglietta. *Esprit*, 104–20.

Alston, P. and Weiler, J. H. H. (1999) An 'Ever Closer Union' in Need of a Human Rights Policy: The European Union and Human Rights, in Alston, P., Bustelo, M. R. and Heenan, J. (eds) *The EU and Human Rights*. Oxford/New York, NY: Oxford University Press.

Amoore, L. (2006) Biometrics Borders: Governing Mobilities in the War on Terror. *Political Geography*, 336–51.

Anderson, B. R. (1991) *Imagined Communities: Reflections on the Origin and Spread of Nationalism*. London/New York: Verso.

Anderson, M. and Apap, J. (2002) *Striking a Balance between Freedom, Security and Justice in an Enlarged Europe*. Brussels: Centre for European Policy Studies.

Apap, J. and Carrera, S. (2003) *Maintaining Security within Borders: Towards a Permanent State of Emergency in the EU?* Brussels: Centre for European Policy Studies.

Appadurai, A. (2001) *Globalization*. Durham, NC: Duke University Press.

Arditi, B. (2008) On the Political: Schmitt contra Schmitt. *Telos*, 7–28.

Austin, J. (2002) *Lectures on Jurisprudence, or the Philosophy of Positive Law*. Bristol: Thoemmes Press.

Austin, J. L. (1975) *How to Do Things with Words*. Cambridge, MA: Harvard University Press.

Badiou, A. (1995) *Metapolitics*. London: Verso.

Balakrishnan, G. (2000) *The Enemy: An Intellectual Portrait of Carl Schmitt*. London/New York: Verso.

Balibar, E. (2004) *We, the People of Europe? Reflections on Transnational Citizenship*. Princeton, NJ: Princeton University Press.

Balzacq, T. (2005) The Three Faces of Securitization: Political Agency, Audience and Context. *European Journal of International Relations*, 11, 171–201.

Balzacq, T. (ed.) (2010) *On Securitization: The Design and Evolution of Security Problems.* London: Routledge.

Bamyeh, M. A. (2000) *The Ends of Globalization.* Minneapolis, MN: University of Minnesota Press.

Barkan, E. (2000) *The Guilt of Nations: Restitution and Negotiating Historical Injustices.* New York: Norton.

Barroso, J. M. (2005) Fighting Terrorism Together in the EU. Speech in the EU Parliament, 10 March.

Barry, J. A. (1998) *The Sword of Justice: Ethics and Coercion in International Politics.* Westport, CT: Praeger.

Baudrillard, J. (1995) *The Gulf War Did not Take Place.* Bloomington, IN: Indiana University Press.

Bauman, Z. (1997) *Postmodernism and its Discontents.* Oxford: Blackwell.

Bauman, Z. (1998) *Globalization: The Human Consequences.* New York, NY: Columbia University Press.

Bauman, Z. (2001) *Community: Seeking Safety in an Insecure World.* Cambridge: Polity Press.

Beck, U. (1992) *Risk Society: Towards a New Modernity.* London: Sage Publications.

Beck, U. (1999a) Die 'Warum-nicht-Gesellschaft'. *Die Zeit.*

Beck, U. (1999b) *Was ist Globalisierung? Irrtümer des Globalismus – Antworten auf Globalisierung,* Frankfurt am Main, Surhkamp.

Beck, U. (2000) *What is Globalization?* Cambridge: Polity Press.

Beck, U. (2004) *Der kosmopolitische Blick oder: Krieg ist Frieden,* Frankfurt am Main, Suhrkamp.

Beck, U. (2006) *Cosmpololitan Vision.* Cambridge: Polity Press.

Beck, U., Giddens, A. and Lasch, S. (eds) (1994) *Reflexive Modernization: Politics, Tradition and Aesthetics in the Modern Social Order.* Cambridge: Polity Press.

Beck, U. and Grande, E. (2007) *Cosmopolitan Europe.* Cambridge: Polity Press.

Bellamy, R. and Castiglione, D. (1997) Building the Union: The Nature of Sovereignty in the Political Architecture of Europe. *Law and Philosophy,* 16, 421–45.

Berger, T. U. (1996) Norms, Identity, and National Security in Germany and Japan, in Katzenstein, P. J. (ed.) *The Culture of National Security: Norms and Identity in World Politics.* New York, NY: Columbia University Press.

Bigo, D. (2000) When Two become One. Internal and External Securitisations in Europe. *International Relations Theory and the Politics of European Integration: Power, Security and Community.* London: Routledge.

Bigo, D. (2002) Security and Immigration: Toward a Critique of the Governmentality of Unease. *Alternatives,* 27.

Biscop, S. (2005) The European Security Strategy and the Neighbourhood Policy: A New Starting Point for a Euro-Mediterranean Security Partnership? Conference convened by ECFA and RIIR, which analyzed the three dimensions of the Barcelona Process: political, economic and cultural. Cairo.

Bleiker, R. (2001) *The Ethics of Speed: Global Activism after Seattle.* The Hague: Institute of Social Studies.

Bourdieu, P. (2000) *Les structures sociales de l'economie.* Paris: Éditions du Seuil.

Bull, H. (1977) *The Anarchical Society: A Study of Order in World Politics.* London: Macmillan.

Burgess, J. P. (1997) On the Necessity and the Impossibility of a European Cultural

Identity, in Burgess, J. P. (ed.) *Political Culture and Cultural Politics in Postmodern Europe*. Amsterdam: Rodopi.

Burgess, J. P. (2000) Coal, Steel and Spirit: The Double Reading of European Unity (1948–1951), in Stråth, B. (ed.) *Europe and the Other and Europe as the Other*. Brussels: P.I.E.-Peter Lang.

Burgess, J. P. (2001a) The Conceptual History of European Space. *Culture and Rationality: European Frameworks of Norwegian Identity*. Kristiansand: Norwegian Academic Press.

Burgess, J. P. (2001b) *Culture and Rationality: European Frameworks of Norwegian Identity*. Kristiansand: Norwegian Academic Press.

Burgess, J. P. (2001c) Identity and Multiplicity: The Norwegian, the Scandinavian and the European. *Culture and Rationality: European Frameworks of Norwegian Identity*. Kristiansand: Norwegian Academic Press.

Burgess, J. P. (2002) What's so European about the European Union? Legitimacy between Institution and Identity. *European Journal of Social Theory*, 5, 467–81.

Burgess, J. P. (2003) The Abduction of 'The Abduction of Europe', in Burgess, J. P. (ed.) *Museum Europa: The European Cultural Heritage between Economics and Politics*. Kristiansand: Norwegian Academic Press.

Burgess, J. P. (2007a) Gender, Risk and Uncertainty. Chicago, IL: Annual Conference of the International Studies Association.

Burgess, J. P. (2007b) L'éthique politique du principe de précaution (in manuscript).

Burgess, J. P. (2008) Insecurity of the European Community of Values. Paper presented at the International Studies Association. San Diego, CA.

Burgess, J. P. (2010a) La nouvelle éthique politique de l'insecurité. *Ethiques et économiques*, 7(2).

Burgess, J. P. (2010b) Security and the Ethics of Uncertainty. Paper presented at VALDOR annual conference. Stockholm.

Burgess, J. P. (2010c) Special section on the the Evolution of International Security Studies, in Burgess, J. P. (ed.) *Security Dialogue*.

Burgess, J. P. (2011) The Time of Security, paper presented at the annual convention of the International Studies Association, 19 March, Montreal.

Burgess, J. P. and Stråth, B. (1999) Money and Political Economy. From the Werner Plan to the Oelors Report and Beyond, in Magnusson, L. and Strath, B. (eds) *In Search of a Political Economy for Europe*. Brussels: PUI.

Burgess, J. P. and Stråth, B. (2001) Money and Political Economy: From the Werner Plan to the Delors Report and Beyond, in Stråth, B. and Magnusson, L. (eds) *From the Werner Plan to the EMU: The Economic-Political Embedding of Labour Markets between Europe and the Nation in Historical View*. Brussels: PUI.

Burke, A. (2002) Aporias of Security. *Alternatives*, 27, 1–28.

Bush, G. W. (2002) The National Security Strategy. Washington, DC.

Butler, J. (1988) Performative Acts and Gender Constitution: An Essay in Phenomenology and Feminist Theory. *Theatre Journal*, 40, 519–31.

Butler, J. (1990) *Gender Trouble: Feminism and the Subversion of Identity*. New York, NY: Routledge.

Butler, J. (1991) A Note on Performative Acts of Violence. *Cardozo Law Review*, 13, 1303–4.

Butler, J. (1997a) *Excitable Speech: A Politics of the Performative*. New York, NY: Routledge.

Butler, J. (1997b) *The Psychic Life of Power*. Stanford, CA: Stanford University Press.

Butler, J. (2003) Violence, Mourning, Politics. *Studies in Gender and Sexuality*, 4, 9–37.

Butler, J. (2004) *Precarious Life: The Powers of Mourning and Violence*. London: Verso.

Butler, J. (2005) *Giving an Account of Oneself*. New York, NY: Fordham University Press.

Butler, J. (2009) *Frames of War. When is Life Grievable?* New York/London: Verso.

Butler, J., Žižek, S. and Laclau, E. (2000) *Contingency, Hegemony, Universality: Contemporary Dialogues on the Left*. London: Verso.

Buzan, B. (1991) *People, States, and Fear: The National Security Problem in International Relations*. Boulder, CO: Lynne Rienner.

Buzan, B. and Hansen, L. (2009) *The Evolution of International Security Studies*. Cambridge: Cambridge University Press.

Buzan, B., Wæver, O. and de Wilde, J. (1998) *Security: A New Framework for Analysis*. Boulder, CO: Lynne Rienner.

Buzan, B., Wæver, O., Kelstrup, M. and Lemaitre, P. (1993) *Identity, Migration, and the New Security Agenda in Europe*. New York, NY: St. Martin's Press.

Cairns, W. (1997) *Introduction to European Union Law*. London: Cavendish Publications.

Campbell, D. (1993) *Politics without Principle: Sovereignty, Ethics, and the Narratives of the Gulf War*. Boulder, CO: Lynne Rienner.

Campbell, D. (1998a) *National Deconstruction: Violence, Identity, and Justice in Bosnia*. Minneapolis, MN: University of Minnesota Press.

Campbell, D. (1998b) *Writing Security: United States Foreign Policy and the Politics of Identity*. Minneapolis, MN: University of Minnesota Press.

Campbell, D. and Dillon, M. (1993) *The Political Subject of Violence*. Manchester/New York, NY: Manchester University Press.

Campbell, D. and Shapiro, M. J. (1999) *Moral Spaces: Rethinking Ethics and World Politics*. Minneapolis, MN: University of Minnesota Press.

Canguilhem, G. (1988) *Ideology and Rationality in the History of the Life Sciences*. Cambridge, MA: MIT Press.

Canguilhem, G. (1999) *The Normal and the Pathological*. New York, NY: Zone Books.

Carlsnaes, W., Carlsnaes, W., Sjursen, H. and White, B. (2004) *Contemporary European Foreign Policy*. London/Thousand Oaks, CA: Sage.

Carrino, A. (1999) Carl Schmitt and European Juridical Science, in Mouffe, C. (ed.) *The Challenge of Carl Schmitt*. London: Verso.

c.a.s.e. Collective (2006) Critical Approaches to Security in Europe: A Networked Manifesto. *Security Dialogue*, 37, 443–87.

c.a.s.e. Collective (2007) Europe, Knowledge, Politics: Engaging with the Limits. The c.a.s.e. Collective Responds. *Security Dialogue*, 38, 558–74.

Cassese, A. (2001) *International Law*. Oxford: Oxford University Press.

Chalmers, D. and Szyszczak, E. M. (1998) *European Union Law*. Aldershot/Brookfield, VT: Ashgate/Dartmouth.

Churchill, W. (1994) The Tragedy of Europe, in Nelsen, B.F. (ed.) *The European Union. Readings on the Theory and Practice of European Integration*. Boulder, CO: A. Stubb.

Cochran, M. (1999) *Normative Theory in International Relations: A Pragmatic Approach*. Cambridge/New York, NY: Cambridge University Press.

Cohen, A. P. (1985) *The Symbolic Construction of Community*. London/New York, NY: E. Horwood/Tavistock Publications.

Cohen-Jonathan, G. (1989) *La convention européenne des droits de l'homme*. Paris: Hamaritain.

Connolly, W. E. (1991) *Identity/Difference: Democratic Negotiations of Political Paradox.* Ithica and London: Cornell University Press.

Conze, W. (1984) Sicherheit, Schutz, in Koselleck, R., Brunner, O. and Conze, W. (eds) *Geschichtliche Grundbegriffe: Historisches Lexikon zur politisch-sozialen Sprache in Deutschland, Band 5.* Stuttgart: Klett-Cotta.

Council of the European Union (2002) Council Framework Decision of 13 June 2002 on Combating Terrorism.

Council of the European Union (2003) A Secure Europe in a Better World: European Security Strategy. Brussels: European Council.

Council of the European Union (2004) Conceptual Framework on the European Security and Defence Policy (EDSP) Dimension of the Fight against Terrorism.

Council of the European Union (2005a) The European Union Counter-Terrorism Strategy. Brussels.

Council of the European Union (2005b) JHA Council Declaration on the EU Response to the London Bombings. UK Presidency of the EU, 2005.

Council of the European Union (2006) Updated EU Action Plan for Combating Terrorism. European Union.

Council of the European Union (2010) Draft Internal Security Strategy for the European Union: 'Towards a European Security Model'. Brussels.

Cowles, M. G., Caporaso, J. A. and Risse, T. (2001) Europeanization and Domestic Change: Introduction, in Cowles, M. G., Caporaso, J. A. and Risse, T. (eds) *Transforming Europe: Europeanization and Domestic Change.* Ithaca, NY: Cornell University Press.

Crawford, A., Lister, S., Blackburn, S. and Burnett, J. (2005) *Plural Policing: The Mixed Economy of Visible Patrols in England and Wales.* Bristol: Policy Press.

Crawford, N. C. (2002) *Argument and Change in World Politics: Ethics, Decolonization, and Humanitarian Intervention.* Cambridge/New York, NY: Cambridge University Press.

Daase, C. and Kessler, O. (2006) Knowns and Unknowns in the War on Terror: Uncertainty and the Political Construction of Danger. *Security Dialogue,* 38(4), 411–34.

de Benoist, A. (1999) *What is Sovereignty?* e-book, www.alaindebenoist.com, pp. 99–118.

de Benoist, A. (2003) *Schmitt in France,* e-book, www.alaindebenoist.com, pp. 133–52.

de Benoist, A. (2004) *On Identity,* e-book, www.alaindebenoist.com, pp. 9–64.

de Hert, P. (2005a) Balancing Security and Liberty within the European Human Rights Framework: A Critical Reading of the Court's Case Law in the Light of Surveillance and Criminal Law Enforcement Strategies after 9/11. *Utrecht Law Review,* 1, 68–96.

de Hert, P. (2005b) Biometrics: Legal Issues and Implications. Sevilla, Institute of Prospective Technological Studies.

de Hert, P. and Gutwirth, S. (2003) Making Sense of Privacy and Data Protection: A Prospective Overview in the Light of the Future of Identity, Location based Services and the Virtual Residence. Security and Privacy for the Citizen in the Post-September 11 Digital Age: A Prospective overview: Report to the European Parliament Committee on Citizens' Freedoms and Rights, Justice and Home Affairs (LIBE). Sevilla: Institute for Prospective Technological Studies.

de la Grange, T. K. (2002) On the Postmodern Nomos. *Telos,* pp. 140–51.

de la Grange, T. K. (2004) The Theory of the Partisan Today. *Telos,* pp. 169–75.

de Rougement, D. (1966) *The Idea of Europe.* New York, NY/London: Macmillan.

Deering, M.-J. (1991) *Denis de Rougement, l'européen*. Lausanne: Fondation Jean Monnet pour l'Europe.

Delanty, G. (1999) *Social Theory in a Changing World*. Cambridge: Polity Press.

Delanty, G. (2000) *Modernity and Postmodernity*. London: Sage.

Delanty, G. (2003) *Community*. London/New York, NY: Routledge.

Delanty, G. and Rumford, C. (2005) *Rethinking Europe: Social Theory and the Implications of Europeanization*. London/New York, NY: Routledge.

Deleuze, G. (1983) *Nietzsche and Philosophy*. New York, NY: Columbia University Press.

Deleuze, G. and Guattari, F. (1994) *What is Philosophy?* London: Verso.

Delouche, F. (1992) *Illustrated History of Europe*. Paris: Hachette.

den Boer, M. and Monar, J. (2002) 11 September and the Challenge of Global Terrorism to the EU as a Security Actor. *Journal of Common Market Studies*, 40, 11–28.

Der Derian, J. (1987) *On Diplomacy: A Genealogy of Western Estrangement*. Oxford/New York, NY: Blackwell.

Der Derian, J. (1992) *Antidiplomacy: Spies, Terror, Speed, and War*. Cambridge, MA: Blackwell.

Der Derian, J. (1995) The Value of Security: Hobbes, Marx, Nietzsche, and Baudrillard, in Lipschutz, R. D. (ed.) *On Security*. New York, NY: Columbia University Press.

Der Derian, J. (2001) *Virtuous War: Mapping the Military-Industrial-Media-Entertainment Network*. Boulder, CO/Oxford: Westview Press.

Der Derian, J. and Shapiro, M. J. (1989) *International/Intertextual Relations: Postmodern Readings of World Politics*. Lexington, MA: Lexington Books.

Derrida, J. (1978) Force and Signification. *Writing and Difference*. Chicago, IL: University of Chicago Press.

Derrida, J. (1982) Signature, Event, Context. *Margins of Philosophy*. Chicago, IL: University of Chicago Press.

Derrida, J. (1987) *Psyché : inventions de l'autre*. Paris: Galilée.

Derrida, J. (1992a) Force of Law: The Mystical Foundation of Authority, in Cornell, D. and Rosenfeld, M. (eds) *Deconstruction and the Possibility of Justice*. London: Routledge.

Derrida, J. (1992b) *The Other Heading: Reflections on Today's Europe*. Bloomington and Indianapolis, IN: Indiana University Press.

Derrida, J. (1992c) Oxford Amnesty Lecture, with Montefiore, A. (ed.). Oxford.

Descartes (1996) *Meditations Métaphysiques*. Paris: J. Vrin.

Desch, M. C. (1998a) Culture Clash: Assessing the Importance of Ideas in Security Studies. *International Security*, 23, 141–70.

Desch, M. C. (1998b) Culture Clash: Assessing the Importance of Ideas in Security Studies. *International Security*, 23, 141–70.

Deutsch, K. W. (1957a) *Political Community and the North Atlantic Area*. Princeton, NJ: Princeton University Press.

Deutsch, K. W. (1957b) *Political Community and the North Atlantic Area: International Organization in the Light of Historical Experience*. Princeton, NJ: Princeton University Press.

Dillon, M. (1992) Security, Philosophy and Politics, in Featherstone, M., Lash, S. and Robertson, R. (eds) *Global Modernities*. London: Sage.

Dillon, M. (1996) *Politics of Security: Towards a Political Philosophy of Continental Thought*. London/New York, NY: Routledge.

Dilthey, W. (1957) *Philosophy of Existence: Introduction to Weltanschauungslehre*. Translation of an essay with introduction. New York, NY: Bookman Associates.

Dilthey, W. (2002) *The Formation of the Historical World in the Human Sciences*. Princeton, NJ: Princeton University Press.

Donnelly, J. (1992) Twentieth-Century Realism, in Nardin, T. and Mapel, D. R. (eds) *Traditions of International Ethics*.

Dower, J. (1986) *War with Mercy: Race and Power in the Pacific War*. New York, NY: Pantheon.

Doyle, M. W. and Ikenberry, G. J. (1997) *New Thinking in International Relations Theory*. Boulder, CO: Westview Press.

Duchêne, F. (1972) Europe's Role in World Peace, in Mayne, R. (ed.) *Europe Tomorrow: Sixteen Europeans Look Ahead*. London: Fontana.

Dueck, C. (2006) *Reluctant Crusaders: Power, Culture, and Change in American Grand Strategy*. Princeton, NJ: Princeton University Press.

Durkheim, É. (2004) *Sociologie et philosphie*. Paris: Presses Universitaires de France.

Duroselle, J.-B. (1990) *L'Europe: Histoire de ses peuples*. Paris: Perrin.

Dyzenhaus, D. (1998) *Law as Politics: Carl Schmitt's Critique of Liberalism*. Durham, NC: Duke University Press.

Edel, A. (1988) The Concept of Value and its Travels in Twentieth-Century America, in Murphey, M. G. and Berg, I. (eds) *Values and Value Theory in Twentieth-Century America: Essays in Honor of Elizabeth Flower*. Philadelphia, PA: Temple University Press.

Ekengren, M., Matzen, N. and Svantesson, M. (2006) The New Security Role for the European Union – Transnational Crisis Management and the Protection of Union Citizens. Stockholm: Swedish National Defense College.

Eriksen, T. H. and Nielsen, F. S. (2001) *A History of Anthropology*. London: Pluto Press.

European Commission (1973) Declaration on European Identity. General Report of the European Commission. Brussels.

European Commission (2003) *A Secure Europe in a Better World: European Security Strategy*.

European Commission (2005) Communication from the Commission. A Strategy on the External Demension of the Area of Freedom, Security and Justice.

European Court of Justice (1962a) Costa/ENEL.

European Court of Justice (1962b) Van Gend en Loos.

Evans, A. (1998) *A Textbook on EU Law*. Oxford: Hart Publishers.

Featherstone, M. (1990) Global Culture: An Introduction, in Featherstone, M. (ed.) *Global Culture: Nationalism, Globalization and Modernity*. London: Sage.

Ferry, J.-M. (2000) *La question de l'Etat européen*. Paris: Gallimard.

Finkielkraut, A., Badinter, R. and Daniel, J. (2000) *La morale internationale entre la politique et le droit*. Paris: Éditions de Tricorne.

Fiore, R. N. and Nelson, H. L. (2003) *Recognition, Responsibility, and Rights: Feminist Ethics and Social Theory*. Lanham, MD: Rowman and Littlefield.

Foucault, M. (1975) *Surveiller et punir*. Paris: Gallimard.

Foucault, M. (1981) *The Will to Knowledge: The History of Sexuality, Volume I, Introduction*. Harmondsworth: Penguin.

Foucault, M. (1989) *Madness and Civilization: A History of Insanity in the Age of Reason*. London: Routledge.

Foucault, M. (1994a) A propos de la généalogie de l'éthique: un aperçu du travail en cours, in Ewald, F. and Defert, D. (eds) *Dits et écrits*. Paris: Gallimard/Seuil.

Foucault, M. (1994b) Usage des plaisirs et techniques de soi, in Defert, D. and Ewald, F. (eds) *Dits et écrits*. Paris: Gallimard.

Foucault, M. (1997) Subjectivity and Truth, in Rabinow, P. (ed.) *Ethics: Subjectivity and Truth*. New York, NY: The New Press.

Foucault, M. (1999) Foucault, in Faubion, J. (ed.) *Aesthetics, Method and Epistemology*. New York, NY: The New Press.

Foucault, M. (2003a) *The Birth of the Clinic: An Archaeology of Medical Perception*. London: Routledge.

Foucault, M. (2003b) *Society Must Be Defended*. Lectures at the Collège de France 1975–1976. New York, NY: Picador.

Fraser, N. (2001) Recognition without Ethics? *Theory, Culture and Society*, 18, 21–42.

Frattini, F. (2005) *Internal and External Dimension of Fighting Terrorism*. Berlin.

Freud, S. (1990) *The Ego and the Id*. New York, NY: Norton.

Freud, S. (1961) *Beyond the Pleasure Principle*. New York, NY: Liveright Pub. Corp.

Friedman, J. (1999) The Hybridization of Roots and the Abhorrence of the Bush, in Featherstone, M. and Lash, S. (eds) *Spaces of Culture*. London: Sage.

Fukuyama, F. (1992) *The End of History and the Last Man*. New York: Avon Books.

Gare, A. (2002) Narratives and Culture: The Role of Stories in Self-Creation. *Telos*, pp. 80–100.

Gasper, D. (2001) *Global Ethics and Global Strangers: Beyond the Inter-national Relations Framework: An Essay in Descriptive Ethics*. The Hague: Institute of Social Studies.

Gautron, J.-C. (1999) *Droit européen*. Paris: Éditions Dalloz.

Gay, P. (1977) *The Enlightenment: An Interpretation of the Science of Freedom*. New York, NY: Norton.

Germain, R. D. and Kenny, M. (2005) *The Idea of Global Civil Society: Politics and Ethics in a Globalizing Era*. London/New York, NY: Routledge.

Giddens, A. (1990) *The Consequences of Modernity*. Cambridge: Polity Press.

Giddens, A. (1991) *Modernity and Self-Identity*. Cambridge: Polity Press.

Gottfried, P. (1998) Modern Liberalism and the 'Fascist' Comeback. *Telos*, pp. 173–9.

Gottfried, P. (2008) Gloomy Observations about the Political Present. *Telos*, pp. 185–92.

Gouldner, A. (1970) *The Coming Crisis of Western Sociology*. New York, NY: Equinox.

Goux, J.-J. (2000) *Frivolité de la valeur: essai sur l'imaginaire du capitalisme*. Paris: Blusson.

Grabbe, H. (2000) The Sharp Edges of Europe: Extending Schengen Eastwards. *International Affairs*, 76, 519–+.

Graham, G. (1997) *Ethics and International Relations*. Oxford/Cambridge, MA: Blackwell.

Gregg, R. W. (1998) *International Relations on Film*. Boulder, CO: Lynne Rienner.

Grimm, D. (2000) Das Andere darf anders bleiben. Wieviel Toleranz gegenüber fremder Lebensart verlangt das Grundgesetz? *Die Zeit*.

Guild, E. (2004) The Variable Subject of the EU Constitution, Civil Liberties and Human Rights. *European Journal of Migration and Law*, 6, 381–94.

Guild, E. (2007) *Security and European Human Rights: Protecting Individual Rights in Times of Exception and Military Action*. Nijmegen: Wolf Legal Publishers.

Guittet, E.-P. (2006) Military Activities with National Boundaries: The French Case. *Illiberal Practices of Liberal Regimes: The (In)security Games*. Paris: L'Harmattan.

Gupta, A. and Ferguson, J. (1997) *Culture, Power, Place: Explorations in Critical Anthropology*. Durham, NC and London: Duke University Press.

Haack, S. (2006) Constitutional Concepts within the Process of European Integration. *Futures*, 38, 180–96.

Haacke, J. (2005) The Frankfurt School and International Relations: On the Centrality of Recognition. *Review of International Studies*, 31, 181–94.

Habermas, J. (1998a) *Die postnationale Konstellation: Politische Essays.* Frankfurt am Main: Suhrkamp.

Habermas, J. (1998b) *The Inclusion of the Other: Studies in Political Theory.* Cambridge, MA: MIT Press.

Hall, S., Held, D. and McLennan, G. (1992) Introduction, in Hall, S., Held, D. and McGrew, T. (eds) *Modernity and its Futures.* London: Polity Press.

Hannay, D. (2000) Europe's Foreign and Security Policy: Year 1. *European Foreign Affairs Review*, pp. 275–80.

Hansen, T. B. and Stepputat, F. (2005) *Sovereign Bodies: Citizens, Migrants, and States in the Postcolonial World.* Princeton, NJ: Princeton University Press.

Harbour, F. V. (1999) *Thinking about International Ethics: Moral Theory and Cases from American Foreign Policy.* Boulder, CO: Westview Press.

Harré, R. (1998) *The Singular Self.* London: Sage.

Harris, J. W. (2003) *Legal Philosophies.* Oxford: Reed Elsevier.

Hart, H. L. A. (1997) *The Concept of Law.* Oxford/New York, NY: Clarendon Press/Oxford University Press.

Hassner, P. and Rupnik, J. (1999) Que devient l'idée d'Europe? *Esprit*, 74–80.

Hegel, G. W. F. (1977) *Phenomenology of Spirit.* Oxford: Oxford University Press.

Hegel, G. W. F. (2008) *Philosophy of Right.* New York, NY: Cosimo.

Heidegger, M. (1962) *Being and Time.* New York, NY: Harper and Row.

Heidegger, M. (1993) What Calls for Thinking, in Krell, D. F. (ed.) *Basic Writings.* San Francisco, CA: HarperCollins.

Hobsbawm, E. J. (1994) *The Age of Extremes: A History of the World, 1914–1991.* New York, NY: Pantheon Books.

Höffe, O. (1999) *Demokratie im Zeitalter der Globalisierung.* München: C.H. Beck.

Hoffmann, S. (2000) Towards a Common European Foreign and Security Policy? *Journal of Common Market Studies*, 38, 189–98.

Honneth, A. (1995a) *The Fragmented World of the Social.* New York, NY: State University of New York Press.

Honneth, A. (1995b) *The Struggle for Recognition: The Moral Grammar of Social Conflicts.* Cambridge, MA: Cambridge University Press.

Honneth, A. (1996) *The Struggle for Recognition: The Moral Grammar of Social Conflicts.* Cambridge, MA: MIT Press.

Howorth, J. (2001) European Defence and the Changing Politics of the European Union: Hanging Together or Hanging Separately? *Journal of Common Market Studies*, 39, 765–89.

Hunnings, N. M. (1996) *Encyclopedia of European Union Law: Constitutional Texts.* London: Sweet and Maxwell.

Hurrell, A. (2002) Ethics and Norms in Internatioanl Relations, in Carlsnaes, W., Risse, T. and Simmons, B. A. (eds) *Handbook of International Relations.* London: Sage.

Hutchings, K. (1992) The Possibility of Judgment: Moralizing and Theorizing in Interanational Relations. *Review of International Studies*, 18, 51–62.

Hutchings, K. (1999) *International Political Theory: Rethinking Ethics in a Global Era.* London/Thousand Oaks, CA: Sage.

Jabri, V. and O'Gorman, E. (1999) *Women, Culture, and International Relations*. Boulder, CO: Lynne Rienner.

Jaspers, K. (1981) *Nietzsche*. Berlin: Walter de Gruyter.

Joas, H. (1997) *Die Entstehung der Werte*. Frankfurt am Main: Suhrkamp.

Joas, H. (1998) The Autonomy of the Self: The Median Heritage and its Postmodern Challenge. *European Journal of Sociology*, 1, 7–18.

Joas, H. (2000) *Kriege und Werte. Studein zur Gewaltgeschichte des 20. Jahrhunderts*, Gåottingen: Verbrück Wissenschaft.

Johnson, J. T. (1999) *Morality and Contemporary Warfare*. New Haven, CT: Morality and Contemporary Warfare.

Johnston, L. and Shearing, C. D. (2005) Justice in the Risk Society. *Australian and New Zealand Journal of Criminology*, 38, 25–38.

Kant, I. (1983a) An Answer to the Question: What is Enlightenment? *Perpetual Peace and Other Essays*. Indianapolis, IN: Hackett Publishing.

Kant, I. (1983b) Idea for a Universal History with a Cosmopolitan Intent. *Perpetual Peace and Other Essays*. Indianapolis, IN: Hackett Publishing.

Kant, I. (1983c) To Perpetual Peace: A Philosophical Sketch. *Perpetual Peace and Other Essays*. Indianapolis, IN: Hackett Publishing.

Kant, I. (1996) *The Metaphysics of Morals*. Cambridge, MA: Cambridge University Press.

Kant, I. (2007) *Critique of Pure Reason*. London: Penguin.

Katzenstein, P. J. (1996) *The Culture of National Security: Norms and Identity in World Politics*. New York, NY: Columbia University Press.

Kier, E. (1995) Culture and Military Doctrine: France Between the Wars. *International Security*, 19, 65–93.

Kier, E. (1997) *Imagining War: French Military Doctrine between the Wars*. Princeton, NJ: Princeton University Press.

Kitchen, V. M. (2009) Argument and Identity Change in the Atlantic Security Community. *Security Dialogue*, 40, 95–114.

Klossowski, P. (1997) *Nietzsche and the Vicious Circle*. London: Continuum.

Kolm, S.-C. (1996) *Modern Theories of Justice*. Cambridge, MA: MIT Press.

Koskenniemi, M. (2002) *The Gentle Civilizer of Nations: The Rise and Fall of International Law, 1870–1960*. Cambridge/New York, NY: Cambridge University Press.

Kristeva, J. (1988) *Étrangers à nous-mêmes*. Paris: Grasset.

Kristeva, J. (1990) *Lettre ouverte à Harlem Désir*. Paris: Grasset.

Kuhn, H. (1975) Werte – eine Urgegebenheit, in Gadamer, H.-G. and Vogler, P. (eds) *Neue Anthropologie*. Stuttgart: Georg Thieme.

Kuhn, T. (1972) *The Structure of Scientific Revolutions*. Chicago, IL: Chicago University Press.

Kuijper, P. J. (2004) The Evolution of the Third Pillar from Maastricht to the European Constitution: Institutional Aspects. *Common Market Law Review*, 41, 609–26.

Lacan, J. (1937) The Looking-Glass Phase. *International Journal of Psychoanalysis*, I.

Lacan, J. (1966a) L'agressivité en psychanlyse. *Écrits*. Paris: Éditions du Seuil.

Lacan, J. (1966b) Le stade du miroir comme formateur de la fonction du 'je'. *Ècrits*. Paris: Éditions du Seuil.

Lacan, J. (1966c) Propos sur la causalité psychique. *Écrits*. Paris: Éditions du Seuil.

Lacan, J. (1973) *Les quatres concepts fondamentaux de la psychanalyse*. Paris: Éditions du Seuil.

Lacan, J. (1975) *De la psychose paranoïaque dans ses rapports avec la personnalité*. Paris: Éditions du Seuil.

Lacan, J. (1988a) *Freud's Papers on Technique, 1953–1954.* New York, NY: W.W. Norton.

Lacan, J. (1988b) *The Seminar of Jacques Lacan. Book 2.* New York, NY: Norton.

Lacan, J. (1992) *The Ethics of Psychoanalysis, 1959–1960.* New York, NY: Norton.

Lacan, J. (1999) The Mirror Stage as Formative of the I. New York, NY/London: W. W. Norton.

Lacan, J. (2009) The Function and Field of Speech and Langauge in Psychoanalysis *Ecrits.* New York, NY/London: W. W. Norton.

Latour, B. (1993) *We Have Never Been Modern.* Cambridge, MA: Harvard University Press.

Le Barron, F. (2000) *La croyance economique.* Paris: Éditions du Seuil.

Lefever, E. W. (1998) *The Irony of Virtue: Ethics and American Power.* Boulder, CO: Westview Press.

Levinas, E. (1961) *Totalite et Infini, essai sur l'exteriorite.* La Haye M. Nijhoff.

Levinas, E. (1972) *Humanisme de l'autre homme,* [Montpellier], Fata Morgana.

Levinas, E. (1974) *Autrement qu'etre ou au-dela de l'essence,* La Haye M. Nijhoff.

Levinas, E. (1998) *Éthique comme philosophie première.* Paris: Rivages Poches.

Liberatore, A. (2007) Balancing Security and Democracy, and the Role of Expertise: Biometrics Politics in the European Union. *European Journal on Criminal Policy and Research,* 13, 109–37.

Liddel, H. G. and Schott, R. (1940) *A Greek–English Lexicon.* Oxford: Clarendon Press.

Linklater, A. (1998) *The Transformation of Political Community.* Cambridge: Blackwell.

Lepenies, W. (1981) *Geschichte der Soziologie: Studien zur kognitiven, sozialen und historischen Identität einer Disziplin.* Frankfurt am Main: Suhrkamp.

Locke, J. (1967) *Essay on Human Understanding.* London: Polity Press.

Lyon, D. (2008) Identification and Surveillance. *Bioethics,* 22, 499–508.

McCormick, J. P. (1997) *Carl Schmitt's Critique of Liberalism: Against Politics as Technology.* Cambridge/New York, NY: Cambridge University Press.

MacIntyre, A. C. (1984) *After Virtue: A Study in Moral Theory.* Notre Dame, IN, University of Notre Dame Press.

MacIntyre, A. C. (1988) *Whose Justice? Which Rationality?* Notre Dame, IN: University of Notre Dame Press.

MacLean, R. M. (2000) *Law of the European Union.* London: Old Bailey Press.

Malanczuk, P. (1997) *Modern Introduction to International Law.* London/New York, NY: Routledge.

Manners, I. (2002) Normative Power Europe: A Contradiction in Terms? *Journal of Common Market Studies,* 40, 235–58.

Manners, I. and Whitman, R. (2003) The 'Difference Engine': Constructing and Representing the International Identity of the European Union. *Journal of European Public Policy,* 10, 235–58.

Marder, M. (2008) Carl Schmitt's 'Cosmopolitan Restaurant': Culture, Multiculturalism, and Complexio Oppositorum, 29–47.

Maréchal, J.-P. (2001) Critique d'un lieu commun: l'economie comme science. *Esprit,* 129–40.

Massumi, B. (2007) Potential Politics and the Primacy of Perception. *Theory and Event,* 10.

Mattern, J. B. (2001) The Power Politics of Identity. *European Journal of International Relations,* 7, 349–97.

Mauss, M. (1989) Une catégorie de l'esprit human: la notion de personne, celle de 'moi'. *Sociologie et anthropologie.* Paris: PUF.

McElroy, R. W. (1992) *Morality and American Foreign Policy: The Role of Ethics in International Affairs*. Princeton, NJ: Princeton University Press.

Melluci, A. (1996) *The Playing Self: Person and Meaning in the Planetary Society*. Cambridge, MA: Cambridge University Press.

Mesure, S. (1998) *La rationalité des valeurs*. Paris: Presses Universitaires de France.

Monnet, J. (1952) Allocutions prononcées par M. Jean Monnet, President de la Haute Autorite, à la premiere seance de la Haute Autorite, le 10 aout 1952 à Luxembourg; à la premiere session de l'Assemblée le 11 septembre 1952 à Strasbourg. Strasbourg, Communaute europeenne du charbon et de l'acier.

Nathan, L. (2006) Domestic Instability and Security Communities. *European Journal of International Relations*, 12, 275–99.

Niess, F. (2001) *Die europäische Idee. Aus dem Geist des Widerstands*. Frankfurt: Suhrkamp.

Niethammer, L. (2000) *Kollektive Identität. Hemiliche Quellen einer unheimlichen Konjunktur*. Hamburg: Rowohlt.

Nietzsche, F. W. (1968) *The Will to Power*. New York, NY: Vintage Books.

Nietzsche, F. W. (1994) *On the Genealogy of Morality*. Cambridge: Cambridge University Press.

Nietzsche, F. W. (1996) *Human, All too Human*. Cambridge/New York, NY: Cambridge University Press.

Nietzsche, F. W. (1997) *Daybreak: Thoughts on the Prejudices of Morality*. Cambridge/New York, NY: Cambridge University Press.

Nietzsche, F. W. (2002) *Beyond Good and Evil: Prelude to a Philosophy of the Future*. Cambridge: Cambridge University Press.

OED (1971) *Oxford English Dictionary*. Oxford: Oxford University Press.

O'Neil, P. (2005) Complexity and Counterterrorism: Thinking about Biometrics. *Studies in Conflict and Terrorism*, 28, 547–66.

Ogilvie, B. (2005) *Lacan: La formation du concept du sujet (1932–1949)*. Paris: Presses Universitaires de France.

Olsen, J. P. (2004) Survey article: Unity, Diversity and Democratic Institutions: Lessons from the European Union. *Journal of Political Philosophy*, 12, 461–95.

Oppenheim, F. E., Carter, I. and Ricciardi, M. (2001) *Freedom, Power, and Political Morality: Essays for Felix Oppenheim*. Basingstoke/New York, NY: Palgrave.

Outram, D. (1995) *The Enlightenment*. Cambridge: Cambridge University Press.

Pageden, A. (2002) Europe: Conceptualizing a Continent, in Pageden, A. (ed.) *The Idea of Europe from Antiquity to the Europe Union*. Cambridge: Cambridge University Press.

Passerini, L. (2002a) From Ironies of Identity to the Identities of Irony. in Pageden, A. (ed.) *The Idea of Europe from Antiquity to the Europe Union*. Cambridge: Cambridge University Press.

Passerini, L. (2002b) *Il mito d'Europa. Radici antiche per nuovi simboli*. Firezne: Giunti.

Pogge, T. (1992) Cosmopolitianism and sovereignty. *Ethics*, 103, 48–73.

Poggi, G. (1993) *Money and the Modem Mind. Simmel's Philosophy of Money*. Los Angeles, CA: University of California Press.

Polanyi, K. (2001) *The Great Transformation of the Political and Economic Origins of our Time*. Boston, MA: Beacon Press.

Price, R. and Tannenwald, N. (1996) Norms and Deterence: The Nuclear and Chemical Weapons Debate, in Katzenstein, P. J. (ed.) *The Culture of National Security: Norms and Identity in World Politics*. New York, NY: Columbia University Press.

Purvis, T. and Hunt, A. (1999) Identity versus Citizenship: Transformations in the Discourses and Practices of Citizenship. *Social Legal Studies*, 8, 457–82.

Qizilbash, M. (2009) Identity, Community, and Justice: Locating Amartya Sen's Work on Identity. *Politics, Philosophy, Economics*, 8, 251–66.

Rawls, J. (1971) *A Theory of Justice*. Cambridge, MA: Harvard University Press.

Rawls, J. (1996) *Political Liberalism*. New York, NY: Columbia University Press.

Ricœur, P. (1990) *Soi-même comme un autre*. Paris: Éditions du Seuil.

Ricœur, P. (1991) Tolérance, intolerance, intolerable. *Lectures I. Autour du politique.* Paris: Éditions du Seuil.

Rieker, P. (2006) From Common Defence to Comprehensive Security: Towards the Europeanization of French Foreign and Security Policy? *Security Dialogue*, 37, 509–28.

Risse, T. (2005) Neofunctionalism, European Identity, and the Puzzles of European Integration. *Journal of European Public Policy*, 12, 291–309.

Robinson, F. (1999) *Globalizing Care: Ethics, Feminist Theory, and International Relations.* Boulder, CO: Westview Press.

Rosencrance, R. (1998) The European Union: A New Type of International Actor, in Zielonka, J. (ed.) *Paradoxes of European Foreign Policy*. The Hague: Kluwer Law International.

Ross, A. and Jain, A. K. (2007) Human Recognition Using Biometrics: An Overview. *Annales Des Telecommunications-Annals of Telecommunications*, 62, 11–35.

Roudinesco, E. (1990) *Jacques Lacan & Co.: A History of Psychoanalysis in France, 1925–1985*. Chicago, IL: University of Chicago Press.

Salmon, T. (2006) The European Union: Just an Alliance or a Military Alliance? *Journal of Strategic Studies*, 29, 813–42.

Sandel, M. J. (1982) *Liberalism and the Limits of Justice*. Cambridge/New York, NY: Cambridge University Press.

Schmitt, C. (1930a) Das Problem der innerpolitischen Neutralität des Staates. *Verfassungsrechtliche Aufsätze*. Berlin: Duncker and Humblot.

Schmitt, C. (1930b) *Hugo Preuss: Sein Staatsbegriff und seine Stellung in der deutschen Staatslehre*. Tübingen: J.C.B. Mohr.

Schmitt, C. (1957) Die Lage der europäischen Rechtswissenschaft (1943/44). *Verfassungsrechtliche Aufsätze*. Berlin: Duncker & Humblot.

Schmitt, C. (1991) *Völkerrechtliche Großraumordnung mit Interventionsverbort für Reichsbegriff im Völkerrecht*. Berlin: Duncker & Humblot.

Schmitt, C. (1993) The Age of Neutralizations and Depoliticizations, in Konzen, M. and McCormick, J. P. *Telos*, 130–42.

Schmitt, C. (1996) *Roman Catholicism and Political Form*. Westport, CO: Greenwood Press.

Schmitt, C. (2003) *The Nomos of the Earth in the International Law of the Jus Publicum Europaeum*. New York, NY: Telos Press.

Schmitt, C. (2004) *Legality and Legitimacy*. Durham, NC: Duke University Press.

Schmitt, C. (2007) *The Concept of the Political*. Chicago, IL: University of Chicago Press.

Schultz, P. F. I. (1994) Hidden Killers: The Global Landmine Crisis. Office of International Security and Peacekeeping Operations. United States Department of State. Bureau of Political-Military Affairs.

Schuman, R. (1950) Declaration of 9 May 1950. Brussels: European Commission.

Schuman, R. (1964) Pour l'Europe. Paris: Les Editions Nagel.

Seckinelgin, H. and Shinoda, H. (2001) *Ethics and International Relations.*

Basingstoke/New York, NY: Palgrave, in association with *Millennium Journal of International Studies.*

Segers, R. T. and Viehoff, R. (1996) Die Konstruktion Europas. Überlegungen zum Problem der Kultur in Europa, in Segers, R. T. and Viehoff, R. (eds) *Kultur Identität Europa. Über die Schwiergikeiten und Möglichkeiten einer Konstruktion.* Frankfurt am Main: Suhrkamp.

Segesvary, V. (1999) *From Illusion to Delusion: Globalization and the Contradictions of Late Modernity.* San Francisco, CA: International Scholars Publications.

Selznick, P. (1992) *The Moral Commonwealth: Social Theory and the Promise of Community.* Berkeley, LA/London: University of California Press.

Shaw, M. (1999) *Politics and Globalisation: Knowledge, Ethics and Agency.* London/New York, NY: Routledge.

Sheptycki, J. (1998) Policing, Postmodernism and Transnationalization. *British Journal of Criminology,* 38, 485–503.

Sheptycki, J. (2004) Criminal Justice and Political Cultures: National and International Dimensions of Crime Control. *Social and Legal Studies,* 13, 557–9.

Simmel, G. (1978) *The Philosophy of Money.* London/Boston, MA: Routledge and Kegan Paul.

Simmel, G. (1989) *Einleitung in die Moralwissenschaft. Eine Kritik der ethischen Grundbegriffe.* Berlin: W. Hertz.

Simmonds, N. E. (2002) *Central Issues in Jurisprudence: Justice, Law and Rights.* London: Sweet and Maxwell.

Sjursen, H. (2004) The EU as a 'Normative Power': How Can this Be?

Slaughter, A.-M. (1995) International Law in a World of Liberal States. *European Journal of International Law.*

Slaughter, A.-M. (1997) The Real New World Order. *Foreign Affairs,* 176, 183–97.

Sleinis, E. E. (1994) *Nietzsche's Revaluation of Values: A Study in Strategies.* Urbana, IL: University of Illinois Press.

Smith, A. D. (1971) *Theories of Nationalism.* London: Duckworth.

Smith, H. (2000) *Democracy and International Relations: Critical Theories/Problematic Practices.* Basingstoke/New York, NY: Macmillan Press/St. Martin's Press.

Smith, K. (2003) *European Union Foreign Policy in a Changing World.* Cambridge: Polity Press.

Smith, K. and Light, M. (2001) *Ethics and Foreign Policy.* Cambridge/New York, NY: Cambridge University Press.

Stråth, B. and Magnusson, L. (2001) *Money and Political Economy: From the Werner Plan to the Delors Report and Beyond.* Brussels: P.U.I.

Stritzel, H. (2007) Towards a Theory of Securitization: Copenhagen and Beyond. *European Journal of International Relations,* 13, 357–83.

Sutch, P. (2001) *Ethics, Justice, and International Relations: Constructing an International Community.* London/New York, NY: Routledge.

Taleb, N. N. (2007) *The Black Swan: The Impact of the Highly Improbable.* London: Penguin.

Taylor, C. (1989) *Sources of the Self: The Making of the Modern Identity.* Cambridge, MA: Harvard University Press.

Taylor, C. (1995) *Philosophical Arguments.* Cambridge, MA: Harvard University Press.

Taylor, C., A. Gutmann & ebrary Inc. (1994) *Multiculturalism: Examining the Politics of Recognition.* Princeton, NJ: Princeton University Press.

Teschke, B. (2003) *The Myth of 1648: Class, Geopolitics and the Making of Modern International Relations.* London/New York, NY: Verso.

Treaty of the European Union (1992) *Treaty of the European Union*. Brussels: European Commission.

Treaty of the European Union (2008) *Treaty of the European Union*. Luxemburg: Office of Official Publications of the European Communities.

Thomas, W. (2001) *The Ethics of Destruction: Norms and Force in International Relations*. Ithaca: Cornell University Press.

Tönnies, F. (2002) *Community and Society*. Mineola, NY: Dover Publications.

Tonra, B. (2003) Constructing the Common Foreign and Security Policy: The Utility of a Cognitive Approach. *Journal of Common Market Studies*, 41, 731–56.

Trachtenberg, M. (1991) *History and Strategy*. Princeton, NJ: Princeton University Press.

Varga, V. (2007) *Cartographia: Mapping Civlisations*. New York, NY: Little Brown & Co.

Väyrynen, R. (1998) Global Interdependence or the European Fortress? Technology Policies in Perspective. *Research Policy*, 27, 627–37.

Von Busekist, A. (2004) Uses and Misuses of the Concept of Identity. *Security Dialogue*, 35, 81–98.

Wæver, O. (1995) Securitization and Desecuritization, in Lipschutz, R. (ed.) *On Security*. New York, NY: Columbia University Press.

Wæver, O. (2005) Security: A Conceptual History for International Relations. *Journal of International Relations*, 11(3), 307–33.

Wæver, O. (2008) Peace and Security: Two Evolving Concepts and their Changing Relationship, in Al., H.G.N.B.E. (ed.) *Globalization and Environmental Challenges: Reconceptualizing Security in the 21st Century*. Munich: Springer Verlag.

Wagner, P. (1994) *A Sociology of Moderntity: Liberty and Discipline*. London: Routledge.

Walker, N. (2000) *Policing in a Changing Constitutional Order*. London: Sweet and Maxwell.

Walker, R. B. J. (1993) *Inside/Outside: International Relations as Political Theory*. Cambridge, MA: Cambridge University Press.

Walker, R. B. J. (2007) Security, Critique, Europe. *Security Dialogue*, 38, 95–103.

Wallon, H. (1931) Comment se développe chez l'enfant la notion de corps propre. *Journal de Psychologie*, 28, 705–48.

Walters, E. G. (1987) *The Other Europe : Eastern Europe to 1945*. Syracuse, NY: Syracuse University Press.

Walzer, M. (1983) *Spheres of Justice: A Defense of Pluralism and Equality*. New York, NY: Basic Books.

Weber, C. (1995) *Simulating Sovereignty: Intervention, the State and Symbolic Exchange*. Cambridge: Cambridge University Press.

Weller, M. (1999) *The Crisis in Kosovo 1989–1999: From the dissolution of Yugoslavia to Rambouillet and the Outbreak of Hostilities*. Cambridge: International Documents and Analysis.

Wessel, R. A. (2003) The State of Affairs in EU Security and Defence Policy: The Breakthrough in the Treaty of Nice. *Jornal of Conflict and Security Law*, 8, 265–88.

Williams, M. C. (1998) Identity and the Politics of Security. *Alternatives*, 4, 204–55.

Williams, M. C. and Neumann, I. B. (2000) From Alliance to Security Community: NATO, Russia, and the Power of Identity. *Millennium – Journal of International Studies*, 29, 357–87.

Winn, N. (2003) Towards a Common European Security and Defence Policy? The Debate on NATO, the European Army and Translantic Security. *Geopolitics*, 8, 47–68.

Winter, G. (1996) *Sources and Categories of European Union Law: A Comparative and Reform Perspective.* Baden-Baden: Nomos.

Witte, B. D. (1999) Direct Effect, Supremacy, and the Nature of the Legal Order, in Craig, P. and Búrca, G. D. (eds) *The Evolution of EU Law.* Oxford: Oxford University Press.

Wivel, A. (2005) The Security Challenge of Small EU Member States: Interests, Identity and the Development of the EU as a Security Actor. *Jcms-Journal of Common Market Studies,* 43, 393–412.

Wolff, L. (1994) *Inventing Eastern Europe: The Map of Civilization on the Mind of the Enlightenment.* Stanford, CA: Stanford University Press.

Yúdice, G. (1988) Marginality and the Ethics of Survival. in Ross, A. (ed.) *Universal Abandon? The Politics of Postmodernism.* Minneapolis, MN: University of Minnesota Press.

Žižek, S. (1991) *For They Know not what They Do: Enjoyment as a Political Factor.* London/New York, NY: Verso.

Žižek, S. (1992) *Looking Awry: An Introduction to Jacques Lacan through Popular Culture.* Cambridge, MA: MIT Press.

Žižek, S. (1993) *Tarrying with the Negative: Kant, Hegel, and the Critique of Ideology.* Durham, NC: Duke University Press.

Zupancic, A. (2000) *The Ethics of the Real.* New York, NY/London: Verso.

Index